“英语周计划系列丛书”是针对我国读者的英语学习特点开发的，以“周”为谋篇布局单位、以“日”为具体实施单元的极具特色的英语辅导用书，具有思维创新、规划科学、目标明确、讲练结合、直击实战等特点。《4周全面突破BEC综合备考周计划（中级）》是本系列针对BEC的一个分册。

本书主要针对报考BEC中级的考生。涵盖了BEC中级考试的所有题型：阅读、写作、听力和口语，并将这四种题型依次安排在4周学习。导学部分对BEC考试的基本情况和最新动态做了介绍。书后附录有两套最新模拟题，供考生在综合备考结束后检验学习效果。本书荟萃众多英语培训机构及各类相关书籍的精华，考生在增强应试能力的同时可以提高英语结合运用水平，真正做到“一书在手，全部拥有”。

图书在版编目（CIP）数据

4周全面突破BEC综合备考周计划（中级）/于春艳，张凤主编. —北京：机械工业出版社，2015.12
（英语周计划系列丛书）
ISBN 978-7-111-53061-9

Ⅰ.①4… Ⅱ.①于… ②张… Ⅲ.①商务英语-自学参考资料 Ⅳ.①H31

中国版本图书馆CIP数据核字（2016）第037650号

机械工业出版社（北京市百万庄大街22号 邮政编码100037）
策划编辑：孙铁军 责任编辑：王庆龙
版式设计：张文贵 责任印制：李 洋
三河市国英印务有限公司印刷
2016年6月第1版·第1次印刷
185mm×245mm·15.5印张·416千字
标准书号：ISBN 978-7-111-53061-9
定价：36.80元

丛书序

本丛书由全国知名培训机构——环球卓越联手众多一线辅导名师编写而成。

随着中国经济的发展及全球化趋势的加剧，BEC 考试（剑桥商务英语证书 Business English Certificate）已经成为越来越多职场人士的首选之一。终生有效的 BEC 证书，正像磁石一样吸引着越来越多的人加入到这个队列当中。但是如何在有限的时间里科学规划、理性备考，则是一个困扰众多考生的问题。为解决这些问题，本丛书应运而生！

“英语周计划系列丛书”是机械工业出版社的一个品牌图书，该品牌涵盖了多个考试领域，BEC 是其中之一。本套“4 周攻克 BEC 周计划系列”共 13 本，分别是：《4 周攻克 BEC 词汇 6000 周计划》（初级）、《4 周攻克 BEC 词汇 8000 周计划》（中级）、《4 周攻克 BEC 词汇 10000 周计划》（高级）、《4 周全面突破 BEC 综合备考周计划》（初级）、《4 周全面突破 BEC 综合备考周计划》（中级）、《4 周全面突破 BEC 综合备考周计划》（高级）、《4 周攻克 BEC 听力周计划》（中级）、《4 周攻克 BEC 口语周计划》（中级）、《4 周攻克 BEC 写作周计划》（中级）、《4 周攻克 BEC 阅读周计划》（中级）、《BEC 标准预测试卷 10 +2》（初级）、《BEC 标准预测试卷 10 +2》（中级）、《BEC 标准预测试卷 10 +2》（高级）。可以说，本系列丛书有着鲜明的特色，具体说来有以下六点：

一、4 周合理规划，科学有序备考

每本书均严格按照 4 周布局，依据考试分值比例及重难点程度，科学划分时间，便于考生摒弃盲目和无序，从一开始就是有针对性、有目的、有规划地复习备考。

二、级别分类清晰，高效针对备考

本丛书严格按照 BEC 考试级别，即初级、中级、高级进行划分的，级别清晰，层次分明，便于各个级别的考生能够一目了然地明确自己的考试需求，从而达到直接针对的目的。

三、点面统筹结合，人性服务备考

本丛书既有详细的专项训练（听、说、读、写），又有全面周密的专业词汇书，还有重点、考点集于一体的综合辅导教程，同时还有标准预测试卷。既满足了不同基础考生的不同需求，又将专项训练、综合辅导及模拟实战综合于全套书中，便于考生循序渐进，步步为营。相信本丛书体现的人性服务将助考生一臂之力。

四、讲练配置周密，直接把握备考

本丛书注重讲练结合，在章节讲解完毕后，辅以针对性极强的习题，部分习题就是历年真题的再现。讲练结合的分寸恰到好处，便于考生更好地把握住所学知识，直接备考。

五、真题处处剖析，实战演练备考

本丛书的可贵之处是，合理利用了历年真题的精华之处，并巧妙地让这些真题以不同的方式出现在不同的场合下，让考生随时随地熟悉 BEC 考试，真正达到实战模拟的效果。

六、编写讲求独特，市面独一无二

本丛书的编写讲求实用、周到、全面，并力求科学量化。如词汇，直接将初级、中级、高级的总词汇量合理量化到每周的每天。这样的体贴设置，让考生面对茫茫书海再也不必不知所措，这是市面绝无仅有的一大特色！

最后，衷心祝福所有的考生考试顺利！

环球卓越

2016 年 5 月

前 言

《4周全面突破BEC综合备考周计划》（中级）主要针对报考BEC中级考试的学员。本书涵盖了BEC中级考试的所有题型：阅读、写作、听力、口语。本书共分四周的学习内容，将每个题型根据大纲样题的要求，依照历年真题的难度，深刻剖析命题思路，总结归纳命题规律，为考生备考指引方向，真正实现“知己知彼，百战不殆”。同时本书荟萃了众多英语培训机构特色及各类相关书籍的精华，使考生在增强应试能力的同时提高英语综合运用水平。本书内容丰富全面，包括阅读、写作、听力、口语等各类题型的解题技巧、专项练习和仿真试题，真正做到了“一书在手，全部拥有”。

本书主要有以下几方面特色：

计划明确：把学习内容科学地分为4周，有利于考生有条不紊地安排复习，以“周”计划、“天”安排和“周”总结的形式安排复习内容，既突出了重点，又有针对性及计划性。

内容全面：针对不同题型，分别提供试题精讲、精准模拟和综合训练，环环相扣，稳步提升答题技巧。

解析到位：针对不同题型的命题规律及出题特点，讲解解题思路与备考策略，逐步明确复习重点。

高仿模拟：提供两套完整的模拟试题，完全按照真题体例及出题难度编排，解析精准，巩固备考效果。

总结完整：特设“高频词汇”及“参考译文”等栏目，提高复习效率，全面提升英语水平。

本书在编写过程中，参考了相关的词汇书籍和相关的培训机构网站一些内容，无法一一注明，在此表示感谢！本书虽已经过仔细的编审和校订，但仍恐有疏漏之处，欢迎广大读者批评指正。

祝所有考生都能顺利通过考试！

编 者

导 学

考生须知

本书适用于准备参加剑桥大学考试委员会外语考试部（Cambridge ESOL）商务英语证书中级考试的考生。

考试介绍

商务英语证书（BUSINESS ENGLISH CERTIFICATE）是我国教育部考试中心和英国剑桥大学考试委员会合作，于1993年起举办的考试。BEC共分三个等级：BEC初级（BEC Preliminary Level，缩略为BEC P），BEC中级（BEC Vantage Level，缩略为BEC V），BEC高级（BEC Higher Level，缩略为BEC H）。

该系列考试是一项语言水平考试，根据公务或商务工作的实际需要，从听、说、读、写四个方面对考生在一般工作环境下和商务活动中使用英语的能力进行全面考查，对成绩合格者提供由英国剑桥大学考试委员会颁发的标准统一的成绩证书。该证书由于其颁发机构的权威性，在英国、英联邦各国及欧洲大多数国家的企业和教学机构获得认可，成为确认证书持有者英语能力证明的首选证书，同时也是在所有举办该项考试的国家和地区求职的"通行证"。

剑桥商务英语证书考试（BEC）由中英双方合办。英国剑桥大学考试委员会负责命题、阅卷、颁发证书。中国教育部考试中心负责报名、印制试卷和组织考试。

BEC考试报名无开始时间，即任何时间都可以报名，但有截止时间。报名截止的具体时间以考点公布的时间为准。欲了解各考点的具体报名事宜，可与各考点联系。目前BEC考试在全国共设有63个考点，每个考点也为报名点。报名不受年龄、性别、职业、地区、学历等限制，任何人均可持本人身份证件到当地考点报名。欲了解考试收费标准请咨询当地考点。考生在报名后可得到一本内容包括考试范围、考试题型和样题的《考生手册》，供考生参照复习。

该等级考试每年举行三次，时间为每年五月的第三个周六；每年11月的第三个周六。2011年新增一次考试。上午笔试，下午口试，口试进度慢的，延至第二天。如考试时间有变化，以考点当年公布的为准。考试地点即报名地点，具体考场由各考点张榜公布。

考试答题卡由教育部考试中心海外考试处汇集后寄英国剑桥大学考试委员会评卷。评出成绩后（BEC中级分Pass with Merit、Pass、Level A2、Fail四等），打印成绩通知单（包括不及格的D、E、Fail）和成绩证书，寄至教育部考试中心后寄发各考点向考生颁发，成绩证书终生有效。

报考须知

2015年上半年商务英语考试时间是：3月28日，5月16、23和30日。下半年考试时间是：11月14、21和28日。

考试流程

报名（确认报名）→准考证领取→考试→成绩查询→证书领取。

能力描述

	听力/口语	阅读	写作
能力描述	在日常工作中能记录和传递大部分信息 能够参加日常会议或是就熟悉议题进行讨论，通过提问或回答交流客观信息 能够表达个人意见，在一定范围内参与辩论	能理解订单、投诉、约会、问询等方面的标准信函，并将这些信息传递到相关人员以采取进一步行动 能理解工作报告的大意，如关于建议的报告 在自己工作范围之内能理解指令、程序等	能撰写工作范围内的非日常工作信函及报告；若报告超出其工作范围，则需检查和修改 能起草简单明了的指令、规定等

考试题型

阅读和写作	105 分钟
听力	40 分钟（左右）
口语	14 分钟

考试分两个阶段进行。第一阶段为笔试，包括阅读、写作和听力；第二阶段为口试。考试时间分别为：BEC 中级阅读、写作 105 分钟，听力约 40 分钟（含填写答题卡时间），口试 14 分钟。

阅读测试：BEC 中级阅读试题总共分为五部分，共有 45 道题。题型为多选项搭配题（两部分）、多选项选择题（两部分）和错误辨认题（一个部分）。考试时间为 60 分钟。第一部分是搭配题，包括七个问题和四篇短文，或将一篇较长的文章分为四节。第二、三、四和五部分分别是句子填空题、阅读理解题、完形填空题和改错题。在这四个部分中各有一篇较长的文章，均摘选自报纸、商业杂志、商务信件、图书、广告页及商业手册等，都与日常工作相关，用以测试各种阅读能力和技能。

写作测试：这部分试题要求考生写两篇作文。第一篇：给公司内部的一位或数位同事写一个便条、留言、备忘或电子邮件。第二篇：给公司以外的某个人写一封商务函件、一份简短的报告或者一项建议。

第一篇要求考生写 40 ~ 50 个单词。第二篇要求考生写 120 ~ 140 个单词。按照任务的完成情况、词汇量大小和用词的准确性、语法结构、组织、内容和语域与格式是否适当进行评分。

听力测试：这部分试题由三部分共 30 个问题组成。采取的形式为完形填空题、多项选择题和进一步的多项选择题。第一部分有三段简短的谈话。第二部分包括 10 段很短的摘录。第三部分为一篇较长的文字。体裁取自各种不同来源的听力录音，包括访谈、打电话、面对面的交谈和纪录片。内容与商务相关，用以测试听力技巧和技能。

口语测试：共三个部分，形式为面试，涉及商务话题的简短谈话和讨论。考生两人一组，有两位考官，一位提问，一位评分。评分的考官（assessor）按以下四个标准评分：语法和词汇、谈话组织、发音、互动式交流。提问的考官（interlocutor）对整个测试给出总分。

评分标准

BEC 的分数由听、说、读、写四部分组成，各占总分的 25%，只要求总分及格。通过成绩（Passing Grades）有 2 个：优秀（Pass with Merit）和通过（Pass）；未通过成绩（Failing Grades）有 2 个：Level A2 和不及格（Fail）。

通过标准：

Passing Grades:

Pass with Merit	80% and above
Pass	65% to 79%

Failing Grades:

Level A2	45% to 64%
Fail	44% and below

BEC 中级试卷的 4 个部分总分为 120 分，每项各为 30 分。考生的总体级别以四部分所得的总分为基础，并不需要所有四个部分都达到令人满意的水平才能通过考试。每位考生都会得到一份测试成绩报告单，报告单上对他们在每部分的成绩给以评述，根据优秀、良好、合格、薄弱等标准来划分，表明考生在每个部分的相对成绩。

目　录

第一周

阅读部分

本周展望

在BEC考试中，阅读首当其冲，并占了考试总分的四分之一的分数。要在一个小时的时间里出色地完成五个部分，首先要对题型的特点有较为充分翔实的认识。BEC考试由英国剑桥大学考试委员会和中国教育部考试中心联合举办，英国人出题一向以严谨著称，语法、词汇、句子结构、上下文逻辑等都甚为严密，针对这一民族性的特征，我们可以对症下药，抓住主要思路和方法，尽可能发挥自己的最佳水平。

BEC属于英国剑桥大学考试委员会推出的商务英语考试。其阅读部分的风格正如雅思等一系列“剑桥出品”：题型丰富，技巧性强。BEC中级部分共有五种题型，分别是搭配题、填句子、阅读理解、完形填空和改错。从能力要求上看，前三类题型考查的都是考生快速阅读及寻找与之匹配的关键点的能力，而后两类题型则是考查考生的语法运用能力。每部分都有不同的技巧，考生通过反复练习，即可熟悉并掌握这些技巧。

我们将对每个题型用一周的时间进行逐个深入分析和讲解，着重带领考生探索并归纳BEC中级阅读试题的审题方法、做题步骤以及规律等，就大部分应试者在考试中普遍感到困难且不易拿分的几部分给出一些关键分析和解题技巧。通过经典样题分析和模拟练习的集中训练，适当补充一些常用词汇、句型的分析，相信可以帮助考生用短短一周的时间掌握BEC中级阅读技巧的高效途径，建立起更广泛的知识网络，增强取胜的信心。进而使考生借助这一跳板，取得BEC考试最终成功。

周一　搭配题的一个中心、两个基本点

一、题型分析

（一）命题规律

BEC 阅读中级第一部分由 7 个问题和 4 个段落组成。即给出 7 个句子，要求找到每句话对应的段落。其中的 4 个段落可以是一篇较长文章中选出的 4 个相关段落，也可以是相关主题的 4 篇短文章。并且此题所涉及的文章大部分是商业环境中的文章，例如产品广告、招聘广告等。

题目特点：在此题中，所给的 7 个句子一般比较简单，容易理解。4 个段落则相对于 7 个问题要难一些。一般来说，句子中会有明显的同义词转换，可以和段落匹配。比较难的题目不容易发现匹配，而要通过理解句义来思考哪段会讲这个问题，以此来选择答案。

题目的难度属中等。第一部分主要更侧重于对具体的信息或具体的细节的辨认，很少涉及或考到主旨部分。

（二）解题技巧

1. 先看文，再看题。在真正考试时，拿到阅读部分第一题—搭配题时，考生应该先阅读全文，然后再回头阅读所给的选项。
2. 先抓中心，后找要点。“抓住每段的中心，结合逻辑和匹配两个关键点”。也就是说，先快速浏览原文，掌握每段的中心思想，并且在阅读的过程中划出四个段落的关键语句。在阅读时要保留一个短期记忆，带着这个记忆阅读 7 句话。一般来说，句子中会有明显的同义词转换，可以和原文匹配。比较难的题目不容易发现匹配，而要通过理解句义，来思考哪段会讲这个问题，以此来选择答案。常用技巧即看逻辑关系。简单来说，也就是顺接和转折，和找到的答案是否吻合。
3. 单词相同要慎重，单词相似很可能。主要说的是考生在最后选择时，如果选项中的某些关键词与原文段落中的词相同，选择往往是错误的。而如果两个词意思相似，那么答案正确的可能性比较大。
4. 带回原文验对错。考生在选择完答案后，应代入原文中验证答案的对错。

（三）考试准备

该部分阅读要求考生平时多积累一些商务环境下的文章，如职位描述、展望或发展史等。多做有关这方面的针对练习，注重总结归纳，增加熟练度和敏感度，为 BEC 中级阅读考试这部分打下良好的基础。

二、典型样题

Questions 1-7

- Look at the statements below and the article about the development of future business leaders on the opposite page.

- Which section of the article (**A**, **B**, **C** or **D**) does each statement (**1-7**) refer to?
- For each statement (**1-7**), mark one letter (**A**, **B**, **C** or **D**) on your Answer Sheet.
- You will need to use some of these letters more than once.

Example:

0 Take notice of your boss's life away from work.

0	A	B	C	D
	▬	▭	▭	▭

1 Managers need to take action to convince high-flyers of their value to the firm.

2 Organizations need to look beyond the high-flyers they are currently developing.

3 There is a concern that firms investing in training for high-flyers may not gain the benefits themselves.

4 Managers need expert assistance from within their own firms in developing high-flyers.

5 Firms currently identify high-flyers without the support of a guidance strategy.

6 Managers are frequently too busy to deal with the development of high-flyers.

7 Firms who work hard on their reputation as an employer will interest high-flyers.

The Stars of the Future

A Existing management research does not tell us much about how to find and develop high-flyers, those people who have the potential to reach the top of an organization. As a result, organizations are left to formulate their own systems. A more effective overall policy for developing future leaders is needed, which is why the London Business School has launched the Tomorrow's Leaders Research Group (TLRG). The group contains representatives from 20 firms, and they meet regularly to discuss the leadership and development of the organizations' high-flyers.

B TLRG recognizes just how significant line managers are in the process of leadership development. Unfortunately, with today's flat organizations, where managers have functional as well as managerial responsibilities, people development all too often falls victim to heavy workloads. One manager in the research group was unconvinced by the logic of sending his best people away on development courses, "only to see them poached by another department or, worse still, another firm". This fear of losing high-flyers runs deep in the organizations that make up the research group.

C TLRG argues that the task of management is not necessarily about employee retention, but about creating "attraction centers". "We must help line managers to realize that if their companies are known as ones that develop their people, they will have a greater appeal to high-flyers," said one advisor. Furthermore, selecting people for, say, a leadership development program is a sign of commitment from management to an individual. Loyalty can then be more easily demanded in return.

D TLRG has concluded that a company's HR specialists need to take action and engage with line managers individually about their role in the development of high-flyers. Indeed, in order to benefit fully from training high-flyers as the senior managers of the future, firms must actually address the development of all managers who will be supporting the high-flyers. Without this, managers will not be in a position to give appropriate advice. And when eventually the high-flyers do move on, new ones will be needed to replace them. The next challenge will be to find a new generation of high-flyers.

答案解析

▶ **文章大意**

全文探讨的是公司未来接班人，也就是潜力股的培养问题。整篇文章分为四个部分，层层递进，有很强的逻辑性。

A段主要阐述了TLRG这个贯穿全文的研究组织诞生的原因，即现行的研究满足不了需要，于是大多数公司只能自己探索发掘接班人的模式。

B段强调了直属经理对于发掘接班人须从基层抓起的重要性，以及经理们的一些疑虑。

C段讲述的是对公司来说，接班人问题非常重要，院线经理们也应该了解并关注这一点。

D段是针对前面列出的问题，提出相应的解决方法或建议，例如专家协助等。

1 C。第一题的意思是“经理们必须采取措施，使潜力股们相信他们对公司的价值”，也就是C段原文中所说的creating“attraction centers” 和loyalty，即要让潜力股们对公司忠诚。

2 D。第二题的意思是“组织必须把目光投向正在培养中的潜力股以外的地方”，对应的是D段最后两句话：“And when eventually the high-flyers do move on, new ones will be needed to replace them. The next challenge will be to find a new generation of high-flyers.”也就是寻找新一代的潜力股。

3 B。第三题的意思是“担心培养潜力股的投入收不回成本”。与B段的最后一句话如出一辙：“This fear of losing high-flyers runs deep in the organizations that make up the research group.”其中，runs deep in是“积怨甚深于……”的意思。

4 D。第四题讲的是“对于开发潜力股这一问题，经理们需要在公司内部得到专家支持”。与之对应的是原文D段的第一句话：公司的人力资源专家需要采取行动。其中，HR specialists就是expert。

5 A。第五题讲的是“公司目前是在没有指导策略的支持下辨别潜力股”。与之对应的是A段的第一句Existing management research does not tell us much about how to find and develop high-flyers，其中，“Existing management ... find and develop high-flyers”被currently identify high-flyers所替换。

6 B。第六题讲的是“经理们太忙以至于无暇顾及潜力股的发展”。B段中提到heavy workloads，即高负荷量的工作，可以理解为too busy。所以答案是B段的：Unfortunately, with today's flat organizations, where managers have functional as well as managerial responsibilities, people development all too often falls victim to heavy workloads.

7 C。第七题讲的是“公司好的雇主形象可以吸引潜力股”。与之对应的是C段中的if their companies are known as ones that develop their people, they will have a greater appeal to high-flyers。如果公司是以开发员工而著称的话，将会对潜力股有更大的吸引。在问题中，以interest代替了原文C段中的短语have a greater appeal to。

词汇点津

line manager	直属经理
flat organization	扁平化的组织
poach	*vt.* 剽窃，挖角
run deep	根深蒂固
fall victim to	成为……的受害者
retention	*n.* 保留（在文中指留住员工。是风险管理中常见的专业名词。）

三、实战演练

Questions 1-7

Look at the statements below and the article about the development of future business leaders on the opposite page.

- Which section of the article (**A**, **B**, **C** or **D**) does each statement (**1-7**) refer to?
- For each statement (**1-7**), mark one letter (**A**, **B**, **C** or **D**) on your Answer Sheet.
- You will need to use some of these letters more than once.

1 Business card has its own complicated characteristic.
2 The westerners pay more attention to the practical function of the business card.
3 The proper use of the business card can be a representation of high status in the past.
4 The materials of the business cards differ according to their owner.
5 The function of the business card is very simple in business in ancient time.
6 Exquisite business card indicates the owner's ability to do what he wants to.
7 A business card may be not necessary for a head of a department.

A Little Big Card

A Business cards used to be an indispensable attribute of the etiquette and the rules of their use were as sophisticated as those of cutlery. At that time business cards belonged to the notions of such consequence like title, rank, land, horses, etc. First businessmen used their cards as marks of distinction and thus introduced the first modifications in their design. Later, as the growing demand for the cards boosted the development of the printing industry, more and more sophisticated card design patterns appeared.

B For business card design in the modern, with its developed professional conventions, one can still detect the two conflicting approaches, the fanciful and the functional one. The purpose of the first approach is to show that there is nothing impossible for the card's owner. The more striking by its design and materials and the more sophisticated in its manufacturing technology, the card will be the better. What matters is the card's uniqueness. The content of the card does not matter much either.

C The other approach, on the contrary, emphasizes functionality. It is the one that rules in the pragmatic West. And the English name of the item — "business card" —also focuses on its specific functionality. These cards are essential for those company workers that interact with clients. That is why, on the one hand, you can see a small clerk, a service engineer or even a heaver with his own business card and a head of the department without such if he or she does not interact with clients.

D Business cards used to be made exclusively of stiff paper (card), but today come in materials from plastics to thin metals and even glass! A name or business card reflects the owner — it should represent visually the company or the person passing it. Take the time to have a closer look at your own cards and decide if they really suit you and your company.

答案解析

▶ 文章大意

全文主要是讲名片（**business cards**）的两大相互矛盾的特点，即装饰性与功能性。其中开头还涉及部分名片的历史由来，结尾部分也提到制作名片所需要的材料等。内容比较贴近生活，比较容易理解。

A 段主要讲的是过去名片是礼节上一个不可缺少的组成部分，而且它们的使用规则像餐具的使用规则那样复杂。在那个时候，名片犹如头衔、等级、土地、马匹等一样重要。

B段说的是在现代名片设计中，随着其职业习惯的发展，人们仍然可以察觉到互相矛盾的两个方面：装饰性与功能性。并简单介绍了名片的装饰性特点。

C段则说的是其另一个方面恰恰相反，强调功能性。注重实效的西方崇尚这一点。小职员可能拥有自己的名片，而大老板却没有名片。

D段主要讲了制作名片的材料的发展，及不同的材质的名片反映主人或所属公司的风格特征。

1 B。第一题意为“名片本身就具有其复杂的特点”。与之相对应的是B段中的第一句“... one can still detect the two conflicting approaches, the fanciful and the functional one.”其中，“two conflicting approaches”与“its own complicated characteristics”意思基本一致。所以答案为B。

2 C。第二题可译为“西方人更注重名片的实际功能”。与此题相关的是C段中的第二句：“It is the one that rules in the pragmatic West.”在此句中，one是代替上文中提到的functionality，它与pragmatic共同和问题中的practical function相对应。而在问题中，原文中的动词“rule”被转换为词组“pay more attention to”。in the pragmatic West与the westerners相对应。所以答案是C。

3 A。第三题的意思是“在古代能够合理地使用名片是地位高的象征”。与之相对应的是A段中的一句话“At that time business cards belonged to the notions of such consequence like title, rank, land, horses, etc.”其中，high status与原文中的title和rank相对应。在问题中只是把具体的概念抽象化。所以答案为A。

4 D。第四题说的是“制作名片的材料是根据不同主人而选定的”。与之对应的是D段中的第一句和第二句。第一句中提到的“materials from plastics to thin metals and even glass”以及第二句中的“a name or business card reflects the owner”与问题中的The materials和differ according to their owners相照应。所以答案为D。

5 A。第五题的意思是“最初的时候，名片的功能是相对单一的”。与之对应的是A段中的“First businessmen used their cards as marks of distinction and thus introduced the first modifications in their design.”，也就是说，第一批商人主要是用名片来区别彼此，所以说功能比较单一。答案为A。

6 B。第六题的意思是“精湛的名片暗示着它的主人可以做他想做的一切”。与之相关联的是B段的“The purpose of the first approach is to show that there is nothing impossible for the card's owner”这句话。此句中的the first approach指的是fanciful approach。而且nothing impossible for the card's owner的意思也就是the owner's ability to do what he wants to。所以答案为B。

7 C。第七题的意思是“部门经理也可能没有持有名片的必要”。与之相对应的是C段中的最后一句“a head of the department without such if he or she does not interact with clients”。所以答案是C。

周二　三遍攻克句子填空题

一、题型分析

（一）命题规律

BEC 中级阅读试题的第二部分为句子填空题。主要是由留有可填写一句话的空的一篇字数为 450 ~ 580 的正文加上 7 个选项句子所组成的。所选的文章大部分是商业类报刊文章或报告中的文章，经出题者根据考试要求略微修改即可。

题目特点：出题者在这一部分给出的是一篇有 6 个空的文章和 7 个选项，可是由于第一个空格一般都是作为 example 给出，其答案为 G，所以实际上考生只需填 5 个空，即只需 6 选 5。通过联系前后文，主要根据语义和逻辑两方面填写最相关联的句子，选出适合的选项。

题目难度较大。第二部分主要侧重考查考生把握文章段落大意和文章框架的能力，以及如何以语篇逻辑关系为准则，准确地对篇章进行组织衔接的能力。

（二）解题技巧

1. 第一遍带例子快读全文。考生应该把题目所给的例子放入原文中，然后通读全文。
2. 第二遍两个兼顾找位置。这部分的解题思路是两个兼顾——“前后兼顾，语义结构兼顾”。具体地说就是，先浏览一遍全文，掌握文章大意。再掌握空格前后的句子的大意，然后看前后文的结构关系。结构主要看两方面，即顺接还是逆接。如果是顺接，就要进一步看句子是并列结构、前因后果、推理还是递进等等；如果是逆接，看是否有显性的标志词，如 however 等，如果是隐性逆接，那么就要考查逻辑上的合理性。如果最后还是有不确定的选项，建议考生将其分别代入空内，逐一排除，最后得出正确选项。
3. 第三遍代句子试错。也就是把所选择的句子代入原文中，看语义结构是否顺畅。但切记要速战速决，不可浪费过多的时间。

（三）考试准备

由于本部分中的文章大部分是摘自商业类报刊文章或报告，然后经过出题者根据考试要求稍加改动而成的，所以考生应在正式参加考试前多关注这类书籍或报刊，特别是对某领域的成功的介绍，在商业领域中某一现象的重要性，或某一商业概念的简介以及其他商业领域的一些重要问题，以便为正式的考试打下良好的基础，迈出成功的第一步。

二、典型样题

Questions 8-12

- Read the extract below from an article about the coffee industry.
- Choose the best sentence from the list on the opposite page to fill each of the gaps.

- For each gap **8-12**, mark one letter (**A-G**) on your Answer Sheet.
- Do not use any letter more than once.
- There is an example at the beginning (0).

0	A	B	C	D	E	F	G
	▭	▭	▭	▭	▭	▭	▬

Finding the Right People

When a small company grows, managers must take on many new roles. Besides the day-to-day running of the business, they find themselves responsible for, among other things, relations with outside investors, increased levels of cashflow and, hardest of all, recruitment.

For most managers of small and medium-sized enterprises, the job of searching for, interviewing and selecting staff is difficult and time-consuming.

(**0**) ___G___. Interviewing, for example, is a highly skilled activity in itself.

"We have found the whole process very hard," says Dan Baker, founding partner of a PR company. "In seven years we have grown from five to eighteen staff, but we have not found it easy to locate and recruit the right people." (**8**) ________. As Dan Baker explains, "We went to one for our first recruitment drive, but they took a lot of money in advance and didn't put forward anybody suitable. In the end we had to do it ourselves."

Most recruitment decisions are based on a pile of CVs, a couple of short interviews and two cautious references. David Rowe, a business psychologist, studied how appointments were made in five small companies. He claims that selection was rarely based on clear criteria. (**9**) ________. This kind of approach to recruitment often has unhappy consequences for both employers and new recruits.

Small companies often know what kind of person they are looking for. (**10**) ________. According to David Rowe, this means that small company managers themselves have to devote more time and energy to recruitment. It shouldn't be something that is left to the evenings or weekends.

Many companies start the recruitment process with over-optimistic ideas about the type of person that will fit into their team. "It's very easy to say you must have the best people in the top positions," says Alex Jones, managing partner of an executive recruitment company. "But someone who is excellent in one company may not do so well in another environment. (**11**) ________. You can never guarantee a successful transfer of skills."

Whatever the candidate's qualifications, their personal qualities are just as important since they will have to integrate with existing members of staff. This is where, the recruitment industry argues, they can really help.

According to Alex Jones, "A good recruitment agency will visit your company and ask a lot of questions. (**12**) ________. They can ask applicants all sorts of questions you don't like to ask and present you with a shortlist of people who not only have the skills, but who are likely to fit in with your company's way of doing things."

A Finance director in a big company, for example, will often make a terrible small company finance director because he or she is used to having a team doing the day-to-day jobs.

B More often than not, the people making the choice prioritised different qualities in candidates or relied on guesswork.

C Recruitment would seem an obvious task to outsource, but the company's experience of recruitment agencies was not encouraging.

D They need paying for that, of course, but you will have them working for you and not for the candidate.

E They are usually in very specific markets and the problem they face is that recruitment agencies may not really understand the sector.

F This means that companies cannot spend more than the standard ten minutes interviewing each applicant.

G Yet few are trained and competent for all aspects of the task.

答案解析

▶ 文章大意

这篇文章主要是讲规模小的公司在刚刚起步的发展阶段找到合适的人才是有一定难度的，但同时又非常重要。身兼数职的小公司的经理们为找不到合适的人选而发愁。文章还介绍了寻找合适的人选时不应该过度寄希望于招聘机构和中介公司等，以及一些在找人时所需要注意的问题，例如在大公司表现很优秀的员工并不一定会在规模小的公司有所作为。

A 项的意思是“比如说一个大公司的财务总监在小公司往往表现得很糟糕，因为他或她早已习惯有一个团队来进行日常的工作”。

B 项的意思是“通常决策人会将候选人身上的不同素质按优先顺序排列，或者就仅仅依赖于猜测”。

C 项的意思是“招聘这件事似乎应该完全是外包办理的任务，但是这个公司与招聘机构打交道的经历并不怎么愉快”。

D 项的意思是“当然小公司需要付给招聘公司一定的费用，但是小公司是想让招聘公司为他们而不是为候选人服务”。

E 项的意思是“那些小公司通常处在某一特定的市场上，他们面对的难题是，招聘机构并不真正了解这一行业”。

F 项的意思是“这也就意味着这些公司不可能花比标准的 10 分钟一个面试者还多的时间来面试”。

G 项的意思是“但是很少人培训过并且还能够胜任各种任务”。

8 C。第八题所给空的前一句说“规模小的公司招到合适的人是非常困难的”，后一句中提到 Dan Baker 说他们曾经求助于招聘机构，但是花费了金钱和人力却没有能为公司找到合适的人。所以根据前后文可以看出，小的公司是想找合适的人选，所以找到了招聘机构，但结果并不太理想。从语义的角度看，所给的空处的句子应该是关于招聘或招聘机构的。而且从结构来看，后一句中出现的“but”是明显的逆接中的转折。所以说所选的句子应该带有否定的意思。C 项既提到了招聘，也提到了招聘机构，而且后半句的 not encouraging 对结果进行了否定，所以正确答案为 C。

9 B。此题所在的段落主要是说：招聘人才时，没有相对好的标准和依据，结果也就不够理想。第九题空的前一句就是说这部分的选择没有明确的标准，空的后一句是讲这种面试方法只能导致 unhappy consequences for both employers and new recruits。由此可推测第九空的内容可能是这种不科学的招聘方法的进一步或具体阐述，而且是为后面 unhappy consequences 做铺垫，所以也应是否定的。B 选项符合这一条件：通常决策人会将候选人身上的不同素质按优先顺序排列，或者就仅仅依赖于猜测。

10 E。此题的前一句说“Small companies often know what kind of person they are looking for”，后面一句主要说这意味着小公司自己要多花时间和精力在招人上。这里的 this means 的指示代词 this 值得注意，由此可以推断出第十题的空涉及的是导致公司不得不付出更多的不利条件。所以说正确答案为 E 选项：那些小公司通常处在某一特定的市场上，他们面对的难题是招聘机构并不真正了解这一行业。

11 A。此题所在的这段主要是讲所招聘的人是否真正适合公司。第 11 题空的前一句说的是在一家公司表现优秀的职工并不一定能在另一个环境里干的好，空的后一句“You can never guarantee a successful transfer of skills”是对前一观点的进一步说明。由此可以推测第 11 题的内容就是与此相关的。从结构上看，前后句没有转折关系。根据以上分析，正确答案为 A 选项：比如说一个大公司的财务总监在小公司往往表现得很糟糕，因为他或她早已习惯有一个团队来进行日常的工作。

12 D。最后一段都是和招聘机构相关的内容。第 12 题空的前一句“A good recruitment agency will visit your company and ask a lot of questions.”说的是招聘机构如何上门服务。这一空的后一句具体讲招聘机构是通过何种方式帮助招人的。由此可以推断出第 12 题空所填的内容也是有关招聘机构的招聘的。选项 D 中，They need paying for that 的指示代词 that 指代前面的上门服务，而且 D 项的后半句也呼应了空后面的句子，所以说正确答案是 D。

词汇点津

finance director	财务总监
outsource	*vt.* 把……外包 *vi.* 外包
outsource world	外包世界
outsource income	代购代销收入
outsource services	外包服务
more often than not	通常

三、实战演练

Questions 8-12

- Read the extract below from an article about Bankers' Bonuses.
- Choose the best sentence from the list on the opposite page to fill each of the gaps.
- For each gap **8-12**, mark one letter (**A-G**) on your Answer Sheet.
- Do not use any letter more than once.
- There is an example at the beginning (0).

0	A	B	C	D	E	F	G
	▭	▭	▭	▭	▭	▭	▬

Bankers' Bonuses

Lord Myners, the City minister, is allegedly worth £30m ($47m). He is an unlikely tribune of the people. (**0**) ___G___. Derivatives traders are not footballers with unique talents and "should not be paid as though they are", he said last month. More recently he has railed against "market failure"; accusing big clients of investment banks of not challenging the fees and margins they are charged. (**8**) ________. Lack of transparency makes them seem the more villainous. "The nation is angry about this. I'm angry," says Lord Myners.

(**9**) ________. "We are not an incomes regulator," says Hector Sants, chief executive of the Financial Services Authority (FSA). The watchdog's only sanction is to demand more regulatory capital from those banks whose pay policies appear to be putting their firms at greater risk.

The Treasury could influence matters at RBS and Lloyds Banking Group, two big banks in which it has substantial shareholdings, but is reluctant to micromanage. (**10**) ________. The government worries that any attack on bankers'pay could drive financiers offshore, depriving the exchequer of much revenue. City bonuses, which dropped from £ 10 billion in 2007 to £ 4 billion in 2008, could bounce back to £ 6 billion this year, says the Centre for Economic and Business Research (CEBR), a consultancy.

They mirror the health of a financial-services sector that in the good times brought in up to £ 67 billion in annual tax revenues, estimates PwC, an accounting firm. This fiscal year the figure could drop to £ 39 billion, says Douglas McWilliams at the CEBR, although banks' recently buoyant business may increase it. (**11**) ________. So could the slightly softer option of preventing banks from offsetting past losses against future tax bills.

The reluctance to bash bankers' bonuses stems from recognition that wholesale finance is a global business. Bankers are highly mobile, says Marcus Agius, chairman of Barclays. He argues that banks in Britain must be free to pay as much as those elsewhere, but says he is "agnostic" about what that level should be. National and international proposals to reform pay at regulated financial firms are similarly agnostic. They mostly do not spell out how much public disclosure there should be of big pay packages, other than those for board members. (**12**) ________. It requires a detailed breakdown of the remuneration of "employees whose actions have a material impact on the risk exposure of the firm". Yet that measure is unlikely to be implemented, even though the big British banks and the London-based operations of global investment banks have agreed to it.

The FSA, for its part, is not bothered about public disclosure as long as it has the information itself. Sir David Walker, a former central banker charged with an official review of bank-governance practices, has suggested that bands of remuneration for heavy hitters outside the boardroom be disclosed. It seems that banks, in the absence of much more than appeals to their better nature, will be setting their own benchmarks as and when they please. Barclays began a review of its remuneration policies in 2008. It remains unfinished.

A But such attempts at moral persuasion are not working, and those in authority seem reluctant to do more.

B A windfall tax on profits, discussed by both government and opposition, might put any recovery at risk.

C The opportunity to take an equity position at a bargain price has been missed.

D The crisis does not seem to have affected the way bankers are rewarded.

E An exception is the communiqué from the Group of 20 (G20) big countries in September.

F There was not a murmur when RBS hired a head trader for a rumoured £7m in total.

G Yet he has been sounding off, more vociferously than his colleagues, about "unacceptable" pay deals for bankers.

答案解析

▶ **文章大意**

这篇文章是关于银行家的津贴的发放问题。文中介绍了银行家们的薪金都是不透明的。无论经济发展是进步还是危机，银行家们的薪金都不会受其影响。文中通过几个例子，来阐述了这一不公平的社会现象。

A 项的意思是“但是尝试着用道德伦理去劝说是一点作用也没有的，而且当权者似乎不情愿做出更多的努力”。

B 项的意思是“执政党和在野党讨论的对既得利润征收暴税可能对复苏存在风险”。

C 项的意思是“在这场价格战中，取得公平位置的机会已经失去”。

D 项的意思是“这次危机似乎并没有影响到银行家们的收入方式。”

E 项的意思是“一个例外是九月份 G20 的集体公告”。

F 项的意思是“当苏格兰皇家银行以 700 万欧元雇用了一名首席交易员时，表面没有丝毫异议”。

G 项的意思是“然而他却直言不讳，而且在关于银行家“难以接受”的收入上比他的同僚们表现得更强烈”。

8 D。在这一题中，根据原文的后一句中的“Lack of transparency makes them seem the more villainous”，不透明让他们显得尤其邪恶，这里的“他们”指的是银行家们。关键词则是 more villainous，“更加邪恶”表明前一句很可能也是消极方面的描述。所以与之相符的应该是选项 D: The crisis does not seem to have affected the way bankers are rewarded. 这次的危机威胁到了大部分人，却对银行家的收入没产生任何影响。可见，其不公平性很明显地存在着。所以，正确答案是 D。

9 A。此题空格所在的位置是本段的句首，所以应该对其逻辑性进行考查，看关键的连接词是顺接还是逆接。根据上下文的意思，上文说了很多不公平的待遇使他们显得邪恶，而后面却说“我们需要这样的人”，前后是转折关系。而在所给的句子中，恰巧“But such attempts at moral suasion are not working, and those in authority seem reluctant to do more”中的 but 明确指出转折关系，且代入到原文中符合原文，所以正确的答案是 A。

10 F。在解答此题时关键是考查考生对信息的敏感度和细致度。这一空的前一句的前半句，The Treasury could influence matters at RBS and Lloyds Banking Group 中明确涉及了 RBS（苏格兰皇家银行）。而在所给的句子中，只有 There was not a murmur when RBS hired a head trader for a rumoured £ 7m in total 涉及了关键词 RBS。所以说 F 是正确答案，很符合原文的逻辑性。

11 B。联系上下文，后一句“So could the slightly softer option of preventing banks from offsetting past losses against future tax bills”表明，前面句子中所提到的某一现象可以阻止银行用未来的税单抵消以往亏损的这种很容易套利的行为。所以，把剩下的选项代入，可以看出 B 选项很适合。因此 B 选项是正确答案。

12 E。前一句指出“They mostly do not spell out how much public disclosure there should be of big pay packages, other than those for board members”，他们基本上不向公众披露其不计其数的薪酬数量，除了那些国外的成员。而后一句却说：It requires a detailed breakdown of the remuneration of “employees whose actions have a material impact on the risk exposure of the firm”，要求“为可能会对公司产生重大影响的雇员”提供一个薪酬细目。很明显此空是对前面不披露薪酬具体数目的否定。所以选项 E 中的关键词 An exception，即“一个例外”符合以上的分析，故是正确答案。

周三　两手抓、两手都要硬，挑战阅读理解题

一、题型分析

（一）命题规律

BEC 中级阅读试题的第三部分由 1 篇文章和 6 个选择题组成。并且这 6 道题目都是 4 选 1 的单项选择题。出题者所选文章的字数一般在 450 到 550 之间。文章的选材一般是涉及商务领域的书籍，如国际贸易实务、商务营销等，或者文案，如某个职位的企划案，或者是管理类的话题，如经营管理。另外，出题者有可能会根据出题要求修改原文。

题目的主要特点：所给出的文章一般附有标题，而 6 个选择题则是我们熟悉的和高考等重要考试都很相似的阅读理解的单项选择题。所以说这一题型对考生来说并不陌生。

题目的难度较大，从透彻理解文章大意及文中细节两方面的能力进行全面的考查。需要考生在正确的方法指导下，进行反复的练习，养成中心和细节两手抓的好习惯。加上合理的推理或猜测，对考生这一部分的提高有良好的辅助作用。

（二）解题技巧

1. 中心和关键点两手抓。这就要求考生在答题时，首先要理解全文的中心意思，并且抓住文中的关键点。
2. 推断和猜测并用。虽然说这一部分是考生们再熟悉不过的测试题中常见的阅读理解题，但是值得注意的是，出题者所出的选项已经不再着重考查对文中事实的对错的判断，而是侧重对文中观点的考查，更多地涉及在原文基础上的合理推理及猜测。

（三）考试准备

考生还应注意平时积累学习，多阅读一些有关商务领域热门话题的报刊、书籍等。结合本书所介绍的方法，及自身的学习特点，总结出自己的经验方法，为正式的 BEC 考试打下良好的基础。

二、典型样题

Questions 13-18

- Read the following article about Department Store Magic, and the questions on the opposite page.
- For each question（**13-18**），mark one letter（**A**，**B**，**C** or **D**）on your Answer Sheet.

Department Store Magic

For most of the 20th century Smithson's was one of Britain's most successful department stores, but by the mid-1990s, it had become dull. Still profitable, thanks largely to a series of successful advertising campaigns, but decidedly boring. The famous were careful not to be seen there, and its sales staff didn't seem to have changed since the store opened in 1908. Worst of all, its customers were buying fewer and fewer of its own-brand products, the major part of its business, and showing a preference for more fashionable brands.

But now all this has changed, thanks to Rowena Baker, who became Smithson's first woman Chief Executive three years ago. Since then, while most major retailers in Britain have been losing money, Smithson's profits have been rising steadily. When Baker started, a lot of improvements had just been made to the building, without having any effect on sales, and she took the bold decision to invite one of Europe's most exciting interior designers to develop the fashion area, the heart of the store. This very quickly led to rising sales, even before the goods on display were changed. And as sales grew, so did profits.

Baker had ambitious plans for the store from the start. "We're playing a big game, to prove we're up there with the leaders in our sector, and we have to make sure people get that message. Smithson's had fallen behind the competition. It provided a traditional service targeted at middle-aged, middle-income customers, who'd been shopping there for years, and the customer base was gradually contracting. Our idea is to sell such an exciting variety of goods that everyone will want to come in, whether they plan to spend a little or a lot." Baker's vision for the store is clear, but achieving it is far from simple. At first, many employees resisted her improvements because they just wouldn't be persuaded that there was anything wrong with the way they'd always done things, even if they accepted that the store had to overtake its competitors. It took many long meetings, involving the entire workforce, to win their support. It helped when they realized that Baker was a very different kind of manager from the ones they had known.

Baker's staff policies contained more surprises. The uniform that had hardly changed since day one has now disappeared. Moreover, teenagers now get young shop assistants, and staffs in the sports departments are themselves sports fans in trainers. As Baker explains, "How can you sell jeans if you're wearing a black suit? Smithson's has a new identity, and this needs to be made clear to the customers." She's also given every sales assistant responsibility for ensuring customer satisfaction, even if it means occasionally breaking company rules in the hope that this will help company profits.

Rowena Baker is proving successful, but the City's big investors haven't been persuaded. According to retail analyst, John Matthews, "Money had already been invested in refurbishment of the store and in fact that led to the boost in sales. She took the credit, but hadn't done anything to achieve it. And in my view the company's shareholders are not convinced. The fact is that unless she opens several more stores pretty soon, Smithson's profits will start to fall because turnover at the existing store will inevitably start to decline."

13 According to the writer, in the mid-1990s Smithson's department store ________.

A was making a loss

B had a problem keeping staff

C was unhappy with its advertising agency

D mostly sold goods under the Smithson's name

14 According to the writer, Smithson's profits started rising three years ago because of ________.

A an improvement in the retailing sector

B the previous work done on the store

C Rowena Baker's choice of designer

D a change in the products on sale

15 According to Rowena Baker, one problem which Smithson's faced when she joined was that ________.

A the number of people using the store was falling slowly
B its competitors offered a more specialized range of products
C the store's prices were set at the wrong level
D customers were unhappy with the service provided

16 According to the writer, many staff opposed Baker's plans because ________.

A they were unwilling to change their way of working
B they disagreed with her goals for the store
C they felt they were not consulted enough about the changes
D they were unhappy with her style of management

17 Baker has changed staff policies because she believes that ________.

A the corporate image can be improved through staff uniforms
B the previous rules were not fair to customers
C customers should be able to identify with the staff serving them
D employees should share in company profits

18 What problem does John Matthews think Smithson's is facing?

A More money needs to be invested in the present store.
B The company's profits will only continue to rise if it expands.
C The refurbishment of the store is proving unpopular with customers.
D Smithson's shareholders expect a quick return on their investments.

答案解析

▶ 文章大意

这篇文章主要讲的是英国的 Smithson 百货公司在三年前上任的第一个女首席执行官 Rowena Baker 的领导下是如何摆脱困境的。

13 D。本题问的是在 20 世纪 90 年代中期 Smithson 百货公司是怎么样一个情况。A 选项说的是公司正在亏损。第一段中虽然提到顾客越来越少地购买本品牌的商品而更加偏爱时尚品牌，但是却没有明确说明公司已经开始亏损了，所以选项 A 不正确。B 选项是说公司留不住员工，显然文中没有涉及。C 选项显然错误。D 选项说的是顾客主要购买的是 Smithson 名下的产品。根据第一段的最后一句中“its customers were buying fewer and fewer of its own-brand products, the major part of its business, and showing a preference for more fashionable brands”可以看出，顾客购买的主要产品是 Smithson 百货公司自己名下的产品。关键是这个地方：its own-brand products, the major part of its business。所以正确选项为 D。

14 C。本题问 Smithson 百货公司的利润从三年前开始增长的原因是什么。选项 A 说的是零售部门的改善，而第二段提到的是英国大多数零售商在 Rowena Baker 上任后，都开始赔钱，与 A 选项没有直接关系，所以这个选项只是用来迷惑考生的。选项 B 的意思是先前对百货商店所做的努力是营业额上升的原因，如果 B 是正确的，也就意味着 Smithson 百货公司没有必要换首席执行官了。选项 C 很明显是正确答案，如第二段所说：she took the bold decision to invite one of Europe's most exciting interior designers to develop the fashion area，她做出了一个大胆的决定，邀请了欧洲最令人激动的室内设计师来开发时尚领域。并且 This very quickly led to rising sales，这很快就使销售额上升了。

15 A。本题问的是 Rowena Baker 加入公司时面临的一个问题是什么。做对这道题的关键在于对关键句和关键词的理解是否透彻。第二段“provided a traditional service targeted at middle-aged, middle-income customers, who'd been shopping there for years, and the customer base was gradually contracting"，这句话的关键在于contracting，它是“缩小，收缩”的意思。整句话是说：它提供的传统服务目标人群是中年中等收入者，这些人已经在那购物多年，并且客户基数逐渐减少。所以正确答案是选项A。

16 A。本题意思是为什么很多员工反对Baker的计划。提到员工的反对，我们应该看第三段中提到的“many employees resisted her improvements because they just wouldn't be persuaded that there was anything wrong with the way they'd always done thing"，意思是员工不认为他们以前的工作方式存在什么问题，也就意味着他们不愿意改变他们工作的方式。所以正确选项为A。

17 C。本题的意思是Baker为什么要改变员工的政策。我们看第四段中Baker所说的话：How can you sell jeans if you're wearing a black suit? Smithson's has a new identity, and this needs to be made clear to the customers. 意思是：员工怎么能穿着黑西服卖牛仔服？Smithson有一个新的身份，这些必须对客户很明确。也就是C选项说的“客户必须能辨别出服务他们的员工”。选项B和D在原文并未有明确声明。选项A显然不正确，文中并没有提到改善公司形象。

18 B。本题主要是说John认为Smithson面临什么问题。我们看最后一段的最后一句中提到“The fact is that unless she opens several more stores pretty soon, Smithson's profits will start to fall because turnover at the existing store will inevitably start to decline.”这句话的意思是说，事实上除非尽快开更多的店，否则会由于现有商店的营业额开始下降，Smithson的利润将会减少。这与B所说的“除非扩张，公司的利润才会继续增长”正好相对应。所以正确选项为B。

词汇点津

contract	v. 缩小，收缩
chief executive	首席执行官

三、实战演练

Questions 13-18

- Read the following article about Flat Out, and the questions on the opposite page.
- For each question (**13-18**), mark one letter (**A**, **B**, **C** or **D**) on your Answer Sheet.

Flat Out

Having seen the damage caused by property bubbles, Hong Kong officials are determined not to have a repeat on their own patch. Last month the territory's de facto central bank pushed banks into increasing the amount of cash they demand of homebuyers. John Tsang, Hong Kong's usually tepid financial secretary, called in big developers to warn of government intervention if the housing market became "unfair" or "unhealthy". On November 2nd the territory's chief executive, Donald Tsang, vowed to cool prices.

The mounting disquiet reflects a huge jump in the price of property, particularly luxury flats. Statistics compiled by CB Richard Ellis, an estate agent, show that prices of high-end flats have risen by 40% since January, and are now just 13% below their 2008 pre-crisis peak. Some are once again priced at record levels. One flat, at 39

Conduit Road, was reported by the developer to have sold in October for HK $71,000 ($9,200) per square foot. The spike in flat sales has propelled shares in property companies higher, too. That, in turn, has prompted a flood of primary and secondary offerings in property-related shares.

The government's warnings may be having an impact. Sale and purchase agreements in the territory fell by 24% month on month in October (though they were still up by 97% year on year). But many flats have been pulled off the market in anticipation of even higher prices, says Diana Lilauwala of At Home, a broker whose business finding homes for expats has been hit by a sudden paucity of supply.

Unlike in 2008, current prices have little to do with expats and everything to do with local and, especially, mainland buyers. The government's restrictions on leverage in property transactions may not help deter these customers. Some of them require mortgages — the percentage of mainland borrowers in Hong Kong has steadily risen over the past three years — but interest rates are low and many are apparently willing to pay cash. According to data from the Hong Kong Monetary Authority, the amount of money approved for mortgages has been declining in recent months even as prices have been going up.

Surging prices have sparked criticism in the local press about the affordability of housing in Hong Kong. They have also put a spotlight on developers' selling practices. The flat at 39 Conduit Road officially occupies the 68th floor, a lucky number for Chinese people, but that is only because 42 other floors were left out of the building's numbering system. (The one just above it is on the "88th" floor, an even more auspicious number). Papers are filled with stories about tricks used to inflate the reported size of flats, in many cases to a multiple of the actual living space.

Most important, the property boom has increased scrutiny of the way the government controls land sales in Hong Kong. The annual production of new flats has been declining for years. In its yearly report on the territory, released on November 3rd, the IMF welcomed hints that the government might release more land for development. But the acquisition of developable plots is largely left to a few companies with lots of pricing power. More competition is needed, as well as more land.

13 The main reason why last month the territory's central bank forced the bank to increase the amount of cash is that ________.

A John Tsang warned the big developers

B Hong Kong officials expected to avoid bad effects by property bubbles

C Donald Tsang claimed that cool prices would be adopted

D the housing market is going to be not fair

14 Why some foreigner cannot find his or her home in Hong Kong?

A The quantity of the flats is so small.

B The broker cannot give good service.

C The low price of the flats.

D Many flats are not on sales for the expectation of higher price.

15 The most important benefit from the boom of property is ______.

A the criticism from the local press about the affordability of housing in Hong Kong

B the raising price of the luxury flats

C the more secured ways of controlling the sale of the flat

D the rise of the percentage of mainland borrowers in Hong Kong over the past three years

16 What mainly makes the trouble sense decline?

A The increasing price of the pain flats.

B The high price of shares in property companies.
C The issuance of the property-related shares.
D The slowing down on quick increasing price of luxury flats.

17 The main reason why that price's raising doesn't bring about the increasing on the number of the mortgage is that ________.
A the residents of Hong Kong are very rich
B the mainland buyers are not necessary to loan money
C the interest rates of the banks are not high
D the percentage of mainland borrowers in Hong Kong has declined over the past three years

18 The percentage of sale and purchase agreements in the territory fell by 24% month on month in October is closely involved in ________.
A the measurement made by the government
B the increase on the percentage of the mortgage
C the low interest rates of the banks
D the unequal competition of the market

答案解析

▶ 文章大意

本篇文章主要讲述了香港楼市房屋告罄的现象。见识过资产泡沫带来的损害之后，香港官员们决意不在自己的土地上重蹈覆辙。上个月香港实际上的中央银行（香港金融管理局）催促各行增加其要求购房者支付的现金数额。一贯温和的香港财政司司长曾俊华，召集了大开发商，警告他们如果房产市场变得“不公正”“不健康”，政府就会加以干预。不断增加的忧虑反映出资产价格，特别是豪华公寓价格的大幅上涨。与2008年不同，现在的房价与外国人无关，而是与当地买家，尤其是大陆买家有关。

政府也采取了相应的措施，希望能够缓解楼价。上涨的房价激起了当地媒体对香港住房负担能力的批评，还把焦点放在了开发商的销售行为上。

13 B。题干问的是“上个月香港中心银行强行让各行增加其要求购房者支付现金数额的原因是什么”。这部分的内容主要在第一段的前两句话，“Having seen the damage caused by property bubbles, Hong Kong officials are determined not to have a repeat on their own patch. Last month the territory's de facto central bank pushed banks into increasing the amount of cash they demand of homebuyers.”很明显可以看出第二句是结果，且与题干意思大致相同。而第一句就是造成这一举措的原因，即害怕 the damage caused by property bubbles，与选项B的 bad effects by property bubbles 大意相同。选项A和C则是这一举措的具体的措施。选项D显然是对第一段倒数第二句的断章取义，也不能选。所以选项B是正确答案。

14 D。题干问的是“为什么有些外国人在香港找不到住处”。此题的关键在关键词的理解上。第三段中的 expats 是“外国佬”的意思，如果能够准确地知道它的意思，我们就很容易找到相关的语句。“But many flats have been pulled off the market in anticipation of even higher prices, says Diana Lilauwala of At Home, a broker whose business finding homes for expats has been hit by a sudden paucity of supply.”后半句的意思是为外籍人士寻找房子的公司受到了冲击。前半句交代了原因，many flats have been pulled off the market，许多公寓延期上市，也就是D中所说的 many flats are not on sales for the expectation of higher price。

15 C。题干问的是“地产繁荣景象所带来的最大益处是什么”。跟原文相匹配的正确答案是C。原文最后一段的第一句话，“Most important, the property boom has increased scrutiny of the way the government controls land sales in Hong Kong.”最重要的是，地产繁荣增强了政府对控制香港土地出售的方式的检查。与选项 C 所说的 The more secured ways of controlling the sale of the flat 相对应，所以正确选项为 C。而选项 A、B、D 都是其他段中的句子，与该题无关。

16 D。题干问的是“主要是什么情况才能使这种忧患感减少”。根据第二段的内容，与这一问题相对应的是第一句话，“The mounting disquiet reflects a huge jump in the price of property, particularly luxury flats.” 不断增加的忧虑反映出资产价格特别是豪华公寓价格的大幅上涨。所以说选项 D 中提到的价格快速增长的减慢会使这种忧患意识得到缓解。我们看选项 A，普通公寓价格的增长在原文中并没有提到这一情况，所以排除 A 选项。选项 B 是说房地产股票的高价格，根据第二段句尾，股票价格升高是由于房屋的价格的不断大幅度攀升，而根据第二段第一句，房屋价格的快速增长会导致忧患感更强烈，所以 B 是错误的。选项 C 同选项 B 一样，都是增加忧患感。

17 C。题干问的是“房价的持续上涨并没有导致贷款额的增加的主要原因是什么”。正确答案是 C。对应的是第四段的中间一句中的 but interest rates are low and many are apparently willing to pay cash，意思是“由于利率过低，所以很多人都愿意付现金”。与 C 所说的 Thc interest rates of the banks are not high 意思相近。A 选项，根据第四段的第一句“Unlike in 2008, current prices have little to do with expats and everything to do with local and, especially, mainland buyers.” 现在的房价与外国人无关，而是与当地买家尤其是大陆买家有关，所以香港居民富裕程度并不是主要因素。选项 B 和 D，根据原文“the percentage of mainland borrowers in Hong Kong has steadily risen over the past three years”，过去三年中大陆借款人的比重在香港稳步上升，所以说，B 中所说的大陆买家没有必要贷款和 D 中贷款率下降都是错误的。

18 A。题干问的是“香港的房屋销售额和购买合同十月份环比下降了 24% 这一现象主要与什么有关”。与题相符的是 A 选项。根据第三段的第一句话，“The government's warnings may be having an impact”，政府的警告可能也有点效果。接着第二句就提到了香港的房屋销售额和购买合同十月份环比下降了 24% 。所以说与这一下降现象密切相关的是 A 选项，政府的相应措施的实施。

词汇点津

have a repeat on	重蹈覆辙
mounting	*adj.* 不断增加的（与 increasing, growing 等是同义词，在商务经济领域出现频率极高。）
propel	*vt.* 推进；驱使；激励；驱策
expat	*n.* 外国佬

周四　瞻前又顾后，解决完形填空题

一、题型分析

（一）命题规律

BEC中级阅读的第四部分是由一篇带空的文章和与文章对应的15道题所组成。正文的字数大概在200到300词左右。当然文章都是在商业的大背景下选择的。

题目特点：此题可以说是选择题形式的完成句子题。所给出的是一篇有15个空格的正文，以及与之对应的15道题，每道题都有4个选项，从中选择一个最适合的选项。一般说来，文章不会太难，比较容易理解。主要的考查点还是在选项上。

题目的难度适中，这一部分主要是检验考生对词汇的掌握程度，以及在特定环境下对词汇的应用能力。

（二）解题技巧

1. 看首句，抓中心。一般情况下首句都是完整的，所以要先弄清首句的意思。
2. 瞻前顾后，看搭配。这部分主要要求考生抓语境。在这一部分中，环境是解题的关键点，在特定的商务环境下，注重词汇的各种搭配，如短语上的搭配等。同时也要注意词汇之间的不同点的学习。
3. 带入选项，查对错。在结合语境选择出答案后，最好代入到原文中，检查是否符合全文的行文特征。

（三）考试准备

这一部分的完形填空题，要求考生对词汇应用有很强的应变能力。所以就要求考生在平时的学习中多接触商务的特定环境，比如说近义词之间的辨析，各种习语的应用等。熟悉多种热点的商务环境，为考生能够在此环境下自由灵活地应用词汇做积极的准备。

二、典型样题

Questions 19-33

- Read the article below about Human Resources Policy.
- Choose the best word or phrase to fill each gap from **A**, **B**, **C** or **D** on the opposite page.
- For each question (**19-33**), mark one letter (**A**, **B**, **C** or **D**) on your Answer Sheet.
- There is an example at the beginning (0).

Example:

A levels　　**B** standards　　**C** guides　　**D** measures

	A	B	C	D
0	▭	▭	▬	▭

Human Resources Policy

CBA Bank was the largest financial institution to sign the employers' "People Come First" code of practice in the early 1990s. In doing so, it committed itself to the highest (**0**) ___C___ in human resources practices such as the communication of company (**19**) ________ to employees, the setting of individual training and personal (**20**) ________ plans, and the holding of regular performance (**21**) ________ for all staff. Like other organizations, CBA is replacing the traditional hierarchy with a flatter organizational structure which gives employees more broadly defined (**22**) ________ within the company. The change is offering employees greater opportunities for work in cross-disciplinary project teams. As a result, interpersonal (**23**) ________ are extremely important.

The policy seems to be working. There is a great deal of goodwill among employees, who (**24**) ________ the fact that customer satisfaction is the organization's chief aim. CBA claims to pursue this aim for its own (**25**) ________ rather than as a means of earning profits for shareholders. An ability to relate to all kinds of people is the most important attribute CBA looks for in (**26**) ________ recruits. Graduates are (**27**) ________ for a two-year period and exposed to all (**28**) ________ of retail financial services. By the end of this training period, they will have taken their Institute of Banking examination and, if they have (**29**) ________ their performance targets, they will have (**30**) ________ a job at the bank.

"On the whole, we are not looking for people straight out of college," says human resources manager Maiy Kemp. "We would prefer that they had (**31**) ________ some experience of life and had taken a year out between school and college to travel or do some kind of work."

The company has recently introduced a new policy on pay, and it is now (**32**) ________ to performance through bonus schemes, with the objective being to (**33**) ________ employees for their achievements and effort.

19	**A** designs	**B** purposes	**C** ends	**D** objectives
20	**A** continuation	**B** extension	**C** development	**D** advancement
21	**A** reviews	**B** trials	**C** revisions	**D** judgments
22	**A** capacities	**B** parts	**C** roles	**D** elements
23	**A** abilities	**B** talents	**C** assets	**D** skills
24	**A** recommend	**B** honour	**C** respect	**D** obey
25	**A** sake	**B** reason	**C** behalf	**D** cause
26	**A** expected	**B** intended	**C** potential	**D** eventual
27	**A** taken on	**B** written in	**C** put on	**D** drawn in
28	**A** fields	**B** areas	**C** regions	**D** parts
29	**A** arrived	**B** done	**C** passed	**D** met
30	**A** secured	**B** reached	**C** confirmed	**D** fixed
31	**A** gained	**B** won	**C** earned	**D** realised
32	**A** attached	**B** linked	**C** combined	**D** joined
33	**A** return	**B** reward	**C** recompense	**D** refund

答案解析

▶ 文章大意

这篇文章主要是讲 CBA 所实施的人力资源政策。首先介绍的是 human resources practices（人力资源实务）的具体分类。然后谈到 CBA 银行的管理结构，是 flatter organizational structure（扁平化的组织结构），而不是hierarchy（等级制公司）。招聘的基本原则是不招应届毕业生，而要有一定的生活经验或者是工作经验的择业者。

19 D。本题考查的是语义相近的两个词：purpose和objective。结合前后文，这句话说的是将公司的发展目标传达给员工。Purpose：the reason you do something，and the thing you want to achieve when you do it. 它是指具体做某件事情的意图或目的。此处“公司目标”为较抽象和正式的场合，用objective而不用purpose。Objective: something that you are working hard to achieve，especially in business or politics.

20 C。personal development plans为固定搭配，意思是“个人发展计划”。

21 A。regular performance review是“定期的表现回顾”的意思，所以应选review。整句的意思是：定期举行员工的表现回顾。

22 C。A是“能力”的意思。B是“部分”。C是“角色”。D是“因素，成分”的意思。根据原文，broadly defined roles才符合原意。整句话的意思是说：扁平化的组织结构可以给员工定义更加广泛的角色。所以正确答案是C。

23 D。人际交往技巧是很重要的。interpersonal skills是地道的说法。参见一个例句：you will need good interpersonal skills.

24 C。A中的recommend是“推荐，建议”，与the fact（事实）不能搭配，故排除A选项。B中的honour是“敬重”的意思，D选项中的obey是“遵守”的意思。C选项中的respect是“尊重，重视”的意思，在这里是“重视或者接受”的意思。该空所在句子的意思很容易理解，说的是：员工们越来越看重或者说是承认一个事实——顾客的满意是组织的主要目标。所以正确答案应该选择C，respect the fact表示“尊重这一事实”。

25 A。固定用法for the sake of something或for something's sake表示“为了……目的；为了……的利益；为了……”。整句话的意思是：银行追求这个目的是为自己的利益，而不是股东挣利润的工具。所以正确答案为选项A。

26 C。整句话的意思是“召集各种各样的人才的能力是CBA寻找潜在新成员所崇尚的最重要的特质”。potential recruits为“潜在新成员”的意思，地道的词应用potential，所以正确答案为C。

27 A。本题考查的是短语take on的一个用法，在此句中是“雇佣”的意思。整句话的意思是：毕业生将被雇佣两年。

28 B。A选项中的field做“领域，范围”讲的时候是指的研究、活动的范围或领域，多用于科研领域；C选项中的region则是指具体的地域；D选项中的parts主要是“部分”的意思。而选项B中的area应用范围比较广泛，既可以是具体的某一地域，也可以是某一抽象的领域，所以选择B。整句话的意思是：把毕业生分配在各个连锁金融服务领域。

29 D。本题是对固定短语的考查。met the targets即“完成目标”，用的是meet。

30 A。完成了目标就可以得到工作。secure指get something by special effort。这个空的选择应该联系上文：完成目标，然后才能确保得到工作。完成目标是所做的努力，所以经过努力得到工作，选择的是A。

31 A。A中的gain的意思是“通过努力获得有用的东西”，借此让自己变得更有优势，或者说是起到了积极的辅助作用，更适合前后的语言环境。整个句子的意思是：招的人已经具有了一定的生活经验。

32 B。本题也是对固定搭配的考查。根据原文的意思，薪酬现在和业绩挂钩。“与……挂钩，与……联系到一起”用link与to搭配。所以正确答案为B。

33 B。本题也是对固定短语的考查。“Reward employees for their achievements and effort”，因为功劳而奖励员工。这里的reward sb. 是“奖励某人”的意思。

三、实战演练

Questions 19-33

- Read the article below about CIT Files for Bankraptcy.
- Choose the best word or phrase to fill each gap from **A**, **B**, **C** or **D** on the opposite page.
- For each question (**19-33**), mark one letter (**A**, **B**, **C** or **D**) on your Answer Sheet.
- There is an example at the beginning (0).

Example:

A and　　**B** but　　**C** so　　**D** then

0	A	B	C	D
	▭	▬	▭	▭

CIT Files for Bankruptcy

CIT, a lender to thousands of small businesses, files for bankruptcy.

The most gut-wrenching failures may be over, (0) the financial crisis continues to claim the occasional big victim. CIT, a lender to small and medium-sized businesses, from clothing retailers to Dunkin' Donuts franchisees, (**19**) ________ for bankruptcy on Sunday November 1st after failing to garner enough support for a debt-restructuring plan. With $71 billion in assets, the century-old firm is only one-ninth the size of Lehman Brothers, which collapsed in September 2008. (**20**) ________, its Chapter 11 filing augurs ill for America's corporate minnows, (**21**) ________ financing options have narrowed dramatically over the past year.

Financial-services firms have a harder time than most bouncing back from bankruptcy, because their business so heavily (**22**) ________ trust, which has a tendency to evaporate in such situations. CIT has improved its chances by securing the support of the vast majority of its bondholders for a "prepackaged" filing that will reduce its debt by $10 billion while (**23**) ________ its subsidiaries to go on operating. Among (**24**) ________ persuaded to come on board is Carl Icahn, a veteran corporate gadfly who had been trying to derail CIT's restructuring in the (**25**) ________ of profiting by picking through its entrails; he has even offered a $1 billion back-up loan. The firm's advisers say it could emerge from bankruptcy by the end of the year.

The pain will be widely felt. Goldman Sachs, Wall Street's savviest and best-connected firm, is (**26**) ________ a hit of sorts. Perhaps mindful that it could do without more bad publicity of the "vampire squid" sort, it renegotiated the terms of a loan facility that would have triggered a $1 billion payment if CIT (**27**) ________ bust. Goldman will now get only $535m, half of that in collateral.

The biggest losers, of course, are shareholders, who will be wiped out (**28**) ________ as creditors take the equity in the new company. Also likely to lose their shirts are preferred shareholders, including the hapless taxpayer, (**29**) ________ handed over $2.3 billion of funds from the Troubled Asset Relief Programme last December.

(**30**) ________, it is hardly cheering news for the thousands of small firms that rely on CIT and its kind for vendor financing, factoring, leasing, insurance and more. Unlike large companies, for whom bond markets have reopened, the small fry find that capital remains scarce (though demand (**31**) ________ loans have also dropped). Other small-business lenders, too, have pulled in their horns pulled in their (**32**) ________. To help keep credit flowing, the Treasury has loosened the requirements for loans backed by the Small Business Administration, a government agency, and has eased (**33**) ________ to public funds for community banks. These moves are yet to show much benefit.

周六　变形题练习一

第一部分：搭配题的变形题型

（一）题目说明

在前面的部分中我们已经了解到，BEC 阅读中级第一部分由 7 个问题和 4 个段落组成。即给出 7 个句子，要求找到每句话对应的段落。其中的 4 个段落可以是一篇较长文章中选出的 4 个相关段落，这一个类型的搭配题我们在前面已经练习并讲解过。接下来我们主要来讲解一下第二种类型，即所谓文章是相关主题的 4 篇短文章。

（二）解题技巧

与前面介绍的题型的相同点是，在此题中，所给的 7 个句子一般比较简单，容易理解。4 个段落则相对于 7 个问题要难一些。题目的难度属中等。第一部分主要更侧重于对具体的信息或具体的细节的辨认，很少涉及或考到主旨部分。在解题技巧上的不同点表现如下：

1. 一抓题目。抓住所给段落的四个题目的意思，可根据题找对应的选项。
2. 二看关键语句。找段落中与选项相关的契合点。
3. 三找关键词。选项和文中的关键词是做题的关键线索。我们可以根据关键词的相互对应来寻找答案。
4. 典型样题。

PART ONE

Questions 1-7

- Look at the statements below and the advertisements on the opposite page.
- Which advertisement does each statement **1-7** refer to?
- For each sentence **1-7**, mark one letter (**A**, **B**, **C**, or **D**) on your Answer Sheet.
- You will need to use some of the letters more than once.

Example:

0 You need to be familiar with a variety of computer software.

0	A	B	C	D
	▬	▭	▭	▭

1 This job involves working for a well-known company.
2 You will meet a wide variety of customers in this job.
3 This post involves responsibility for recruitment.
4 Your work should not be discussed outside the office.
5 In this job you will deal with people's investments.
6 This post has recently been established.

7 Your job description will require you to read some documents very carefully.

A ILT Consultants £ 19, 000 + benefits

Here's an exciting opportunity to combine your presentation skills and organizational abilities, working for a team of systems analysts. You will need to have a good eye for detail as the role involves large amounts of proof reading and checking. The job also involves client liaison at all levels, as well as an element of research.

B John Guild & Son £ 17, 500 + benefits

City finance house seeks a mature person to work for the Secretariat. The post involves: looking after customers' financial assets such as property and possessions; database work; accounting; and organizational responsibilities. The bulk of the workload is highly confidential. A good level and range of PC experience will secure you an interview.

C Hooper's £ 17, 000

Join this household name and play a key part in supporting their Regional Operations Director and marketing team. This is a newly-created position within a well-established firm and there is plenty of opportunity for you to develop your role. You will need to be self-motivated with the ability to prioritise. Some Windows experience essential.

D ITC Investment Consultants £ 18, 000

This is an opening for a bright, part-qualified assistant to work in an investment company's busy personnel department. You will need to have one year's experience of interviewing job applicants, and the confidence to handle appraisals and disciplinary actions. Further training will be offered or the right candidate. Keyboard skills are desirable as you will manage all personal correspondence.

答案解析

▶ **文章大意**

这四段分别介绍了四个招聘的职位。内容涉及职位的薪金待遇、应聘者的要求，如计算机能力等。

1 C。第一句的意思是：这一工作涉及到一家知名的企业工作。此题主要是抓关键词，C 段中提到了 well-established firm，与所给句子中的 a well-known company 意思基本相同，所以 C 符合题意。

2 A。第二句的意思是：在这一工作中，你可以遇到各种各样的客户。在广告 A 中涉及 client liaison（客户联络），判断 A 符合题意。

3 D。第三句的意思是：这一职位涉及招聘这一职责。在广告 D 中含有 interviewing job applicants 的信息，与所给句子中的 responsibility for recruitment 相符，所以 D 符合题意。

4 B。第四句的意思是：你的工作不可以在办公室外面讨论。在广告 B 中涉及关键词 highly confidential（高度保密），与所给句子中的 should not be discussed outside the office 意思相符，所以 B 符合题意。

5 B。第五句的意思是：在这一工作中，你需要处理客人的投资问题。In this job you will deal with people's investments. 在广告 B 中提到 looking after customers' financial assets，也就是照顾客户的金融资产，与本句意思相符，所以选择 B。

6 C。第六句的意思是：这一职位是刚刚建立的。意思与广告 C 中的关键词 newly-created position 相符，所以 C 符合题意。

7 A。第七句的意思是：你的职位描述需要你认真仔细地阅读相关文件。与广告 A 中的 proof reading and checking 相符，所以 A 符合题意。

第二部分：阅读题的变形题型

（一）题目说明

在前面我们已经介绍了 BEC 中级阅读试题的第三部分出现的普遍经典题目是由 1 篇文章和 6 个选择题组成，并且这 6 道题目都是 4 选 1 的单项选择题。所给出的文章一般附有标题，而 6 个选择题则是我们熟悉的和高考等重要考试都很相似的阅读理解的单项选择题。所以说此前讨论过的题型对考生来说并不陌生。

而现在我们所要分析的是变形后的阅读选择题。题目特点是所给的文章同以前一样是一篇完整的文章，但是问题分成了两个部分。第一部分包括 4 个题，把给出的 7 个句子根据关联性，分别归类到所给的四段中。第二部分也是由 4 个问题组成，把所给的 7 个短语准确地填到所给的 7 个句子中。可以说这一变形题对考生的要求更高了。

题目的难度较大，从透彻理解文章大意及文中细节两方面的能力进行全面地考查。

（二）解题技巧

这部分的解题思路依然是"中心和关键点两手抓，推断和猜测并用"。出题者所出的选项已经不再着重考查对文中事实的对错的判断，而是侧重对文中观点的考查。更多地涉及在原文基础上的合理推理及猜测。具体的解题技巧如下：

1. 先读选项和问题，后读全文。建议考生在拿到题时，先认真阅读所给的选项和问题，然后带着选项和问题阅读全文。
2. 中心和细节一起抓。考生在阅读全文时，不仅要注意对中心意思的掌握，还要注重对重点细节的关注。
3. 推理和猜测共用。由于在这部分题中，更多地考察了考生对文中观点的理解，所以考生应该灵活地运用推理和猜测的办法解题。
4. 难选的题可代入选项检验。对于自己不确定的题，考生可以把选项代入到原文中，看其是否与原文的上下文相符，最后确定选项。

（三）典型样题

PART THREE

Questions 13-20

- Read the article below about stress management and answer questions 13-20 on the opposite page.

A Lesson in Stress Management

Demands placed on us at work can often lead to considerable worry and discomfort. There are, however, ways of protecting ourselves from the stress we face at work. We interviewed Jane Collard, a consultant in stress management.

1 In Jane Collard's opinion, stress is becoming an increasingly common feature of the workplace. Stress is a highly individual reaction, which varies considerably from person to person, and it is difficult for some employees to avoid it. Indeed, stress is regarded by many as part of the organizational culture of our institutions: it comes with the job. Recent figures indicate that time taken off work because of stress has increased by 500 per cent since the 1950s. Undoubtedly, changes in working conditions have led to greater pressure at work at all levels. With reductions in staffing, workloads for individual employees have increased. In addition, many employees are left worrying about the security of their jobs.

2 On the stress management courses that she runs, Jane Collard tries to make the trainees realize that stress in itself is not harmful. Everyone needs a certain level of stress to enable them to feel motivated and to perform effectively. A complete absence of stress can be as damaging as overstress, since it can make people lose interest in their work, and even lead to depression. The difficulties occur when the amount of stress rises above a level which is healthy for a particular individual. If this happens, the effects are very obvious and the trainees are taught to recognize the signs. Stress may be expressed physically, for example through headaches and tiredness, or through emotional problems such as depression. A person suffering from stress may also start to behave differently, and can be difficult to deal with.

3 While it may not always be possible to prevent stress, there are a number of ways in which it can be controlled. The first thing that the trainees learn is how to manage their time effectively. This involves, first of all, setting realistic goals for both the short and long term. Once this framework has been established, tasks are then prioritised on a daily basis. The trainees are also reminded that when they are under pressure the less important items should be left, and they should never hesitate to delegate. Everyone is encouraged to look at ways of reducing "wasted time", for example, by grouping similar tasks together or dealing with items immediately.

4 Jane feels that one of the most useful features of the course is that it enables trainees to deal with those demands or deadlines that they regard as unreasonable. They are encouraged to avoid being defensive, but at the same time they are advised not to be afraid of saying "no". They are asked to give reasons only if necessary. The training helps them to foresee difficult situations or unwanted demands, and they learn how to prepare themselves mentally. Everyone is encouraged not to get stuck in negative thought patterns, where stress can feed a circular sense of helplessness. One solution they discuss is to think of a more encouraging alternative for each negative message. They learn, for example, to remind themselves that nothing terrible happens when a demand is refused or a deadline missed. Life goes on.

Section A

Questions 13-16

- For questions **13-16**, choose the best title for each numbered paragraph from the list below.
- For each numbered paragraph **1-4**, mark one letter (**A-G**) on your Answer Sheet.
- Do not use any letter more than once.

13 Paragraph 1

14 Paragraph 2

15 Paragraph 3

16 Paragraph 4

A Higher stress levels among top managers
B Coping with stress through a positive attitude
C Time lost at work through sickness
D Causes of increased stress in the work environment
E Explanations for missed deadlines
F Stress reduction through better organization
G Typical problems associated with stress

Section B

Questions 17-20

- Using the information in the text, complete each sentence **17-20** with a phrase **A-G** from the list below.
- For each question **17-20**, mark one letter (**A-G**) on your Answer Sheet.
- Do not use any letter more than once.

17 Most people agree that the recent increase in stress is due to changes in ________.

18 The trainees are taught that the right level of stress at work is important for good ________.

19 Trainees learn that one way of limiting stress is by deciding up on ________.

20 One of the most important parts of the course is learning how to react to ________.

A levels of performance
B shorter deadlines
C employment practices
D higher levels of sickness
E unfair demands
F successful management structure
G practical targets

答案解析

▶ **文章大意**

本篇文章讲述的压力管理课程有关的内容。我们工作中的各种要求常常会导致很大的忧虑和不安，然而，如何在我们是与工作面临压力时保护自己，其实有很多自我保护的方法。我们采访了 Jane Collard，一个压力管理顾问。

然后介绍了 Jane Collard 对于工作上压力的看法，压力给人们精神和身体上所造成的影响，以及她所开设的压力管理课程的内容等。

Section A

A 高层经理之间压力更大
B 以积极的态度应对困难
C 生病导致工作时间减少
D 工作环境下压力增加的原因
E 错过最后日期的各种解释
F 通过更好的规划来减少压力
G 与压力相关的典型问题

13 D。第一段中 Jane Collard 认为，压力正日益成在工作场所工作时的共同特点。压力有很强的个人特征性，即个别性。不同的人拥有不同的压力，对一些员工来说很难避免。后半部分介绍了压力增加的原因，其中就提到了“changes in working conditions have led to greater pressure at work at all levels”，工作条件的变化导致了工作各方面的更大的压力。D 选项与第一段内容相符，所以 D 是正确答案。

14 G。通过 Jane Collard 开设的针对压力的典型问题的压力管理课程，告诉学员们压力本身并不是什么有害事物，还介绍了合理压力的好处，每个人都需要一定的压力。还涉及了压力表现的不同方式，包括了选项 G 与压力相关的典型问题，所以正确答案是 G。

15 F。第三段主要介绍了控制压力的一些具体方法手段，如制定切实可行的目标、减少浪费时间等。根据原文，选项 F 的内容包括在内。比如说文中提到的制定切实可行的目标，就是合理地安排规划的具体表现。所以正确答案是 F。

16 B。第四段主要讲的是培养学员面对压力时良好的态度。鼓励他们避免过于积极，但同时也鼓励他们尽量不要害怕说“不”、从一个更加令人鼓舞的方向考虑事物而不是从负面消息的角度等。显然选项 B 与前一句中的“从一个更加令人鼓舞的方向考虑事物而不是从负面消息的角度”相对应。所以 B 选项是正确答案。

Section B

A 表现水平
B 更短的最后期限
C 雇佣惯例
D 更严重的疾病
E 不公平的要求
F 成功的管理机制
G 实际目标

17 C。题干：大多数人认为最近压力的提升是由于什么的变化？根据原文第一段中各种应聘条件的改变可以推断出答案是 C，即雇佣惯例的改变。

18 A。题干：学员可以学习到适当的压力有助于发挥好的什么？根据原文，很明显答案是 A，即有助于表现水平的良好发挥。

19 G。题干：学员学到的控制压力的方法之一是决定什么？根据原文第三段，first of all，setting realistic goals for both the short and long term，所以选择的是 G 选项。

20 E。题干：这一压力管理课程最重要的部分之一是教学员如何应对什么？根据原文，很明显正确答案是 E，即如何面对不公平的要求。

周日　变形题练习二

第三部分：改错题的变形题型

（一）题目说明

前面我们已经分析讲解了 BEC 中级阅读试题的第五部分，主要的考查方向同刊物等的校对有一定的相似性，主要目的是找出额外的或不必要的单词。

通常这部分的改错题都是给出 12 个句子，而且其中大多数是存在错误的，只有少数几个是正确的。这些错误主要表现为存在多余的成分或存在语法错误两大方面。12 个句子一般意思清晰，比较容易理解。

改错题的变形题型与之前所给文章的不同点主要是：之前所给的文章都是一篇完整的商业背景下的文章，而改错题的变形题所给出的是与题对应的两篇独立商业背景下的短文。

改错题的变形题型与之前的题型的不同点主要有两方面：一是题型由原来的一种变为了现在的两种独立题型；二是题的数目由原来的 12 个减少为 10 个。虽然题型增加为原来的两倍，可是数量减少了，所以难度可以说是基本不变的。

题目较简单，主要侧重于考生的英语基本功底，比如说基本的词汇、语法、句法等。

（二）解题技巧

根据真题我们可以看出，题型由原来的一种变为了现在的两种独立型：

其一，与原来相同的是，要找出多余的词，共 5 个题目；其二，是与高考题相似的改错词，也是 5 个题目。接下来我们将根据不同的题型进行解题技巧的解析。

第一部分：找出多余的词。这部分的解题思路是挑出多余的词，找不出的即是正确的。

1. 第一步是找多余的词。首先就要通读整个句子，在理解全句的基础上，找出不恰当的词。此处还要注意的是在多余的词中，虚词占很大一部分。
2. 第二步，就是再审视一遍没有找出错误的句子。如果有 2 ~ 3 个没有找出错误的句子，证明此题全部做对的可能性比较大。经统计分析，改错题通常有 2 ~ 3 个正确选项。如果还有多于 3 个或少于 2 个正确的句子，考生就要重新再检查一遍。

第二部分：改错词。这一部分主要是考查基本的语法，如时态，进行时、完成时等；再如常见的短语搭配，如 pay attention to，by means of 等；再如关系代词和关系副词等。这就要求同学们注重平时的基本语法题的反复练习、总结。其实，这部分的错误方式也很有限，所以只需多练、多记即可。

（三）典型样题

PART FIVE

Section A

Questions 36-40

- Read the text below about a special kind of competition.
- In most of the lines **36-40** there is one extra word which does not fit. One or two lines, however, are

correct.

- If a line is correct, write CORRECT on your Answer Sheet.
- If there is an extra word in the line, write the extra word in CAPITAL LETTERS on your Answer Sheet.

Examples:

0 The international Youth Skills Olympics is a vocational skills competition in

0 CORRECT

00 which the young people demonstrate their achievements in a range of areas.

00 THE

Example:	0	C	O	R	R	E	C	T
	00	T	H	E				

36 The competition, which there is held every two years, is organized by the international

37 Training Organization. All U. K. competitors qualify for the team by getting through

38 a tough national competition. Their backgrounds are vary from arts to sciences,

39 and students to the self-employed. Since they do not know which skill area they

40 will be tested in, they must to train for everything before the start of the competition.

Section B

Questions 41-45

- Read the text below about market research.
- In each line **41-45** there is one wrong word.
- For each line **41-45**, write the correct word in CAPITAL LETTERS on your Answer Sheet.

Examples:

0 Your business will only success if customers like your product

0 SUCCEED

00 or service and are prepared to give you money in exchange about it

00 FOR

Market Research

41 Before you start a business, it is importance to undertake market research

42 and to assess the results with great care: you need to finding out about your

43 potential customers and the state of the market, included your competitors.

44 The more detailed your market research are, the more profitable your business

45 is likely to be. Carry out your study thorough, and repeat it to ensure your results are reliable.

文章A大意

36 这一比赛由国际培训组织举办，每两年一次。

37 英国所有的竞争对手晋级队伍都要经过一个艰难的国家选拔赛。

38 他们的背景不同，无论是从科学到艺术，

39 从学生到个体经营者。因为他们不知道哪个技能范围

40 将被测试，他们必须在比赛开始之前，做好所有的训练。

文章B大意

41 在你开始一个业务之前，进行市场调查是很重要的，
42 并细心评估其结果：你需要寻找你的
43 潜在客户和国内的市场，包括你的竞争者。
44 市场调研越详细，业务就越有利可图。
45 彻底地贯彻你的研究，重复进行，以确保你的结果是可信的。

答案解析

Section A

36 THERE。考查的是 which 引导的定语从句的相关语法知识。在所给的句子中，which 指代 the competition，引导状语从句。而 there is 与定语从句在语法上相冲突，所以 there 是多余的。

37 是正确的。

38 ARE。考查的是主谓一致性。所给的句子中，主语 their backgrounds 和动词 vary 是主动关系，可以直接用 vary。从句子本身的结构看，are 和 vary 并列用在语法上是明显错误的。所以，are 是多余的。

39 是正确的。

40 TO。考查的是情态动词 must 的用法。must 后面应该接动词原形，所以说 to 是多余的。

Section B

41 IMPORTANT。考查的是固定短语 it is + *adj.* to do something，表示做某件事是怎么样的。而所给句子中用的 importance 为名词，所以应该把 importance 改为 important。

42 FIND。考查的是固定短语 need to do something “需要做某事”。而所给句子中是 need to finding，在不定式 to 后面接的是动词-ing 形式，所以说，应该把 finding 改为 find。

43 INCLUDING。考查的是非谓语动词做状语的语法知识。所给句子中，动词 include 和句子的主语是主谓关系，所以应该用动词的-ing 形式，而句子中却用了动词的过去分词 included，所以应该把 included 改成 including。

44 IS。考查的是主谓一致问题。market research 是单数形式，所以谓语动词应该用 is，而不是所给句子中的 are。所以应该把 are 改为 is。

45 THOROUGHLY。是对修饰动词的副词进行考查。修饰动词词组 carry out 应该用副词，而所给句子中，却用了形容词 thorough，所以应该把 thorough 改为副词形式 thoroughly。

第二周

写 作 部 分

一、基础知识介绍

（一）格式

在BEC的写作中采用平头式的写法
收信人的姓名和地址置于信纸的左上方
地址、称呼和结束礼词后没有标点符号
日期在右上方
段落从定格开始，段落之间的行距为两行（但在考试中由于受答题卡限制，请酌情考虑）
写信人的名字和头衔在签名下方

（二）称呼语和敬语

称呼的写法遵循下列原则：
Dear Sir or Madam 写信给某一公司，不确定具体的收信人
Dear Sir 对男士，但是你不知道他的具体姓名
Dear Madam 对女士，但是你不知道他的具体姓名
Dear Mr. Smith 对男士
Dear Ms. Smith 对已婚或未婚的女士
Dear Mrs. Smith 对已婚女士
Dear Miss Smith 对未婚女士
Dear John（此处 John 为英语中常用男名）

对朋友或你比较熟悉的人（通常为多年生意伙伴）
称呼与结束礼词存在对应的关系，请特别注意：
Dear Sir or Madam — Yours faithfully
Dear Mr. /Ms. /Mrs. /Miss Smith — Yours sincerely
Dear John — Best wishes

（三）日期

在英国英语中，“天”在前，但是在美国英语中，“月份”在前。所以某些特别的时期容易引起误解。例如：12 06 2003
在英国指的是：6月12日
在美国指的是：12月6日
因此日期要写成：12 June 2003
注释：在BEC考试中，12 06 2003的用法仍然是可以使用的，因为BEC为英版考试。
要记住月份使用大写字母开头；“天”后不必写th、rd、nd或者st。

（四）信函开头、中间、结尾

1. 信件的开头

We are writing to enquire about …
We are writing in connection with …
We are interested in … and we would like to know…

2. 回信的开头

Thank you for your letter of (date) …

We have received your letter of (date) asking if …
enquiring about …
enclosing …
concerning …

3. 信件的结尾

一般结尾：
I look forward to receiving your reply/order/products/ect.
Looking forward to hearing from you.
如果你在信件中提供了信息：
I hope that this information will help you.
Please contact me if you need any further information.
Please feel free to contact me if you have any further questions.
Please let me know if you need any further information.

4. 中间引入主题

引入主题：
With reference to …
Further to …
With regard to …
I am writing in connection with …
注：引入主题的句子可以写在信件的开头，但 with regard to 不能用于信件的开头。
环境：
(How would you start a letter about each of the following?)
An invoice (No. 679) for a photocopier
With reference to Invoice No. 679, we regret to tell you that the product arrived in bad condition.
A meeting you had with the addressee on Jan. 16th
Further to the meeting on 16 January, I am delighted to tell you that we are now able to give you a special offer for our Peach Series computer.
An advertisement in the times newspaper
I am writing in connection with the advertisement in the times newspaper yesterday.
An application for a post as secretary in your company
I am writing in connection with your application for a post as secretary in our company.
A fax order for six computers that you received today
With reference to your fax order for six computers, I regret to tell you that they are out of stock at present.

二、题型概述

海外的考试严谨性和规范性一般来说都是有规律可循的。商务英语写作鼓励人们注意格式，采用套话，模仿优秀的范文。因而，在短时间里还是可以让自己的写作有所改观的。

第一题是写一篇 40～50 词的电子邮件、备忘录、便条等。

小作文主要是写一篇 40～50 字的商务便函、商务便条、商务留言、备忘录和电子邮件等，写作的背景通常是一事、两人、三要点。这一部分主要考查考生按照题目要求完成任务的能力，组织衔接观点的能力，语言表达的能力，词语的丰富性，语法、拼写的准确性等。分值是 10 分，限定时间为 15 分钟。

第二题是写一篇 120～140 词的商务信函、报告或建议书。

大作文是写一篇 120～140 字的商务信函、报告或建议书。出题形式可能是图表、图画作文，即根据图表或者图画的内容写商务信函、报告或建议。分值是 20 分，时间为 30 分钟。

样题举例

Part One

You are Head of Research for an international car manufacturer. You have to make an urgent trip tomorrow to visit Pierre Blanco, a colleague who works for a subsidiary.

Write a memo of **40-50** words to your secretary:

- telling her who you are going to see and when;
- asking her to book flight tickets and accommodation;
- telling her what work you would like her to do in your absence.

参考范文

Memorandum

To: Miss Anny, the secretary
From: Brown Smith, Head of Research
Date: 15 May, 2010
Subject: A Trip Tomorrow to Visit Pierre Blanco

I need to have an urgent meeting with Pierre Blanco of our Paris office tomorrow. Please book a return ticket to Paris and a hotel room for me as soon as possible. During my absence, please keep me informed of the progress of the project. If there is anything urgent, give me a phone call.

Part Two

- The company you work for is expanding rapidly and is looking for new premises. Your Managing Director is interested in Waterside Industrial Park, and has asked you to write a letter to find out more information.
- Read Waterside Industrial Park's advertisement below, on which your Managing Director has already made some notes.
- Then, using all your Managing Director's handwritten notes, write your letter to Rosemary Brown at Waterside Industrial Park.
- Do not include postal addresses.

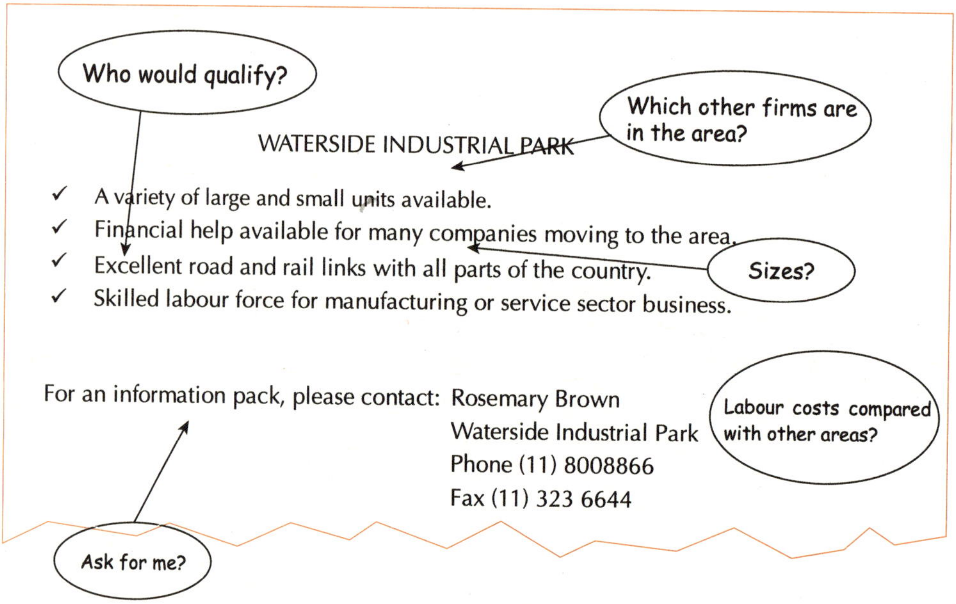

写作思路

这是商务信函中比较常见的询问信息类信函。在商务贸易中，信息交换具有非常重要的作用，往往关系到一笔交易或买卖的成败。在贸易中，为了达到准确交换信息和提出要求、进行新的提案等的目的而进行商务信息咨询。

上题是以图表加注的形式给出了咨询信需要询问的信息内容。在写作过程中，注意商务信函的基本格式。咨询信息类开头：I am writing to enquire about …；With reference to …，I would like to have more information about…；We are writing to enquire about …；We are writing in connection with …；We are interested in … and we would like to know … /asking if …。注意礼貌及简洁。

再根据题中的注脚，写出需要询问的信息内容，注意变换格式，用词谦虚大方，礼貌恭敬，多使用敬语（多感谢对方提供信息）；题中的 5 处注脚，结合简洁原则，最多用五句话完成对信息的咨询。

最后结尾也是套话，常用：I look forward to receive your reply/order/products/etc.；Looking forward to hearing from you.

综上，这封信函最多 7 句话，简洁明了。

参考范文

22 July

Dear Mrs. Brown

Subject: New Premises

With reference to your advertisement in the local newspaper, I would like to have more information about the above.

Could you tell us which other firms are in the area, and what are the sizes of the units available for rental?

Regarding the financial help mentioned, could you inform us who would qualify for it and how to apply?

Another point to clarify is the skilled labour costs compared with other areas.

Finally, we would be grateful if you could send us the information pack to our address.

We look forward to hearing from you soon.

Yours sincerely,

Alya Maideen

三、提升策略

1. 注意商务信函、商务便条、商务报告的写作格式。
2. 加强对各种类型的商务应用文体的格式模仿练习。
3. 积累商务应用知识，对于商业词汇和短语，正确使用信函、传真或电子邮件中的开头和结束语。
4. 加强对词汇和语法结构的积累和运用，在商务写作中，要能够对题目中的信息进行加工并且变换词汇和语法结构，使写作丰富化，不可简单复制原文中的信息，而要经过词汇和语法结构的转化进行叙述。
5. 商务写作要注意礼貌和正式语言风格的使用。

周一　商务便函 Memo

一、商务便函的内容与特点

商务便函（memorandum，简写 memo）是同一商业组织内部广泛使用的书面联系方式，它可以在同事之间、上下级之间、部门与部门之间使用。商务便函的内容通常包括：传达指示、发布通知、任命职务、了解情况、要求合作、汇报工作、提出建议、发表看法、探讨问题或节日安排等。

注：凡是与公司外部进行的正式商务联系，都必须用正规的商务书信。一般公司企业都印有具有自己公司风格的商务便函格式纸。

二、商务便函的基本格式

一般公司式企业都印有具有自己公司风格的商务便函，虽然排列格式不一，但基本组成部分是一样的。如：

Interoffice Memo
To:（收信人） From:（发信人） Date:（日期） Subject:（事由）
Message:（正文）

Memo	
To:（收信人） Company:（公司） Dept:（部门） Location & Ext:（地址与分机号） Subject:（事由）	From:（发信人） Company:（公司） Dept:（部门） Location & Ext:（地址与分机号） Date:（日期）
Message:（正文）	

商务便函一般由以下几个部分组成：

① Memo

Memo 是 Memorandum 缩写，因此也可以用 Memorandum。此外还有 Internal Memorandum 和 Interoffice Memorandum，其意思都是一样的。

② To

这一标题后面应写收信人的姓名与职衔，姓名前可以用尊称或不用。如：

To: Mr. John Smith, Sales Manager

③ From

这一标题后应写发信人的姓名与职衔：职衔可根据需要决定写或不写，但姓名前不要用尊称。如：

From: John Smith, General Manager

④ Date

日期的写法同书信里日期写法的要求完全一样，不要用数字来表示月份。

⑤ Subject

这一标题后是写事由的，即用一个或几个词汇简单概括便函的内容，以便查阅。事由必须简洁明了，不要用完整的句子，如：

Changes in Travel Advance Form

Promotion of Staff

Vacation Schedule

Participation in Training Programmes

⑥ Message

正文常常不需要注明这一标题。

正文与一般书信有所不同，可长可短，往往使用简短的句子和段落，有时只有一句话，有时有好几个段落。为了使阅读者一目了然，各段前还可以写上序号。

便函的内容虽然丰富，但它不像商务书信那样讲究措辞，不用那样注意开头与结尾的表达，只要意思表示清楚即可。

⑦ 除了上述 6 个部分以外，商务便函还可以根据实际需要，在末尾增加发信人的姓名首字母、附件、副本抄送等。

三、商务便函写作的基本要求

※ 倾向于用非正式的、口语化的语言。但给上级的便函语言要正规些。

※ 内容可长可短，但必须紧扣主题，切忌在一封便函中讨论几个不同的话题。

※ 用数码标明段落。层次、问题或用表格等形式有助于文章清晰明了。

※ 常常在一开头将写作目的和盘托出，中间就开头提及的事情进行详细阐述，结尾往往提出要求或征求意见。

※ 在 BEC 考试中，中级写作对收发人、日期、主题等细节不做过多考虑，考生在写作时，直接写正文。

※ 对于答题的要点，在写作前对题目信息进行分析归纳，写作时对信息进行加工，并且恰当使用商务词汇，句式和语法结构也要灵活多变，简洁明了。

四、商务便函实例解析

◇ 告知信息类

（一）常用句式

tell/ notify/ mention /express/ inform/ explain /note/ report/ advise

I am writing to tell/inform you that ...

I am writing to explain ... (tell your boss why you cannot attend)

I am writing to express ... (my regret)

I would like to know that ...

I'm pleased to inform you that...

（二）例题解析

You are the Head Office Manager of a company. You want to ask your secretary to make a budget for office appliances for next season.

Write a memo of **40-50** words to your secretary:

- explaining why the budget is necessary;
- saying what appliances are included;
- telling her the deadline.

谋篇布局

题目思路＋写作要点
1. 本文是办公室的经理写给其秘书的便函，内容是要求秘书写一份下季度的器械预算。 2. 写作中，有三个要点需要包括：该季度预算的必要性或重要性；说明哪些器械是需要预算在内的；告知预算的最后日期。 3. 语言必须简洁，信息不能遗漏，注意格式以及选词的准确合理。

高频词汇

预算	budget
财政预算	budgeting, the budget, budgets
原因表示	as for since because due to the fact that

参考范文

Internal Memorandum

To: Miss Lee, the Secretary **Date:** 1 March, 2011

From: the Header Office Manager, Stephan Smith **Subject:** Appliances Budget for Next Season

I want you to make an appliances budget for next season. You should know such office appliances we need to buy next season as electronic devices, scanners, overhead projectors, computers and you should file these material up to make the budget. Please complete the budget within three days.

范文点评

- 全部完成答题要求，所有内容点：该预算的必要性或重要性（I want you to make, for next season）；给出预算包括的内容（We need to buy next season as electronic devices, scanners, overhead projectors, computer）；完成日期（Please complete the budget within three days.）都已包括在内，并在答题要求

允许的情况下加以发挥。

- 语言规范、自然并且简明扼要。
- 所使用的词汇准确恰当，结构平衡。
- 语域和格式合理。
- 易给读者留下印象。

◇ 布置安排类

（一）常用句式

I plan to/I intend to/I am tempted to/I feel inclined to/I am going to/I am about to / I have decided to

（二）例题解析

You are the Manager of Sale's Department for an international air conditioner manufacturer. You have to hold an urgent meeting tomorrow to arrange the promotion for your new products, while you get serious cold; you ask your sectary to arrange the meeting and promotion tomorrow.

Write a memo of **40-50** words to your secretary:

- informing her to hold the meeting instead of you;
- telling her the arrangements and discussion about the meeting;
- telling her the time, place of the meeting.

谋篇布局

题目思路 + 写作要点
1. 本文是空调制造公司销售部的经理写给他的秘书的便函，内容是告知秘书明天有一个紧急会议需要秘书主持，并且告知其秘书会议主要是关于新产品的促销。 2. 写作中，有三个要点需要包括：告知秘书代替经理主持会议；告知秘书关于会议需要进行讨论的内容及如何安排；告知会议召开的时间和地点。 3. 语言必须简洁，信息不能遗漏，注意格式以及选词的准确合理。

高频词汇

促销	promote, promotion, sales promotion
销售部门	sales department
销售人员	sales staff
销售额	sales volume

参考范文

Memorandum

To: Miss Zhang, the Secretary　　**Date:** 1 March, 2011

From: Jonny King, the Manager of Sale's Department　　**Subject:** An Urgent Promotion Meeting

I will go to see the doctor tomorrow for illness so I want you to hold the meeting of promotion tomorrow. In the meeting tomorrow, you should discuss the prices, advertisements, and sale staff of our new products with other staff, make a record for your discussion and arrangements. The meeting should be arranged at 10 o'clock in the meeting office of our department.

范文点评

- 全部完成答题要求：告知秘书代替经理主持会议（I want you to hold the meeting of promotion tomorrow）；告知秘书关于会议需要进行讨论的内容及如何安排（discuss the prices, advertisements, and sale staff of our new products with other staff, make a record）；告知会议召开的时间和地点（at 10 o'clock in the meeting office of our department），所有内容点都已包括在内，并在答题要求允许的情况下加以发挥。
- 语言规范、自然并且简明扼要。
- 所使用的词汇准确恰当，结构平衡。
- 语域和格式适当合理。
- 易给读者留下印象，易懂易记。

◇ 征求意见类

（一）常用句式

Do you have any suggestions regarding the schedule?
I welcome your suggestions concerning the timetable.
Please let me know if you have any suggestions.
Please provide/offer your advice about the project.

（二）例题解析

You are a Manager of Human Resources Department and you want to train the new staff, but the time is limited. You can just arrange one training course. You want to consult your staff about the course.

Write a memo of **40-50** words to your secretary:

- telling her of training new staff in limited time;
- saying the importance of training;
- requesting suggestions for the arrangements.

谋篇布局

题目思路 + 写作要点
1. 本文是人力资源部的经理写给其秘书的便函，内容是告知秘书他想就对新人进行培训的课程征求同事意见，并且对于培养的安排也要征求同事的意见。 2. 写作中，有三个要点需要包括：告知秘书要进行新员工的短期培训；说明新员工培训的重要性；要秘书搜集关于培训的课程的意见。 3. 语言必须简洁，信息不能遗漏，注意格式以及选词的准确合理。

高频词汇

关于人力资源部门	Personnel department 人事部 staff department/ human resources 人力资源部
征求意见	propose suggestion advise seek for opinions take advise

参考范文

Memorandum

To: Miss Wang, the Secretary **Date:** 1 March, 2011
From: King Clicks, the Manager of Human Resources Department
Subject: Training New Staff

I am writing to inform you that we must train the new staff to let them work better for our company. As for the limited time, we can only arrange one course for them. Please let me know other colleagues' opinions about the course training.

范文点评

- 全部完成答题要求，所有内容点：告知秘书要进行新员工培训并且说明培训的重要性（we must train the new staff to let them work better for our company）；要秘书去搜集其他同事的意见（Please let me know other colleagues' opinions about the course training），要点都已包括在内，并在答题要求允许的情况下加以发挥。
- 语言规范、自然并且简明扼要。
- 所使用的词汇准确恰当，结构平衡。
- 语域和格式适当合理。
- 易给读者留下印象，易懂易记。

◇ 求助申请类

（一）常用句式

Could you please …?
Would you please…?
Is it possible for you to …?
Could you kindly approve … ?
Would you please allow me to …?

（二）例题解析

You are the Manager of Designing Department of an advertisement company. Recently you get a task to scheme new ads for a multinational corporation, but you feel the staff in your department is not enough for completing the task on time. You want to employ a new designer.

Write a memo of **40-50** words to the Manager of Human Resources:

- saying that you need a new designer;
- explaining what happened to your department;
- asking her to approve the request.

谋篇布局

题目思路＋写作要点

1. 本文是公司同事之间的工作便函，内容是请求人力资源经理聘任一位新的设计师，因为设计部门眼下为完成任务人手不够。
2. 写作中，有三个要点需要包括：告知人力资源经理你需要一名新设计师；说明原因；请求人力资源部经理的同意。
3. 语言必须简洁，信息不能遗漏，注意格式以及选词的准确合理。注意语体。因为是不同部门之间的交流便函，所以语气要比较谦恭并且尽量委婉礼貌。

高频词汇

请求	request demand ask beg
同意和允许	approve/approval permit/permission allow enable

参考范文

Memorandum

To: Mrs. Anny Ray, the Manager of the Project　　**Date:** 1 March, 2011
From: Zhang Hua, the Member of the Project
Subject: Asking the Approval of Copying the Material

I am writing to ask for your help to employ a new designer for our department quickly. I found the staff of our department is not enough after accepting the new task. As the new task is essential to our company, could you kindly approve this request?

范文点评

- 全部完成答题要求，所有内容点：告知人力资源经理你需要一名新设计师（to employ a new designer for our department quickly; the new task is essential to our company）；说明原因（I found the staff of our department is not enough）；请求人力资源部经理的同意（could you kindly approve this request），要点都已包括在内，并在答题要求允许的情况下加以发挥。
- 语言规范、自然并且简明扼要。
- 所使用的词汇准确恰当，结构平衡。
- 语域和格式适当合理。
- 易给读者留下印象，易懂易记。

◇ 推荐建议类

（一）常用句式

You'd better ...
You ought to ...
I advise you to...
Maybe you could try...
You should...
I suggest you that you should do...
You may/could ...
I think...
Why not...?

Shall we…?

（二）例题解析

Your company's Human Resources Department Manager, Mrs. Jay, has asked you to employ a new designer for the design department of the company.

Write a memo to Mrs. Jay in the Human Resources Department:

- Agreeing to preside over the job fair and suggesting a time;
- Requesting information about the employment;
- Telling her your own suggestions about the quality of the new designer;
- Write **40-50** words on a separate sheet.

谋篇布局

题目思路＋写作要点
1. 人力资源部经理要求部门员工为公司招聘一名新的设计师，针对这一安排，该员工有一些意见和建议要提出。 2. 写作中，有三个要点需要包括：告知人力资源部经理你接受了该项工作；咨询招聘的新设计师需要具备什么资格；对该项工作提出自己的见解。 3. 语言必须简洁，信息不能遗漏，注意格式以及选词的准确合理，并且注意该便函是下级写给上级的建议函，语气要委婉礼貌，用语要正式。

高频词汇

建议 推荐	suggest recommend make a proposal make a suggestion
招聘会	job fair career fair recruitment fair employment

参考范文

Memorandum

To: Mrs. Anna Jay, the Manager of the Human Resources Department
Date: 1 March, 2011
From: Zhang Hua, the Member of the Department
Subject: New Designer Employment

I would like to accept the task suggested by you and I think the new designer should be more creative than diligent. And I want to ask what I should prepare for the employment? Information of the candidates, quality and criterion of qualified employee, the number of people should be employed is necessary. Please give me some information about the people participating.

范文点评

- 全部完成答题要求，所有内容点：告知人力资源部经理你接受了该项工作（I would like to accept the task）；就该工作提出建议（the new designer should be more creative than diligent）；说明进行该项工作所需要的信息和资料（information of the candidates, quality and criterion of qualified employee, the number of people），要点都已包括在内，并在答题要求允许的情况下加以发挥。
- 语言规范、自然并且简明扼要。
- 所使用的词汇准确恰当，结构平衡。
- 语域和格式适当合理。
- 易给读者留下印象，易懂易记。

周二　商务便条和留言
Note and Message

一、商务便条和留言的内容与特点

便条就是一种简单的书信，内容简短，大多是临时性的留言、要求等。在有急事需告诉别人而又不能面谈时，就可以写便条，如请假条、留言条等，便条一般不写地址，与普通书信基本相同。便条具有用途广泛、形式简单、文字要求不严格的特点。便条都不用邮寄。跟正规的信函相比，便条的语言比较口语化，结束时可不写结尾礼词，只需写上写便条者的姓名。便条的主要目的是为了尽快地把最新的信息、通知、要求或者活动的时间、地点转告给对方。常见的便条有欠条、留言和请假条等。

二、商务便条和留言的基本格式

商务便条因为写作时没有事先准备，因此没有严格的格式要求，但有几点内容是必不可少的，如：

Date/time:
To:
Message:（写信人写在最后）

商务留言的格式大体上和商务便条一致，只有细微差别，如：

Date/time:
To:
Message:（最后用礼词结尾，不需要署名）

商务便条一般包括以下几点：

1. 写信的时间或日期

一般商务便条只写上星期几或者星期几上午或下午。或者具体时刻，日常应用中，一般不写年份，因为便条的内容多半是当日或近日要办的事情。日期一般写在右上角。

2. 收信人

通常商务便条和留言的收信人，通过写信开头的称呼，如 dear Anny，告知收信人。这一要点不需要像 Memo 那样明确说 to sb.，但必须要通过称呼说明。

3. 内容

便条的内容是涉及当天或近日的事情，而且没有经过严格事先计划，所以写作形式比较简单，语言口语化。

留言相对而言比便条要正式，一般都是经过事先考虑或计划的事情，所以写作形式虽简单，但语言相对正式。

4. 结束礼词

便条和留言的结尾跟一般书信一样，有简单的结束礼词，常见的有 Yours faithfully, Yours sincerely, Yours truly, Faithfully yours, Sincerely yours, Truly yours 等。结束礼词第一个词的首字母要大写，最后用逗号。

便条一般可不写结尾礼词，但留言一般要写。

5. 署名

便条结尾写上写信人自己的名字即可。留言一般不注明写信人。

三、商务便条和留言写作的基本要求

- 多用非正式的、口语化的语言。
- 内容较短，但必须紧扣主题，切忌内容空洞、言不达意。
- 词句简洁，尽量避免繁复的应酬语和各种敬语。

四、商务便条和留言实例分析

◇ 请假条

（一）常用句式

I would like to...

I am writing to request time off work to...

Can I ask a day off work to...

Could you tell me if it is possible to...

I am sorry to apply for leave.

简述原因常用句式

In order to..., I hope to attend...

Since... the meeting could be very useful to my work.

Given the fact that... I think...

I have to leave with the time is urgent, as...

（二）例题解析

You have a bad cold and must go to see the doctor and have a good rest.

Write a note to your line manager, Mr. Jack Wilson.

- Requesting time off work to have a rest.
- Saying when you return to company to go on work.
- Hoping the approval.
- Write **40-50** words on a separate sheet.

谋篇布局

题目思路＋写作要点
1. 注意写作形式是 Note，通过便条的形式向你的直属经理 Mr. Jack Wilson 请假休息，是下级写给上级的假条。
2. 写作中，有三个要点需要包括：请求经理允许其请病假回家休息；说明病假时间；希望经理准假。
3. 语言必须简洁，信息不能遗漏，注意格式以及选词的准确合理，并且注意该便函是下级写给上级的建议函，语气要委婉礼貌，用语要相对正式。

高频词汇

请假	leave ask for leave take a leave
看病	see a doctor go to hospital go to the doctor

参考范文

March 24th

Dear Mr. Jack Wilson,

In order to be more efficient in work, I would like to go to see the doctor and have a good rest for three days for my serious cold. Could you tell me if it is possible for me to take time off work? Thank you.

Anny Jay

范文点评

- 全部完成答题要求，注明了请假的原因（be more efficient in work, serious cold）；请求经理允许其请病假回家休息（I would like to go to see the doctor and have a good rest）；说明病假时间（for three days）；希望经理准假（Could you tell me if it is possible to take time off work），比较能让人接受。
- 语言规范、自然并且简明扼要。
- 所使用的词汇准确恰当，对于称呼，使用对方名字尊称而非职务，避免客套但不失礼貌，最后署名的时候也用的全名，显得语气正式。
- 语域和格式适当合理，下级写给上级的便条，简洁但不失正式，礼貌但不客套空洞。
- 易给读者留下印象，容易让人接受请求，且结尾署名使用全名，更显礼貌。

◇ 祝贺

（一）常用句式

I am happy to learn that...

I am pleased to know that...

I want to congratulate you on...

I'd like to congratulate you on...

I want to join in the congratulating you that...

（二）例题解析

Recently, your good friend Jack has got a promotion. Write a note to congratulate him on his success.

- Expressing your happiness on hearing the news.
- Saying good qualities he has own.
- Giving your best wishes to him.
- Write **40-50** words on a separate sheet.

谋篇布局

题目思路＋写作要点
1. 本文是好友得到晋升，你作为好友对此事表示祝贺。 2. 写作中，有三个要点需要包括：表达你得知好消息后感到高兴；赞扬好友的能力；祝福好友工作顺利。 3. 语言必须简洁，信息不能遗漏，注意格式以及选词的准确合理，并且注意该便条是朋友之间的祝贺，语气可以随意一点，省去客套和敬语，但不能少了礼貌。

高频词汇

获得职位/获得工作/晋升	get a position get a job take a position promotion prospect chance of promotion
祝贺	congratulate congratulate on give congratulations to

参考范文

March 15th

Dear Ann,

I am really pleased to learn that you've won the promotion. Please accept my warmest congratulations. You really deserve it because you are so talented and you have worked so hard. I believe you will have a bright future in your work.

George

范文点评

- 全部完成答题要求，表达祝贺以及对朋友获得晋升的肯定，所有内容点都已包括在内，并在答题要求允许的情况下加以发挥。
- 语言规范、自然并且简明扼要。
- 所使用的词汇准确恰当，结构平衡。先说事让对方愉悦，然后表达祝贺，最后表达期望和祝福之前对对方的努力也进行肯定，这是不错的祝贺方式。
- 语域和格式适当合理。
- 易给读者留下印象，亲密但不失礼貌。

◇ 通知留言

（一）常用句式

I'd like to inform you …

I'm writing to inform you …

As I advised you in our last meeting that …

I'd like to remind you that…

What I want to bring to your attention is…

Please note that …

Please notice that …

Please pay attention to the fact that …

（二）例题解析

You are the secretary of design manager. You have received an urgent call from an important client. Write a message to your line manager in the company.

- Saying which client make the call.
- Telling what the client says in the call.
- Explaining the importance of that client.
- Write **40-50** words.

谋篇布局

题目思路＋写作要点
1. 本文是公司秘书写给经理的留言，内容是关于客户打来的紧急电话。 2. 写作中，有三个要点需要包括：说明电话是谁打的；告知电话的内容；解释该客户是公司的重要客户。 3. 语言必须简洁，信息不能遗漏，注意格式以及选词的准确合理，并且注意该留言的内容结构详略分配合理，语言较为正式。注意是下级写给上级的，注意语气。

高频词汇

客户	client correspondence customer

参考范文

March 7

Dear manager,

CCC Company, the biggest cooperative partner of our company, has just given you a call to tell you their unsatisfactory to our advertising design for their company. They inform us to provide a new and creative designing within one week or they will cancel the contract with us.

Sincerely yours,

Anny Smith

范文点评

- 全部完成答题要求，所有内容点：说明电话是谁打的（CCC Company）；告知电话的内容（tell you their unsatisfactory to our advertising design for their company; inform us to provide a new and creative designing within one week or they will cancel the contract）；解释该客户是公司的重要客户（the biggest cooperative partner of our company），要点都已包括在内，并且详略得当、重点突出。

- 语言规范、自然并且简明扼要；三个要点顺序安排流畅合理。
- 所使用的词汇准确恰当，句型和用词富于变化，显得词汇丰富不单调。
- 语域和格式适当合理。
- 逻辑和理由合理。

周三　商务电子邮件 E-mail

一、商务电子邮件的内容和特点

商务电子邮件是目前最为经济、快捷的通信媒介。利用电子邮件发出的商务信函格式与信件形式发出的函件格式基本大同小异，其撰写格式、所用语气和网络礼仪、单词的拼写和用词、语法、标点符号等切不可因求快而随意。商务电子邮件也是非常正式的商务文体，撰写邮件有三种方式：写邮件、回复邮件、转发邮件。

二、商务电子邮件的基本格式

商务电子邮件和普通信件的格式基本一样，如：

Date：（日期）
To：（收信人）
From：（写信人）
Subject：（函件的事由）（相当于标题）
（函件主体）

商务电子邮件一般包括以下几点：

1. 日期

日期的写法同书信里日期写法的要求完全一样，不要用数字来表示月份。

2. 收信人

收信人这一栏必须写明收件人的姓名和电子邮箱的地址。

3. 发件人

这一栏必须写明发件人的姓名和电子邮件的地址。

4. 事由或标题

标题所传递的信息让收件人一眼就能抓住信函的主旨，并且帮助收件人迅速做出如何处理函件的决定：或删除；或保存；或及时回函；或暂时搁置。可见，一个简明扼要、准确传递信息的标题非常重要。

此外，如有副本抄送的话，就放在“事由”的上一行，副本抄送要注明副本收件者的姓名和电邮地址。

5. 函件主体

函件主体基本和纸质信函一样，包括称呼、正文、结束礼词和签名。

注意：虽然电子邮件同信函格式一样，但要注意的是电子邮件的保密性较差，一些机密或敏感性问题不要通过电子邮件传输。

三、商务电子邮件的基本要求

1. 函件的内容尽量不要超过一屏。
2. 内容确实过长的话，就简要概括要点，而详细内容则以附件形式发出。
3. 不可使用单词的缩略形式。
4. 必须使用正式语体，尽量避免使用口语化或随意的语言和词汇。

四、电子邮件实例

◇ 安排会议的通知

（一）常用句式

表示原因：

Because of … / For… / Owing to… / Thanks to… / On account of… / Due to… / As a result of …

表达提出建议：

You'd better… / You should… / I suggest you that you should do… / Maybe you could try… / I advise you to do …

（二）例题解析

You are a customer service manager and you want to arrange a meeting with your team next Monday.

- Write an Email to your team.
- Explaining the purpose and time of the meeting.
- Saying how they should prepare for the meeting.
- Telling them what they should do if they cannot attend.
- Write **40-50** words.

谋篇布局

题目思路 + 写作要点
1. 本文是客服部经理写给客服部成员的一封电邮，内容是关于召开会议的。 2. 写作中，有三个要点需要包括：简述会议的目的和时间；说明要员工如何为会议做准备；说明如有不能参加会议的员工，应该如何处理。 3. 语言必须简洁，信息不能遗漏，态度必须诚恳。

高频词汇

工作人员	employee member staff
召开会议	have a meeting hold a meeting convene a meeting call a meeting

参考范文

Date: March 25th, 2011

To: Martin <Martin@163. com>; Anny <Anny@163. com>; David < David@163. com >...

From: Mike < Mike@yahoo. com. hk >

Subject: Team Meeting

Dear staff,

In order to further improve our customer service, I would like to have a meeting at 9:00 a. m. next Monday. Every team member should give a presentation on his/ her work of the last four weeks and suggestions on the future work. Please let me know in advance if you can not attend the meeting.

Sincerely yours,

Mike

范文点评

- 全部完成答题要求，所有内容点：简述召开会议的原因（In order to further improve our customer service）；说明要员工如何为会议做准备（Every team member should give a presentation）；说明如有不能参加会议的员工，应该如何处理（Please let me know in advance），以及会议的时间。
- 语言规范、自然并且简明扼要。
- 所使用的词汇准确恰当，结构平衡。
- 语域和格式适当合理。
- 易给读者留下印象，易懂易记。

◇ 调整工作时间

（一）常用句式

We now have to change the working hours...

We have to adjust the office hour for a period time.

Due to..., we decide to adjust the working hours...

In order to ..., we have to inform you that we decided to adjust working hours...

（二）例题解析

You are the manager of a company. Your company has decided to change the working hours due to a big order of your company.

- Write an Email to all your staff.
- Giving the reason for the change of working hours.
- Introducing the new office hours.
- Telling staff the change is temporary.
- Write **40-50** words.

谋篇布局

题目思路＋写作要点
1. 本文是一家公司在收到大订单后，经理决定临时更改工作时间并且通知员工这一决定的电子邮件。 2. 写作中，有三个要点需要包括：说明更改工作时间的缘由；说明新的工作时间；告知员工工作时间的变更只是暂时的。 3. 语言必须简洁，信息不能遗漏，注意格式以及选词的准确合理，并且注意该邮件是公司上级写给全体员工的一项决定，所以对于原因的说明要简洁明了。

高频词汇

调整工作时间	adjust working hours change working hours
工作时间	working hours company hours office hours

参考范文

Date:	March 25th, 2011
To:	Phillip < Phillip @ macau. ctm. net >; Martin < Martin @ 163. com >; Anny < Anny @ 163. com >; David < David@163. com >…
From:	John Smith < Smith1220@yahoo. com. hk >
Cc:	Mike < Mike250@ mentongegs. vic. edu. au >
Subject:	Adjust Working Hours

Dear All Staff,

I'm writing to inform you that the office hours will be adjusted before completing the ABC Company's big order from April 2nd to April 20th. The new working hours are 8:00-12:00 in the morning and 13:30-17:30 in the afternoon. Working hours will get back to normal when the big order completes.

Sincerely yours,

John Smith

范文点评

- 全部完成答题要求，所有内容点都已包括在内：说明更改工作时间的缘由（completing the ABC Company's big order）；说明新的工作时间（The new working hours are 8:00-12:00 in the morning and 13:30-17:30 in the afternoon）；告知员工工作时间的变更只是暂时的（will get back to normal）。
- 语言规范、自然并且简明扼要，文体非常正式，语言严谨。
- 所使用的词汇准确恰当。

- 语域和格式适当合理。
- 易给读者留下印象，易懂易记。

◇ 举办庆祝会的通知

（一）常用句式

I'd like to inform you that …

I am happy to advise you …

We are pleased to inform you that …

I am delighted to inform you …

We will hold a celebration …

We will hold a party to celebrate …

We will have a party …

（二）例题解析

You are the manager of a company. The company will hold a small party to celebrate the completing of the big order.

- Write an email to all staff.
- Telling staff the reason for the party.
- Telling staff when and where the party starts and ends.
- Telling staff that all staff should attend the party.
- Write **40-50** words.

谋篇布局

题目思路 + 写作要点
1. 本文是一封公司经理通知员工举办庆祝会的信函。公司完成了大的订单，为了表示庆祝而举办庆祝会是公司内部的正常活动。 2. 写作中，有三个要点需要包括：说明开庆祝会的原因；告知庆祝会的时间和地点；要求所有员工参加。 3. 语言必须简洁，信息不能遗漏，注意格式以及选词的准确合理，用语要正式严谨。

高频词汇

举办庆祝会	hold a celebration hold a party to celebrate have a party have a celebration
盈利	profit earnings make profit

参考范文

Date:	March 25th, 2011
To:	Kitty < Kitty121@yahoo. com. hk >, Phillip < Phillip @ macau. ctm. net >, Martin < Martin@163. com >; Anny < Anny@163. com >; David < David@163. com >…
From:	Anna Wang < wanganna@sina. cn. com >
Subject:	Hold a Celebration

Dear All Staff,

We think you may be interested to know that we will have a party to celebrate completing the last big order and making profit. The party will be held in Pearl Hotel on April 20 from 9:00 to 5:00. I hope all of you attend the party.

Sincerely yours,

Anna Wang

范文点评

- 全部完成答题要求，说明开庆祝会的原因（celebrate completing the last big order and making profit）；告知庆祝会的时间和地点（in Pearl Hotel on April 20 from 9:00 to 5:00）；要求所有员工参加（I hope all of you attend the party.），内容安排较为合理。
- 语言规范、自然并且简明扼要，正式严谨。
- 语域和格式适当合理。
- 易给读者留下印象，并且充满礼貌和期待，易吸引读者。

周四　商务信函
Business Letter（上）

一、商务信函的内容和特点

在商务交往中，信息交换和信息获取非常重要，信息来源以及交换的方式有很多，或口头或书面，而书面形式使用更广，包括信函、电邮和电传等。电邮和电传都是基于电子设备进行传输的信函，所以这一部分就详细介绍信函的写作。

信函既可用于询问对方的资信情况或建立业务关系，也可用于询问对方某种产品的价格、货物装运期、付款条件或订购产品、提出索赔等。因此为了达到准确交换信息和提出要求的目的，商务信函必须使用正式、简洁的语言，语气礼貌友好。

二、商务信函的基本格式

1. 信头（heading）

信头也称为信笺抬头，由寄信人公司名称、地址、电话号码、email 地址和传真构成。信头通常位于信纸的最上端，如：

The Australian Telephone & Telegraph Company
96 Jephon Street, Toowong, QTD　4066 Australia
Tel:（07）23719033　Fax: 23741225

2. 日期（date）

日期顶边写在信头下方的右脚处，距离信头三到四行。
注意年份必须全部写出，
月份最好用英文全拼，不提倡用缩略式，
日期可以用序数词或基数词，
年份前要加逗号，
日期切忌全部用数字表示。
如：1st November, 2008 或 1 November, 2008
不用 2008-11-01 或 01-11-2008

3. 信函编号（reference number）

信函编号是为了便于往来书信的存档和查阅，一般采用 Your Ref.（你方编号）或 Our Ref.（我方编号）。信函编号通常放在日期的上方或与日期平齐靠左的位置，如：

Your Ref. :
Our Ref. :

4. 信内地址（inside address）

信内地址是指写在信内的收信人的姓名、头衔、单位名称、营业地址，和城市、国家名称和邮政编码。书写顺序是由小单位到大单位，每项内容单独成行，如：

Mr. Francis Lawrence
Vice President
Swinton Co.
87 Unico Avenue
Toronto, St9878
Canada
	Mr. Francis Lawrence
	    Vice President
	        Swinton Co.
	            87 Unico Avenue
	                Toronto, St9878
	                    Canada

并列式	斜列式

5. 称呼（salutation）

称呼写在信内地址下方的两行处，紧靠左边边缘。称呼是一种礼貌，用于正文开头前，常用的正式称呼有：

Dear Sir 或 Dear Madam（写给个人）Dear Mr. /Mrs. /Miss/Ms. Smith

Dear Sirs 或 Gentlemen（写给公司）

如果称呼多个男性则用 Messrs. ，如：Messrs. Smith and Hanks

如果称呼多个女性，则在姓名前用 Mmes.，如：Mmes. White and Gray

6. 正文（body）

信函的主体部分。

7. 结束礼词（complimentary close）

用于信函结束时的一种客套，前面也提到过，常用的有 Yours faithfully 等。

8. 签名（signature）

签名通常用手签。

最后的签名一般包括：公司名称、写信人的手写签名、写信人的打印签名、写信人的头衔，如：

Yours truly,

General Trading Co.

(signature)

John Smith

Sales Manager

9. 其他（这部分内容不是必须写的内容，有则写没有就不写）

① 经办人代号（reference notation）

经办人代号是提供信件产生的信息资料，便于必要时查对之用。经办人代号是有信件口授者和秘书的姓名首字母组成，用冒号或斜线号分开，如：

FCM/HL, FCM: HL, FCM/hl, fcm: hl

② 附件（enclosure）

如果信中有附件时，则应在左下角注明 Encl. 或 Enc.，然后标明附件名称、份数及种类。如：

a. Encl.: Order form No. 512

b. Enc.: (3)

1. B/L
2. Invoice
3. Certificate

③ 副本抄送（Carbon copy/C C）

如果寄给对方的信件中有副本寄给另外一个人或单位，则在签名处左下端打上 C C 及副本收件人或公司名。如：

C C：China National Light Industrial Products Imp. & Exp. Corp.

④ 主办人

如果所寄信函需要由对方公司专人处理，则可在信内地址和称呼之间加上如下文字：

Attention: Mr. David Jones, Business Manager

完整格式如下图：正式商务信函的书写格式

Bredgate 51,
DK 1260,
Copenhagen K,
Denmark
Our ref: WFX/SQ
Your ref: JS201/SD707

July 4, 2010
Superbuys Ltd.
Superbuy House
Wolverton Road
London SW 167
The UK
Attention: Mr. David Jones, Business Manager
Dear Sirs,

………
……………………………………………
………
…………………………….

Yours sincerely,

General Trading Co.

(signature)

John Smith

Sales Manager

FCM/HL
Enc.:(3)
1. B/L
2. Invoice
C. C. China National Light Industrial Products Imp. & Exp. Corp.

三、商务信函的基本要求

在 BEC 考试中，一般要求考生书写的内容就是信函的正文主体部分，其他部分作为对商务知识的拓展进行了解即可。主体部分写作要求及注意事项：

1. 研究收信人的兴趣所在
2. 采用恰当的语气

提倡使用体谅对方的态度（You-Attitude）/

避免以自我为中心的态度（I-Attitude or We-Attitude）
3. 语气自然、真诚
4. 言简意赅
5. 有礼有节，善解人意
礼貌用语，如 your kind enquiry，your esteemed order，your valued custom
6. 避免行文冗长
7. 避免陈词滥调
8. 措辞精确有力
（1）选用简单的词汇
（2）保持词语释义的一致性
避免出现一词多义
避免多词一义的错误
（3）用词准确
避免词义不清的表达方式，如 considerable quantity，favourable price，appreciable rise
（4）措辞具体、形象
9. 避免单调贫乏
（1）松散句与掉尾句
（2）长句和短句
（3）语序变化
10. 全盘布局
（1）An opening paragraph referring to the promise made.
（2）A statement that the promise has not been kept.
（3）That the delay is causing your inconvenience.
（4）A closing paragraph requesting completion without further delay.
11. 重视开头和结尾段落，注意多模仿常用的开头结尾句式，多加练习，熟练掌握这些句型。

◇ 开头部分

（1）开头部分要恰到好处。
（2）不要使用否定性的或不礼貌的词语。
（3）要从对方的角度出发体谅对方（You-Viewpoint），而不能以自我为中心（I-Viewpoint）。
（4）开始句一定要切合正题，不要东拉西扯，重复对方明知的信息。
（5）起首段落不宜太长。
（6）起首段落要前后一致，保证连贯性。开始句最好提一下上一次联系的情况，显得自然。

信函的开头部分常用句式：

1. 感谢对方来信

We thank you for …	Your letter (inquiry, telex, email, fax, etc.) of …
Thank you for …	
We appreciate …	
We were pleased to receive …	
Please accept our thanks for …	

2. 对来信进行回复

<table>
<tr><td>We are pleased to reply to …</td><td rowspan="4">Your letter (inquiry, telex, email, fax, etc.) of …</td></tr>
<tr><td>In answer to …</td></tr>
<tr><td>In response to …</td></tr>
<tr><td>In reply to …</td></tr>
</table>

3. 回复来信中的有关问题

<table>
<tr><td>With reference to …</td><td rowspan="4">Your letter (inquiry, telex, email, fax, etc.) of …</td></tr>
<tr><td>In reference to …</td></tr>
<tr><td>Referring to …</td></tr>
<tr><td>We refer to …</td></tr>
</table>

4. 回复来信中提出的要求或指示

<table>
<tr><td colspan="2">As requested …</td><td rowspan="7">In your letter of…</td></tr>
<tr><td colspan="2">As required …</td></tr>
<tr><td colspan="2">As instructed …</td></tr>
<tr><td>According to …</td><td rowspan="4">The request/instruction …</td></tr>
<tr><td>In accordance with …</td></tr>
<tr><td>In compliance with …</td></tr>
<tr><td>In conformity with …</td></tr>
</table>

5. 表达满意和欣喜

<table>
<tr><td>We were gratified …</td><td rowspan="3">To learn from your letter of … that …</td></tr>
<tr><td>We were glad …</td></tr>
<tr><td>It was a pleasure …</td></tr>
</table>

6. 表达遗憾和惊讶

<table>
<tr><td>We regret …</td><td rowspan="3">To learn from your letter of… that …</td></tr>
<tr><td>We were sorry …</td></tr>
<tr><td>We were surprised …</td></tr>
</table>

对于主动和对方联系的商务信函，可以用以下方式开头：

1. 通过别人的介绍了解到对方

Your company has been recommended to us by ...
We have learnt from... that...
The name of your reputable firm has come to us through ...
We have had your name and address given to us by ...

2. 对以前信函的补充或确认

Further to our letter of...
With further reference to our letter of...
Confirming our letter/conversation of...
We confirm that out letter of ... and ...
With further reference to...

3. 通知对方一些情况

This letter is ...	To inform you that ...
We are pleased ...	
We have the honor ...	
We have the pleasure informing you that...	
We regret to inform you that ...	

◇ 结尾段落

(1) 明确指出希望对方采取的行动。
(2) 如果对方不是行动的执行者，一定要指明动作的执行者是谁。
(3) 说明该行动的具体实施细则。
(4) 指明最后的期限。
(5) 赞赏对方，但除非对方曾为你做过什么，否则不要随便道谢。
(6) 避免使用消极性词汇。
(7) 如若需要，表明愿意提供帮助的态度。
(8) 结尾段落不宜过长。

结尾常用句式：

1. 期待对方回复的信件，可以用以下方式结尾：

We shall be glad to have ...	A/an/your reply (answer, favorable news, comment, etc.)
We hope to be favored with ...	
We shall be obliged for ...	
We are waiting for ...	
We shall appreciate ...	
We look forward to ...	

续表

We trust to hear …	From you about / concerning / in this respect / in this matter
We hope to hear …	
We shall be glad to hear …	
Please let us hear …	
Will you let us hear …	

2. 对于无须对方答复的信函，可以用以下两种方式结尾：

a. 表达感谢或希望继续合作的意愿

We thank you for the services you rendered in this matter.
Thank you for your attention to this matter.
We appreciate your patronage and hope that the pleasant relationship established between us will continue.
Your favorable cooperation will be greatly appreciated.

b. 表达歉意

We apologize for the delay in replying to your letter.
We regret the trouble we are causing you …
Please accept our apology for the inconvenience we have caused you …
We regret that we are unable to be of assistance to you.
We regret that we can't meet your requirements.

检查：

在签名之前，请参考下述问题，检查一下所写信函是否准确、恰当。

(1) 布局是否合理？

(2) 拼写是否正确？标点符号用得是否恰当？

(3) 是否包含所有要点？所传递的信息是否准确？

(4) 措辞是否简明、准确、礼貌？

(5) 语言是否自然、真诚？

(6) 是否做到从对方角度出发，体谅对方？

(7) 全文总基调是否合适？能否产生预期的效果？

(8) 如果自己是收信人的话，是否愿意收到这样一封信？

如果所有的答案都是“Yes”，那么就可以放心地签名寄送了。

周五　商务信函
Business Letter（下）

四、商务信函实例分析

◇ 告知变化类

（一）常用句式

I am writing to tell you that ...
I am writing to inform you that ...
I am writing to explain...
I am writing to apologize for/ about...
I am happy to advise you...
We are pleased to inform you ...
We regret that...
I am sorry to inform you ...
I am afraid that we...
I regret to tell you that...

（二）例题解析

- You work in the Sales Department of an international company. Anne Brown, an important client, is visiting your company for a day. There are some changes to the itinerary you sent her last week.
- Write a letter of **120-140** words to Ms. Brown, using the original itinerary and your handwritten notes, informing her of the changes.

Proposed itinerary for one-day visit of Anne Brown
Wednesday 12th December

10:00　Ms. Brown arrives on flight K838 from Singapore
　　　John Smith to meet Ms. Brown at airport
　　　[Original arrival time too]

10:30　Arrival at company
　　　John Smith to give Ms. Brown an introductory tour of company

11:30　Lunch at White Hart Restaurant　[Restaurant full. It's now the Swan Hotel.]
　　　(John Smith, Carol Snape, Sue Smith, Tome White, Connie White, Anne Brown)
　　　[Carol cannot make it. Explain why.]

续表

13:30	Meeting in boardroom (Carol Snape, Sue Smith, Tom White, Anne Brown)
14:30	Coffee break
14:50	Product presentation (Carol Snape, Sue Smith, Tome White, Anne Brown)
	Give some details.
16:30	John Smith to take Ms. Brown to the airport
17:40	Ms. Brown departs on flight R186 to Singapore
	John has to go early. Sue will take Anne to the airport.

谋篇布局

题目思路+写作要点

1. 本文是一封告知变化类的商务信函，是关于顾客对公司进行参观的全程安排，然而因为一些原因，原先的安排有变动，因而要写一封信函告知顾客旅程安排的变动。
2. 写作中，有五个要点需要包括：如题目中所标注的内容；到达公司的时间、就餐地点均有变化，要解释其原因；陪同人员中的 Carol Snape 不能一同就餐，也要解释其原因；对于产品介绍要多给出其内容具体事项等；告知接机人员的安排。
3. 语言必须简洁，信息不能遗漏，注意格式以及选词的准确合理，用语要正式严谨。

参考范文

Dear Ms. Brown,

Further to last week's correspondence, I am writing to inform you that we have to make a few adjustments to the original itinerary for Wednesday 12th December.

In order to allow plenty of time for you to travel from the airport, your tour of the company will be slightly shorter than the hour which we had originally planned. In addition, please note that lunch will be at the Swan Hotel as the White Hart is full on Wednesday. However, Carol Snape will not be joining us due to a previous engagement.

It has been confirmed that Tom Brown will show the sample of the new-styles blouse at 14:50. As John Smith has to learve early, Sue Smith will accompany you to the airport for your evening flight.

Please feel free to contact me if you have any further questions.

Sincerely yours,
XXX

范文点评

- 全部完成答题要求，题目中所标注的内容，到达公司的时间、就餐地点；陪同人员中的 Carol Snape

不能一同就餐；对于产品介绍给出其具体事项等；告知接机人员安排的变动，五点变动一一陈述并且做了合理解释，比较能让人信服。更重要的是，将五点变动的内容连同其原因进行了恰当衔接，使整篇文章连贯有条理。全篇语言规范、自然并且简明扼要，所用词汇和句型均为商务英语专业术语和句式，显得正式严谨。

- 语域和格式适当合理。
- 易给读者留下印象，内容实而不详，吸引对方为获取进一步信息而回复该信函，在商务交往中，是比较常见的方式。

◇ 商务信函回复

（一）常用句式

1. 信件回复的开头：

We thank you for ...	Your letter (inquiry, telex, email, fax, etc.) of ...
Thank you for ...	
We appreciate ...	
We were pleased to receive ...	
Please accept our thanks for ...	

2. 要求提供信息：

Please could you ... We would be grateful if you could ... We would appreciate it if you could ...	give us further details about... inform us (about/if) ... let us know (about/if) ...
We would like to know (about/if) ...	

3. 对相关信息的回复：

With reference to ...
In reference to ...
Referring to ...
We refer to ...

4. 一般结尾：

I look forward to receiving your reply/order/products/etc. Looking forward to hearing from you.

（二）例题解析

- You are the manager of a company. A customer has sent you a letter summarizing a negotiation made 2 weeks ago. You have written some notes on the letter.
- Write a reply to the buyer using the letter and your notes.
- Write **120-140** words.

Mr. Anny Williams
Beauty Clothing
20 Granada Road
Portsmouth

Dear Clare,

It was good to see you again last week and we are delighted that your clothing will be included in our summer catalogue.

As promised, listed below are the points agreed at the meeting.

The contract is for the Anna range of clothing in three styles.

You will grant us exclusive import rights for the toys in the UK.

The quantity will be 10, 000 pieces, with a further option of 4, 000.

The price per piece will be $50. 00 for the first 2, 000. You will confirm the price for the optional 3, 000 pieces.

Payment will be by letter of credit.

The initial order will be ready ex factory by 2nd, September 2011.

I trust you will find this in order. I look forward to your written confirmation in due course.

Best regards,
John Smith
Chief Purchaser

So are we!

Which styles?

We agreed 5,000?

$50.00 for the option pieces

Not possible–15th at the earliest

谋篇布局

题目思路＋写作要点

1. 本文是一封商务回信，在写回信过程中，应注意题目中所给的信息以及标注的内容。
2. 从题目中可以看出，回信需包括五个内容点（5个标注的内容），所以应该根据文中的信息合理安排结构和段落。注意公司往来信件中，涉及公司的商业利益，所以在用词和语言上必须非常慎重，而且随时记住以本公司的立场和利益为重。
3. 语言必须简洁，信息不能遗漏，应注意格式以及选词的准确合理，用语要正式严谨，条理需清晰，层次需分明。

参考范文

Dear Sirs,

We thank you for your letter concerning the negotiation of our contract. We were pleased to know from your letter of your interest in our products and include our clothing in your summer category.

As to the styles you mentioned in your letter, please tell us in detail which styles you want to buy. With reference to the quantity, I remember we agreed on 5, 000 pieces in last negotiation, please check it. As for the price of optional pieces, whether the price is the same as the first 2, 000 pieces?

With reference to the delivery date, we regret to tell you that we are unable to deliver by 2nd September 2011. The earliest date would be 15th September 2011. I hope this will be acceptable for you.

If you find any further questions of information, please contact me.

Your early reply is awaited.

Yours sincerely,

XXX

范文点评

- 全部完成答题要求，对于商务信函的回复，针对题目中的信息进行整合，并且有条理有层次地加以陈述。文中包含了题中所标注的所有内容，语言规范、自然并且简明扼要，所用词汇和句型均为商务英语专业术语和句式，显得正式严谨。
- 语域和格式适当合理。
- 易给读者留下印象，在确认信息的同时细心找出各个存有疑问的信息，并在信函中指出以期望得到对方的肯定确切的回复。在商务交往中，信函的回复注意一定要根据原信函的内容和信息进行整合，并且要确认信息的准确度，信函回复是商务信函往来中最常见的。

◇ 询问

（一）常用句式

May I have an idea of your prices?

Can you give me an indication of price?

Please let us know your lowest possible prices for the relevant goods.

If your prices are favorable, I can place the order right away.

Heavy enquiries witness the quality of our products.

As soon as the price picks up, enquiries will revive.

Enquiries for carpets are getting more numerous.

Enquiries are so large that we can only then allow you 200 cases.

（二）例题解析

- You are an employee of a computer repair workshop. Your manager has received the letter below about a faulty cassette player which he inspected. He has written his comments on the customer's letter and asked you to write a reply.
- Write a letter of 120-140 words to the customer, using the manager's comments and explaining why your company cannot repair the cassette computer.

Mr. D. Mazy
Computer Field,
6 Adelaide Park
London

Dear Mr. Mazy

[Sorry! Technician off sick]

Re: repair of Lenovo Computer

You returned our computer to us on 5th September, after having it in your shop for over a month, saying that you could not repair the following faults:

1. a problem with the volume control —— Needs replacing; part not available

2. difficulty operating the on/ off switch —— Possible to replace but very dear

I was very surprised to hear this, because the equipment is not all that old.

Therefore I would be grateful if you could explain in writing why the equipment is, in your opinion, beyond repair, so that I can discuss this matter with the manufacturers.

Yours sincerely,

Peter Hanks

Manufactured in 1998

Out of business since 2005

谋篇布局

题目思路＋写作要点

1. 本文是一封对服务评价信的回复信函，本题的做答要根据题目中给出的信函标注中的内容进行理解和整合，并且将题目中的信息有条理有层次地整理成连贯得体的信函。
2. 根据题目中的信息，标注了5点内容。在BEC中级考试中，对信函的要求就是写出5点要点，而这5点都是题目中已给的信息。该题的5点内容涉及对电脑修理时间过长的不满进行解释，对设备的两个问题没能解决的回答，以及电脑的新旧、电脑生产商不再生产该类产品进行说明。
3. 考生在写作该信函时要注意，语言必须简洁，信息不能遗漏，注意格式以及选词的准确合理，用语要正式严谨。

常备词句

afford 买得起	authorize 授权
cancel 取消	charge 收取，索要金额
confirm 确认	convince 使……相信
deliver 交货	dispatch 分派
distribute 分销	extend 扩大，延伸
fund 提供资金	install 安装
invest 投资	promise 承诺，许诺
recruit 招募，雇佣	split 分割

参考范文

Dear Mr. Hanks,

We have received your recent letter concerning the faulty computer.

I am sorry that we have kept you waiting for a long time. It is because our technician was ill and had been off work for a month.

As to the problem with the volume control, I'm sorry to tell you it has to be replaced. However, the equipment, manufactured in 1998, is such an old version that the spare part for the volume control is not available.

We are able to replace the on/off switch with a new one, but I should point out that changing it may cost you considerably.

Finally, I regret to inform you that the manufacturers of the product have been out of business since 2005.

I hope that the information will help you.

Yours sincerely,

XXX

范文点评

- 全部完成答题要求，对于评价类信函的回复信函，内容相对而言比较简单。对电脑修理时间过长的不满进行解释，对设备的两个问题没能解决的回答，以及电脑的新旧、电脑生产商不再生产该类产品进行说明，这五点内容均是题目中所给出的标注，很明显的信息，考生将其整合并且运用恰当的关联词进行衔接，层次清晰。
- 语言自然并且简明扼要，所用词汇和句型均为商务英语专业术语和句式，显得正式严谨。
- 语域和格式适当合理。
- 易给读者留下印象。

周六　商务报告 Business Report

一、商务报告的内容和特点

商务报告是商务文书的重要组成部分，在商务交往中起着重要的桥梁作用，尤其是作为对外交流沟通使用的商务报告，在现代企业中使用得特别频繁。在当今经济全球化背景下，熟练掌握商务报告的写作技巧，已是从事商务活动的人员，特别是职业经理人必备的文书处理技能之一，同时也是 BEC 考试中尤为重要的一部分。

根据报告的书写形式，商务报告可分为简式报告和正式报告两种。一般来说，内容单一、篇幅较短的报告宜采用简式报告形式；内容较为详细、论题较为重要、涉及面较广、要求又比较严格的报告宜采用正式报告形式。根据报告的功能，商务报告可分为：日常报告、调查报告、可行性报告、建议报告和商务旅行报告。其中，应用最广的是日常报告、调查报告和可行性报告。

1. routine report

日常报告，是指定期或不定期地向有关部门或上级领导对销售情况、生产情况等所做的汇报，最常见的有周报、月报、季度报告和年度报告。其目的是总结评定过去某一时期的业绩，同时跟踪发展动态及问题。

2. business trip report

商务旅行报告，通常属于非正式报告，一般用个人名义以备忘录的形式发给自己的上司，其目的是使上司及有关人员了解项目、工作或所参加会议的情况。

3. investigation report

调查报告，是指受其他单位或个人委托或本单位指示，对某一情况进行调查后写出的尽量反映客观事实的报告，这类报告是委托人或本单位领导进行决策的重要依据。

4. feasibility report

可行性报告，是指从众多的可选方案中筛选出一种最佳方案的报告。这类报告必须对所提出的方案、意见加以充分的论证。

5. proposal report

建议报告，是指作者为解决某一问题而提出具体建议的报告。它与可行性报告有共同之处，但前者通常只提出一个方案，后者可以列举多种方案，经比较各自的优点后再着重推出最佳方案。

商务报告有自己独特的结构，绝大多数商务报告都可以分为三大部分：引言 introduction，正文 body（主要内容为调查发现 findings），结尾 final section（包括 conclusion 和 recommendation，建议可根据实际内容选择，需要建议的可写；但 conclusion 是必要的内容）。

二、商务报告的基本格式

常用商务报告主要包括以下四部分：

1. introduction

介绍该报告的目的和报告的主题。

2. facts and findings

简述从信息中分析出来的问题、现象。

3. conclusion

根据信息的分析得出结论。

4. recommendation

根据结论提出看法和建议。对于商务报告，recommendation 部分不是必需的内容，

三、报告模板

INTRODUCTION 首句

The purpose of this report is to ...
The objective of this report is to ...
The aim of this report is to ...
This report aims to ...
Mr. X has asked me to report to investigate / evaluate / study / recommend / analyze / give feedback / estimate / assess 重复题目.
As requested by 某人/某部门, ...I am submitting the following report about 重复题目中的目的.
Upon request of 某人/某部门,
As you 或者某人，某部门 requested on November 12, I am submitting the following report on 重复题目.
Here is the report concerning 重复题目要求.
We have done a survey showing that 重复题目要求，或者直接开始阐述数据或者信息.

FINDINGS 首句

According to the recent market research / investigation / survey / the chart above / the table above / undertaken, ...
The recent visit/investigation/survey showed that ...
The table/chart above tells us that ...
From the chart shown, we find/learn/notice that ...
The table/chart above is showing that...

CONCLUSION 首句

According to the findings above, it can be concluded that ...
From the table shown, it can be concluded that...
Therefore, it can be concluded that ...
在有 conclusion 这个 sub-title 的情况下，就直接陈述结论。

RECOMMENDATION 首句

On the basis of the results, I have the following recommendations: ...

续表

On the basis of the analysis, it is reasonable to have the following recommendations: ...
Something is recommended, eg, a change of attitude. A more professional attitude will need to be encouraged through training.
With reference to the facts above, the following recommendations can be made, ...
With reference to the advantages stated above, the following recommendations can be made, ...
Based on the conclusion/analysis above, we recommend that/it can concluded that ...
Sth. should be done.
It is recommended that ...
The following are the recommendations ...
在有 recommendation 这个 sub-title 的情况下，也可以直接陈述结论。注意，recommendation 以及 recommend 后面要用动词原形（虚拟语气）。

四、商务报告的基本要求

1. 在语言方面，首先，商务报告的最大特点在于其简洁性，比其他文体更加注重表达效果的准确性、时效性，客观描述性语句较多，不主张使用修饰夸张性语言。
2. 商务报告，尤其是可行性报告和调查报告多用长句、复合句、并列复合句等句式，并通过使用介词短语、插入语、同位语、倒装句、被动语态等特殊句型，使语句结构更严密，细节更突出，句子的逻辑性更强。
3. BEC 考试中，商务报告的题型一般为图形或图表题，通过图表和图形给出信息，然后基于该信息进行总结，写出符合要求的商务报告。

五、商务报告的四步写作法

1. 收集信息（Collecting information）：通过题目所给出的文字信息或图形图表信息进行筛选分析。
2. 谋篇布局（Planning the structure）：确定报告写作的目的，对收集到的信息进行整理、分类，删除无关信息，然后按照信息的重要程度进行合理排列。
3. 撰写草稿（Writing the draft）：撰写报告的各个部分。
4. 校对编辑（Proofreading and editing）：校对编辑报告是写作的最后一个过程，也是极其重要的一个过程，很遗憾这一过程往往被人忽视。撰写人写完草稿后应对报告进行全面检查，检查的具体内容包括两方面：一是语言，包括语法、拼写、标点符号、语言风格等；二是信息，包括数据、图表、观点等。检查后，应对报告进行编辑，尽量做到报告便于读者阅读。

六、商务报告实例分析

◇ 销售报告

（一）常用句式

This report aims to work out/find out/check out/ figure out the need of ...

续表

This report aims to work out the reasons …
Here is the report concerning …
The objective of this report is to …
The report sets out to …

（二）例题解析

- The sales of your company, Taller Electrical Ltd. , have been falling lately. Your managing director has asked to write a report on this issue.
- Look at the information below, on which you have already made some handwritten notes.
- Then, using all your handwritten notes to write your report.
- Write **120-140** words.

Explain why.

March 2011

Quarterly Report

- Our sales department has reported a fall in sales in the first quarter.
- The lowest level of customer satisfaction in the recent five years.

How to improve.

TVs did the worst.

	Fridges	TVs	Cookers	Heaters
January	2, 000	3, 000	1, 500	3, 000
February	1, 800	2, 500	1, 500	2, 500
March	1, 500	2, 000	1, 500	2, 000

How to increase sales in the next.

Possible reason for this.

谋篇布局

题目思路 + 写作要点
1. 本文是通过图表提供信息，然后基于该信息进行分析的书面文书。 2. 商务报告中，有五个要点需要包括：报告的写作目的，本文中的目的为分析电器销量下降的原因；分析对比电器产品三个月的销售情况；分析出三月份电视机销售最差，热水器销量也不佳，要求解释其原因；结论部分提出如何改善销售不佳的状况；提出增加销量的相关建议。 3. 语言必须简洁，信息不能遗漏，注意格式以及选词的准确合理，用语要正式严谨。

常备词汇

annual report 年度报告	half-year sales report 半年度销售报告

续表

quarterly report 季度报告	inventory 库存，存货
article 商品	operational margins 经营利润
brand leader 畅销品牌	major brand 主导品牌
marketing strategy 营销策略	marketing mix 营销组合

参考范文

Report on: the Fall of Sales

Introduction

The objective of this report is to analyze the current sales situation and suggest some possible solutions as to how to increase sales in the next quarter.

Findings:

The sales in the first quarter of 2009 were unsatisfactory, which might indicate that we have already been deeply affected by the worldwide economic recession.

TVs and heaters performed the worst with a fall of 1,000 in sales respectively. However, the demand for heaters usually falls when spring comes.

It was also reported that the level of customer satisfaction plunged dramatically, which might also trigger the decrease of our sales. As the consumption capacity is shrinking, there is an urgent need for us to improve the after-sales service to win more customers.

Conclusion

The current situation calls for our immediate action to introduce the employee bonus schemes to improve our business performance in sales in the next quarter.

范文点评

- 从内容上讲，该报告涵盖了题目所要求的信息点，并且做出了合理的分析，达到了商务报告的写作目的。
- 本报告的写作目的（analyze the current sales situation and suggest some possible solutions）分析电器销量下降的原因；然后分析对比电器产品三个月的销售情况；分析出三月份电视机销售最差，热水器销量也不佳的原因（Heaters usually falls when spring comes）；结论部分提出如何改善销售不佳的状况并提出增加销量的建议是 to introduce the employee bonus schemes。
- 从语言上讲，用词精确，句子结构严谨而又富于变化，规范且自然，言简意赅。
- 语域和格式适当合理，用语符合商务英语的使用范畴，格式完整地包含了报告的四部分内容，findings 简明清晰地阐述了信息要点，conclusion 和 recommendations 根据分析得出结论，提出建议，衔接得当，条理清晰。

◇ 统计报告

（一）常用句式

This report aims to find out the more appropriate supplier that meets our key needs by comparing ... and ...
This report aims to compare ... and ... ranging from field experience, reputation and reliability to the service flexibility, so that we could select the more appropriate one.

续表

The report aims to contract the more competitive supplier, which meets our exact need perfectly, though the comparison between... and ...

（二）例题分析

- Your line manager has decided to review the staff situation in your department. You have been asked to write a report concerning this.
- Look at the information below, on which you have already made some handwritten notes.
- Then, using all your handwritten notes, write your report.
- Write **120-140** words.

	Number of staff leaving the department	Number of recruitment
2008	2	2
2009	3	2
2010	6	3

What reason?

Not enough

Number of new staff needed: 4

Say what type of staff needed

Possible new recruitment methods: Specialist recruitment agency Local recruitment agency

Compare

Say what effect this will have

To...	All staff
CC...	
Subject:	Training Opportunities
The company decides to provide overseas training opportunities to staff that have stayed at least five years with the company. Please submit your application.	

谋篇布局

题目思路＋写作要点
1. 本文是通过文字和图表提供信息，然后基于该信息进行分析的书面文书。 2. 商务报告中，有四个要点需要包括：报告的写作目的，即评价本部门的员工情况以便进行员工招募；分析需要什么能力的新员工；结论部分，提出相关建议。根据题目所给的信息，进行对比分析，然后进行选择，客观上该报告的结论部分应该给出选择，而提建议的部分则实际上可以省去，所以该报告包含三项内容比较合适。 3. 语言必须简洁，信息不能遗漏，注意格式以及选词的准确合理，用语要正式严谨。

高频词汇

recruitment 招募，聘任	develop team work 开拓团队协作
staff turnover 人员流动率	meet the needs 满足需求
team building 团队建设	attach importance to team building 重视团队建设
stick to the schedule 严格按计划进行	training function 培训职能
follow-up evaluation 后续评估	training opportunity 培训机会

参考范文

Report on: Selecting the Service Supplier

Introduction

This report aims to assess the current staff situation in our department and recommend ways of recruiting staff.

Findings

Our department is experiencing a serious understaffing problem due to the fact that in 2008 we were only able to recruit three new staff whereas six people left our department; it was caused by, as reported by some staff, the fact that employees were unhappy about their career paths here. There is an urgent need for us to employ both administrative staff and IT personnel.

The company is promising to offer overseas training opportunities to loyal staff, which provides a great opportunity for us to attract new employees.

Local recruitment agency

The local agency is good at recruiting skilled office staff but not people with specialist IT skills.

Specialist recruitment agency

The IT recruitment agency deals with the entire application and screening process. Although their costs are high, it would enable the company to recruit more quickly.

Conclusion

I suggest we should employ new qualified staff through specialist recruitment agency and it is urgent for our department to employ new staff to balance the normal work.

范文点评

- 从内容上讲，该报告对本部门缺人并且严重影响部门正常工作的情况进行统计，分析得出需要进行员工招募；对于员工招募，又对比分析了两种途径：Local recruitment agency 和 Specialist recruitment agency，最后得出自己的结论并提出建议，认为通过 Specialist recruitment agency 进行员工招募更好，而且员工招募非常紧急。
- 在对比的基础上选择出合适的招聘机构，达到了商务报告的写作目的。
- 从语言上讲，用词精确，句子结构严谨而又富于变化，规范且自然，言简意赅。分析部分条理清晰，详略得当。
- 语域和格式适当合理，用语符合商务英语的使用范畴，格式完美地包含了报告的三大主体部分内容。findings 简明清晰地阐述了信息要点，对于标注的信息进行了完美的加工，并对结构和形式的处理也使得这部分内容的陈述简短有力，结构明晰。conclusion 根据分析得出结论，回答了通过这份报告挑选出适合的招聘机构，衔接得当，前后呼应，条理清晰。

周日　商务建议书
Business Proposal

一、商务建议书的基本内容和特点

建议书是指单位或个人对某项事业或工作有所研究和思考，进而向有关领导、政府、企事业单位、专业团体提出改进措施和建设性意见所形成的一种书面材料。它也是英文商务写作常见的一种文体，可以将其视为报告类文书之一种，但是它与其他报告相比有其自身特点，因此英文中常用一个特定的名称“Proposal”来界定此类文书。

同商务报告的分类方法一样，商务建议书还可根据其正式程度划分为非正式建议书（Informal Proposal）和正式建议书（Formal Proposal）。商务建议书其具体书写格式和商务报告完全相同，具体可参照上一章节中关于商务报告格式的介绍。

二、商务建议书的基本格式

常用商务建议书主要包括以下三部分：

1. introduction

介绍该建议书的目的和建议的主题。

2. facts and findings

简述从信息中分析出来的问题、现象。

3. conclusion

根据信息的分析得出结论。

4. recommendation

根据信息的分析提出看法和建议。

此外，还有一种常用格式，与商务信函接近，但主体内容则围绕着 findings 和 recommendation 进行书写。

Dear Mr. Lee

Subject:

正文（introduction, findings, recommendation）

Your name

注意：在实际商务写作中，商务报告和商务建议书可以看做是一体的，因为商务报告中往往也包含了建议这一部分，商务建议书中也有结论部分，所以实际写作中，商务报告和商务建议书的写作模式基本一样，但侧重点不同，往往也可以合称为商务报告建议书。

三、商务建议书的基本要求

- 建议书要以事实为根据撰写。
- 提出的建议要具体，操作性要强。
- 对采纳建议能带来的好处既要写得乐观，也要防止吹嘘。
- 建议书与可行性报告相比有共同之处，但“报告”可以列举多种方案，经比较各自的优劣后再推出最佳方案，而在建议书中通常只提出一个方案。

- 书写商务建议书时，注意根据题目的要求组合语言，题目中往往给出了所需要的信息以及建议和看法，需要考生根据题目信息进行整合，将信息和建议能够流畅地贯通起来，使之成为逻辑性强、衔接得当的一篇商务报告书。因此，在 BEC 考试中，商务报告是要求相对简单的，主要考查考生对全文信息的把握以及对语言句式结构变换的能力。

四、商务建议书实例分析

◇ 业务建议

（一）常用句式

This proposal aims to/sets out to ...
This proposal is designed to...
The purpose of this proposal is to...
This proposal recommends a solution and provides budget and time schedule figures.
The suggestion is based on the research I've done in the past few years, and I believe it will work well.
I hope you will adopt this proposal.
What we think is to ...
I recommend that ...
I strongly hope that the next year will promise a brighter prospect for our company.

（二）例题分析

- The staff at your company were recently asked what they thought about working conditions. Your line manager has asked you to write a report summarizing their opinions and suggesting possible improvements.
- Look at the information below, on which you have already made some handwritten notes.
- Then, using all your handwritten notes, write your proposal.
- Write **120-140** words.

I know you had a meeting with staff recently. Can you write a proposal telling me what staff thought about working conditions, what changes can be made, and how the company will benefit from improving conditions?

Better productivity

Give an example

Meeting with employees about working conditions

Staff has some good things to say but they also mentioned these problems:

- The need for more flexible working hours
- Poor condition of some office areas
- Too little paid holiday

Explain why needed

Suggest a solution

Say what the biggest problem is

谋篇布局

题目思路＋写作要点
1. 本文是写给上司的建议书。题目是通过图表的形式提供信息，因此要分析图表内容，根据标注进一步构思建议书的整体框架。
2. 有五个要点需要包括：对公司的好处是提高工作效率；员工对于公司的积极的评价需举例说明；解释需要弹性工作时间的原因；带薪假太少；作出结论并提出建议。当然，建议书不能忘记了要先说明建议书的写作目的。
3. 语言必须简洁，信息不能遗漏，注意格式以及选词的准确合理，用语要正式严谨。

高频词汇

flexible working hours 弹性工作时间	flexible working system 弹性工作制
paid holiday 带薪假	benefit premium 福利津贴
base pay 基本工资	benefit system 福利制度
company performance 公司绩效	performance evaluation 绩效评估

参考范文

Proposal on Staff Opinions about Working Conditions

Introduction

The objective of this proposal is to summaries the results of the last staff meeting.

Findings

1. most of the employees are quite satisfied with the new non-smoking policy, which has substantially improved the working conditions.
2. However, some complained about the inflexible working hours, as they have to leave work early to fetch their children from the school.
3. Apart from the above, the new batch of interns working here has made some office areas too crowded to ensure a quiet and uninterrupted working environment.
4. Finally, the problem of too little paid holiday was also put forward by staff. I would suggest rewarding staff with chances of paid holiday to increase productivity at our workplace.

Conclusion

In my opinion, it is vital for our staff to regularly take some time off to refresh themselves to work better.

Recommendation

It is suggested that providing more chances of paid holiday lead to better productivity and bring benefits to the company in the long run.

范文点评

- 从内容上讲，该建议书基本包含了表格和标注所提供的信息。Findings 四项内容是将图标 2 的四项标注进行整合并且对标注中所提出的问题一一进行解释和说明，考生在写作这一部分时可适当发挥，将标注的信息进行加工和重新组织，使之有条理、连贯并且衔接得当即可。结论部分则是对第一个表内信息和标注的解释，并且也总结了全文。
- 从语言上讲，用词精确，句子结构严谨而又富于变化，规范且自然，言简意赅。分析部分对标注信息的转述和再加工非常成功，体现了用词的丰富性和结构的多样性，使文章看起来不让人感觉乏味。

- 语域和格式适当合理，用语符合商务英语的使用范畴，格式完美地包含了报告的三大主体部分内容。findings 简明清晰地阐述了信息要点，对于标注的信息进行了完美的加工，并对结构和形式的处理也使得这部分内容的陈述简短有力，结构明晰。conclusion 根据分析得出结论，结尾根据分析部分指出的问题提出了自己的建议，即将带薪休假作为对员工的嘉奖来激励员工提高工作积极性，并且给予更多的带薪假机会给员工。衔接得当，前后呼应，条理清晰。

◇ 项目建议

（一）常用句式

This proposal aims to …
The purpose of this proposal is to …
Our policy should cover the following categories of …

（二）例题分析

- The staff at your company were recently asked what they thought about the company canteen. Your line manager has asked you to write a proposal summarizing their opinions and suggesting possible improvements.
- Look at the information below, on which you have already made some handwritten notes
- Then, using all your handwritten notes, write your proposal.
- Write **120-140** words.

How was the information obtained

I know you had a meeting with staff recently. Can you write a proposal telling me what staff thought about the company canteen, why the number of staff using the company canteen at mealtimes has been falling? Can you also suggest some possible ways to encourage staff to use the canteen?

Suggest something

Meeting with employees about the company canteen

Staff mentioned these:

- Menu — Elaborate on this
- Conditions of the canteen — What problem
- Price too high — Compared with whom?

谋篇布局

题目思路＋写作要点

1. 本文是写给上司的改善公司餐厅就餐环境的建议书。题目是通过图表的形式提供信息，因此要分析图表内容，根据标注进一步构思建议书的整体框架。
2. 有五个要点需要包括：阐明建议书的意图；员工对公司餐厅的看法；建议和看法（这一部分内容，题目中标注内容已经给出相关信息，需要进行整合）；对餐厅的菜单、就餐环境以及价格进行比较详细的说明。本文在写作时可根据建议书格式和题目要点构思全文。
3. 语言必须简洁，信息不能遗漏，注意格式以及选词的准确合理，用语要正式严谨。

高频词汇

company image 公司形象	company culture/ enterprise culture 公司文化
company values 公司价值观	pro-business environment 对商务有利的 环境
staff complaints 员工投诉	benefits 效益
productivity 生产力	working efficiency 工作效率

参考范文

Proposal on the Low Utility Rate of Staff Canteen

Introduction

The purpose of this proposal is to examine key reasons why our employees prefer other lunch venues as opposed to our staff canteen and suggest possible ways for improvement. Semiformal interviews with 20 staff members were conducted to obtain the following opinions.

Findings

Menu: it was pointed out by many employees that the menu failed to offer any variety. Set menus can no longer cater to their needs for healthy and balanced diet.

Conditions of the canteen. The main problem is that the canteen is too crowd at peak hour.

Price too high. Compared with many other fast food restaurants within a five-minute walking distance from our premises, our food is too expensive.

Conclusion

Some minor adjustment in environment of company canteen should bring better effects.

Recommendation

It is strongly suggested that we should introduce flexible opening hours to avoid too many people dining at peak hour and provide cheaper, more healthy and diversified meals to attract our employees.

范文点评

- 从内容上讲，该建议书基本包含了图表和标注所提供的信息。阐明建议书的意图；员工对公司餐厅的看法；建议和看法（这一部分内容，题目中标注内容已经给出相关信息，需要进行整合）；对餐厅的菜单、就餐环境以及价格进行比较详细说明均是将标注的信息进行加工和重新组织，使之有条理、连贯并且衔接得当。
- 从语言上讲，用词精确，句子结构严谨而又富于变化，规范且自然，言简意赅。分析部分对标注信息的转述和再加工非常成功，体现了用词的丰富和结构的多样，使文章看起来不让人感觉乏味。
- 语域和格式适当合理，用语符合商务英语的使用范畴，格式完美地包含了报告的三大主体部分内容。findings 简明清晰地阐述了信息要点，对于标注的信息进行了完美的加工，并对结构和形式的处理也使得这部分内容的陈述简短有力，结构明晰。conclusion 根据分析得出结论，结尾根据分析部分指出的问题提出了自己的建议，将公司餐厅改为弹性时间，错开就餐高峰期导致的拥挤和用餐时间浪费现象，并且建议餐厅提供更加丰富的、物美价廉的、健康的饮食来吸引员工就餐。衔接得当，前后呼应，条理清晰。

第三周

听 力 部 分

本周展望

在这一周里，我们安排了剑桥商务英语考试听力部分的内容。剑桥商务英语中级的听力考试分三部分，我们将分别对每部分题型进行了解，每个题型分两天学习，前一天侧重理论讲解，后一天侧重练习。希望通过本周的学习，大家可以对剑桥商务英语中级的听力题型有所熟悉。

题型介绍

BEC 中级听力考试分为三个部分：第一部分为短对话填空；第二部分为搭配题；第三部分为长对话。分数与题数分配如下：

短对话填空	四道题	4 分
搭配选择	五道题	5 分
长对话	八道题	8 分

周一　填空题三步走

一、题型分析

（一）命题规律

这部分有三段交谈或电话留言，每段对应一篇留有空格的文字，每篇文字上下文关系非常清楚，有四个空格需要填写一两个单词或一个数字，留有空格的文字可能包括表格、日记摘录、发票、留言簿等。每段谈话或留言，考生可以听两遍，要求在听的过程中填写空格。

这部分听力测试集中在获取事实性信息，考生仔细听录音的同时，借助试卷上的提示找出所缺的信息。例如，他们可能需要记下人名，如果录音中拼读了人名，答案也必须正确地拼写。他们也可能需要听出房间号码或者电话号码、一项指示或者一个最后期限。这部分问题的答案很少是简单的听写，为了找到正确的答案，需要将所提示的材料重新做出确切的表达。

（二）应试方法

1. 读题预判断：

这部分听力测试集中在获取事实性信息，考生拿到试卷后应抓紧时间将题目看一遍，根据文字信息，揣测空格中所要填的词的词性。一般来说，这部分要填的内容是：公司名称、人名、号码（电话号码、订单号码等）、日期、一项指示等，这一题主要是考考生的辨别词汇的能力。在听力开始之前，对听力和填空内容有大致的判断，有助于提高听力的准确性，对提高听力效率非常重要。

预读目标：获取听力内容大致方向，基本把握填空内容词性、类别。

2. 初次填写：

仔细听录音的同时，借助试卷上的提示找出所缺的信息。在听第一遍时，考生要尽可能记下有关的名称、地点、号码等关键内容。对于较长的一时难以写完整的单词，可用汉字或不完整单词简单标注，待听力结束后再补充完整。对于不确定的填空内容，切忌在一处犹豫不决，浪费时间，简单标示后，要继续仔细听后续内容，不确定处在第二遍检查时再行填写。

初填目标：确定听力内容大意，填写70%以上填空内容。

3. 再次检查：

听第二遍时检查所填内容，补充完善所填信息。听第二遍时，一定要集中精力核对所填写的内容，有目的、有针对性的仔细听写核对。对于填写完成的答案，要保证其正确性。对于实在填写不上的内容，不必纠结，迅速调整心态，完成后续听力部分，切忌因小失大。

再检目标：完成全部填写，确保填写内容准确无误。

二、典型样题

练习一

Conversation One
(Questions 1-4)

- Look at the note below.
- You will hear a woman calling a colleague about a customer visit.

Customer Visit Schedule

Visitors are five European (1) ________
8:30am meet visitors at the (2) ________
Visit to the (3) ________ firstly
Visit to the (4) ________ after the coffee

对话大意

生产部的 Nash 打来电话想要 Jane 帮出差在外的 Sophie 带领从欧洲各国来的技术经理参观公司。首先安排在办公室见面，然后参观生产线，喝过咖啡后在午饭前去供货处参观。

答案解析

(1) tech-managers。此处填名词“技术经理”，要求考生在平时应熟练掌握各种职位的英文表达。注意在录音中，tech-manager 之前出现了一个 representative（代表），此为干扰信息。
(2) office。从录音中“I thought you could meet them at eight thirty in the office”一句可得知，男士要求女士在办公室接待参观者。
(3) produce line。女士首先询问了应该带客户参观什么，并且提出参观产品，男士说他们已经参观过，并提议首先参观生产线。“Maybe you could take them around the produce line instead?”此句为关键信息句。
(4) delivery yard。注意题中的时间标志 after coffee，在录音中听到这个时间时注意后面出现的重点内容，便可直接得到答案。

听力原文

Woman: Hello. This is Jane speaking.
Man: Hello. It's Nash here, from production. Sophie should be taking some customers around next Monday, but she's on business and will be back until next Friday. So I was wondering…
Woman: … if I'd do it?
Man: You are right.
Woman: No problem. Who are the customers representatives from Paris again?
Man: Not this time. It's the tech-managers. There are about five. They are from Germany, Italy… all around Europe.
Woman: And the schedule?
Man: I thought you could meet them at eight thirty in the office. I would suggest meeting at reception, but it'll be busy then.

Woman: Do you want me to show them around the product first?

Man: I think they've seen it before. Maybe you could take them around the produce line instead?

Woman: Good idea. What about after coffee?

Man: The delivery yard maybe? There's a lot going there and visitors usually find it interesting — I'm not sure they'd like it, especially not before lunch.

Woman: I agree.

Man: Thanks again.

小结

本段录音内容考查重点是对录音中的职位名称、工作地点以及具体细节信息的掌握。从题干中根据所要填的答案在句子中的成分可以推断出是表示人物或者地点的名词。

练习二

Conversation Two

(Questions 5-8)

- Look at the note below.
- You will hear a woman calling about a claim for furniture that she ordered.

TELEPHONE MESSAGE

Caller's name: Sally from Hamorson Company

Subject: Talking about a claim.

Notes :

- The purpose is to (**5**) ________ the claim.
- For the reason of (**6**) ________ given by an expert, the buyer has to (**7**) ________ a claim first.
- The seller thinks (**8**) ________ is not clear, so he refuse to make any compensation.

对话大意

Hamorson 公司的 Sally 打电话到 Lazen 出口公司去解决关于订购家具的索赔问题。Lazen 公司要 Homorson 公司提供凭证。Homorson 公司请商品检验局的专家检查了货物，说明是由于包装不当引起的损坏，Lazen 公司认为应该是在海上运输的时候导致的损坏，不接受索赔。

答案解析

(**5**) settle。从对话中的 I'm calling to 可知打电话的目的，之后出现的 settle 一词即为真正的目的——解决索赔问题。"I'm calling to settle the claim for the furniture we ordered." 此句为关键信息句。

(**6**) deficient packing。从题干中的 for the reason of 可以推断出所填的答案应该是事情所发生的理由，从句子"The result shows that damage was caused by deficient packing." 可知，文中女士反映到检验局的检验结果是由于包装不当造成了商品的损坏。

(**7**) lodge。"lodge a claim" 为"提出索赔"之意。如果考生有充分的商务背景知识可以直接判断出，买方在收到了不符合规格的产品并且造成了损失之后，一般是会提出索赔要求的，故此处应填写的答案就是索赔。另外我们也可以根据题干中的空白处在句子中所做的成分判断出应该填写的词是动词。

(**8**) liability。从录音中男士的谈话内容可知，他说检验的结果不能最终决定哪一方应该承担责任，而且在运输途中发生的损失是无法控制的，因此可知责任并不是很明确，故填 liability（责任）。其中，句子"your findings can't be the only way to determine who should hold the liability" 为关键信息句，与题干中的 not clear 在表述上意思一致。

听力原文

Man: Good morning. Lazen Export Corporation. Can I help you?

Woman: Hello. This is Sally from Hamorson Company. I'm calling to settle the claim for the furniture we ordered.

Man: Oh, yes, we've received your notice of claim. You said that nearly half of the goods are broken. Do you have any evidence?

Woman: Sure, the goods have been inspected by an expert in Commodity Inspection Bureau. The result showed that damage was caused by deficient packing. So we have no choice but to lodge a claim for losses.

Man: But I can assure you that the goods were in excellent condition when we shipped in New York. I guess other factors, such as the excessive moisture at sea, may be the cause of the damage.

Woman: I don't agree. I think we should respect the inspection analysis.

Man: Well, your findings can't be the only way to determine who should hold the liability. In fact, we can't take control over the loss occurring on unexpected condition and thus cannot accept your claim.

小结

本题主要考查对细节信息的掌握。考生可以通过对题干的分析确定所填的答案的词性，第一个答案为动词，第二个答案为名词，第三个是动词，最后一个在句子中做主语，也应为名词，这样可以在录音中抓住主要的信息进行判断，从而更加准确快速地得出答案。

商务背景知识扩展

理赔（settlement of claims）是指违约方受理受损方提出的赔偿要求。

在理赔时应注意：

1. 要认真细致地审核买方提出的单证和出证机构的合法性；
2. 要认真做好调查研究，弄清事实，分清责任；
3. 要合理确定损失程度、金额和赔付办法。

保险理赔程序：

1. 立案查验；
2. 审核证明和资料；
3. 核定保险责任；
4. 履行赔付义务。

保险理赔的原则：

1. 重合同，守信用；
2. 坚持实事求是；
3. 主动，迅速，准确，合理。

周二　填空题巧应试

一、实战应用

（一）方法总结

1. 三步法牢记：

在周一的解题技巧中，已经总结了完形填空的三步法，“一预读二初填三检查”，在实际做题时，一定要按照上述三步法，严格把握时间，按照一二三一步一步执行。

2. 时间决定成败：

考试中，时间就是分数，每个题型，每道题，都是有严格的时间，容不得一点犹豫和浪费。听力更是如此，在填空题中，一个填空浪费了时间，下面的听力就难以听全。一定要珍惜时间，果断填写，切忌为一题一空之得失，而至满盘皆输。

3. 快听快写：

听力重在听，听的速度一定要跟得上录音的语速，这在于平时的练习。听力的完形填空，不仅要听得快，写得也要快，更要会用简单的标记法表示复杂的单词，以满足完型填空的时间要求，这在平时练习中要多多注意。平时听力练习一定要像考试一样认真对待。

（二）实战心态

在听力考试时，往往容易由于考试的环境和压力，导致听力效果不如平时练习时好。为了克服这一问题，在平时练习时一定要注意，练习时最好不要戴耳机，也不要把声音调的特别大。正常音量下，在适当空旷的环境下练习听力，有助于听力的提高。在听力水平不错时，在周围有点噪音时，如果依旧能正常听写，那么考试时周围环境的影响就会大大减小。为了克服考试时的心理压力，不妨在平时练习时多给自己一点压力，强迫自己紧张，使自己在紧张状态下依旧能保持正常听写。

二、典型样题

练习一

Conversation One
(Questions 1-4)

- Look at the note below.
- You will hear a message about a man calling about a deal.

Message

For: Mr. Green

Mr. Zhang phoned about the (**1**) ________ of our products.

He's contacted other (2) ________ who are/ is willing to supply similar goods.
He wanted to negotiate if we can offer a reduction of (3) ________ and he really hope the (4) ________ can be reached.

对话大意

这是一通关于要求降价的电话对话。男子联系了其他的供应商，发现他们能提供低于该商品价格 10% 的类似产品，遂要求降价 5%，并希望能达成他们之间的第一次交易。考生在做这道听力题时要注意题中出现了两个数字，仔细分析哪个符合题意。

答案解析

(1) reduction。从题目上看，本题应该填名词，由原文 "I want to negotiate with your manager if you can offer a reduction of 5%" 可知道本题应该填 reduction。
(2) supplies。由原文 "We have contacted other suppliers who are willing to supply similar goods at the price about 10% lower than yours" 可知答案。
(3) 5%。由原文 "I want to negotiate with your manager if you can offer a reduction of 5%" 可知答案。
(4) transaction。由原文 "I sincerely hope to reach a transaction." 可知答案。

听力原文

Woman: Marketing Manager's Office. Can I help you?
Man: Mr. Green, please.
Woman: Sorry, he is out. Can I take a message?
Man: I think it's better for me to leave a message. This is Mr. Zhang. It is very difficult to market your products in our market at the price you offered.
Woman: The price offered is very reasonable.
Man: We have contacted other suppliers who are willing to supply similar goods at the price about 10% lower than yours.
Woman: Really? Have you compared our products with theirs? They are definitely not in the same class.
Man: The quality of your product is better, but the price gap cannot be ignored. It shouldn't be as big as 10%, so I want to negotiate with your manager if you can offer a reduction of 5%.
Woman: OK. I see. I will pass the message.
Man: Oh, one more thing — you must ship the goods as contracted. Since this is the first contract between us, I sincerely hope to reach a transaction.
Woman: All right. Goodbye.
Man: Goodbye.

练习二

Conversation Two
(Questions 5-8)

- Look at the form below.
- You will hear a man asking a partner for something about a former staff.

- You have 15 seconds to read through the form.

INFORMATION OF EMPLOYEE

Frank is asking some information about a staff called (**5**) ________.
The staff worked in (**6**) ________.
His post (**7**) ________.
His monthly earning (**8**) ________ pounds.

对话大意

生产部的 Frank 打电话到人事部寻问 Stephen Grate，是因为税务办公室有一封关于他的信。人事部查询信息后告知 Frank Grate 的住址为 Barnfield 街 180 号，是客户部的一名办公室助理，月薪为 530 美元。

答案解析

(**5**) Stephen Grate。本对话是男士向女士询问关于一名员工的信息，从男士对人名的拼读就可以知道他的姓是 Grate，名字是 Stephen，考试应该熟悉英文人名的表达方法。其中 surname 是“姓”。
(**6**) Customer Services。文中女士问是否这名员工在生产部工作时，男士回答的是客户服务部。
(**7**) office assistant。男士问到他的职位时，注意女士的回答，可直接得到答案。其中，题目中的 post 是职位的意思，与录音中的 job title 是同义词。
(**8**) 530。女士在回答关于这名员工的月薪时，她第一次给出了一个干扰信息（635），后面的才是正确的数字。

听力原文

Woman: Personnel...
Man: Hello, it's Frank here, from Production.
Woman: Hi, Frank.
Man: I've had a letter from the tax office about a worker who worked here last summer — I wonder if you could look him up in your records.
Woman: Sure, what's the name?
Man: The surname's Grate. First name Stephen.
Woman: How does he spell his surname?
Man: G-R-A-T-E. Got that?
Woman: Oh yes, here we are... lives at a hundred and eighty-three School Road, Barnfield...
Man: Yes, that's the one.
Woman: And you say he was working in Production?
Man: Uhm, Customer Services, actually.
Woman: Aah — they had lots of workers working for them last summer.
Man: Well, the tax people want to know his exact job title — I'm not sure why.
Woman: Mm, let me see... He was an office assistant.
Man: Right, got that. They also want to know about his monthly earnings.
Woman: Let's have a look... six hundred and thirty-five pounds a month... Oh, sorry, he was a new one, so that's five hundred and thirty pounds. Anything else?
Man: That's fine, thanks. I'll send them the information today...

商务背景知识扩展

公司部门分类

行政部 Administrative Department
财务部 Financial Department
质量管理部 Quality Control Department
营销部 Sales Department
营运部 Operation Department
技术部 Technology Department
维修部门 Maintenance Department
人力资源部 Human Resources Department
客户服务部 Customer Service Department

周三　搭配题三步走

一、题型分析

（一）命题规律

这部分分为两组，每组的形式安排都一样：考生听到 5 段简短的独白，必须将每个独白与一组标有 A-H 字母的选项对应起来。在每一组里，8 个选项的内容大致相似，总的主题或议题将在题目的提示中清楚说明。例如，考生可能听到 5 个人的谈话，必须判断这些人是从事什么工作的，因此这组 A-H 的选项将包括一系列的工作名称；这些选项也可能由 8 个地点、论题、收件人、目的等组成。两组题目总是测试不同的内容，所以，如果第一组重点为议题，第二组将侧重在其他方面，比如功能。

这部分听力测试的是考生的总体听力技能和推断能力、获取主旨和理解主要思想的能力。为了成功地回答问题，考生需要在听的过程中逐步构思，提炼构思并得出答案。"字对字"是不行的，考生不要指望听到这种明显的线索。然而，总会有个"正确"答案，并不要求考生写出"最佳"答案。

（二）应试方法

1. 读题预判断：考生在听录音前，先快速阅读各选项，弄懂各个选项的意思。这有利于在听力过程中掌握关键词，将录音与各部分的意义联系起来，再结合提供的选项进行取舍。

2. 一听初选择：在第一遍听力时，要根据选项中的 key words 找到对应选项，对答案有个初步的判断。在听录音时要特别抓住 key words，找到试题选项中和录音中的近义词或同义词。

3. 二听定结果：在第二遍听力时，辩明独白所要表达的主要意思，然后确定选择结果。在作答过程中，考生应注意命题者制造的一些陷阱，慎重选择。需要当心的是：有些单词听上去似乎是答案，但别忙着确定，一定要等听完该段独白的全部录音才能最后定答案。

二、典型样题

练习一

Section One
（**Questions 13-17**）

- You will hear five short recordings.
- For each recording, decide what the speaker's idea is in managing the company.
- Write one letter（**A-H**）next to the number of the recording.
- Do not use any letter more than once.
- After you have listened once, replay the recordings.

(13) ________

(14) ________

(15) ________

(16) ________

(17) ________

A	Don't appear to take things personally.
B	Be the first to state a opinion.
C	Prepare for the worst.
D	Let people know your plans.
E	Win widespread support for your ideas.
F	Understand each person's motivation.
G	Don't respond to others immediately.
H	Be flexible in your approach.

原文大意

(**13**) 原文意思为：在公司里工作，应该正确应对抱怨，被别人看出你被别人的评论所干扰是致命错误，暴露你的弱点容易被别人利用，因此失去支持。

(**14**) 原文提到这几年的经验并在和同事的相处中学会如何避免失败的管理。无论处在什么职位，都应准备好应对反对的意见。这样就能够在别人给你反对意见时能够让他们保持安静。

(**15**) 原文提到在对待员工方面坚持一种想法并且任何场合都是如此是很严重的错误。有的时候需要严厉，但有时候更需要和蔼的劝告，一味地严厉只会让员工反感。

(**16**) 工作中要清楚地知道是在和谁交流，不能够弄清楚员工的动力是最糟糕的，无论是金钱、地位还是其他的，弄清楚了这些就能保证有效地沟通与激励员工。这将会决定应对别人的方式，也能更好地控制局面，达到想要的结果。

(**17**) 想要控制局面的话，就是让别人跟得上每个阶段的进度。即使有人批评你，但是如果能做到这点，就能够创造一种氛围，让每个人都觉得他是其中的一部分。

答案解析

(**13**) A。整体分析原文，如果你在工作中很容易被别人的抱怨所干扰，你就会暴露出你的性格上的弱点…… 说明了应该避免在处理问题时感情用事。(take things personally)

(**14**) E。文中 "it's important to anticipate this by getting as many colleagues as possible on your side" 意思是让尽可能多的同事站在自己这边是很重要的，与题目中的 "win widespread support for your ideas" 在意义上一致。

(**15**) H。文中 "The worst thing you can do is stick to one strategy and apply it to every situation." 说明了只坚持一种方法而且任何条件下都用它是很糟糕的，也就是需要处理问题的时候灵活一些，这与题目中的 be flexible（灵活的）是一致的。

(**16**) F。在原文中 "The worst mistake you can make is to fail to find out what drives them — money, status or whatever." 提到最大的错误就是不能弄清楚什么驱使了他们，是钱、地位还是别的什么。其中，关键词 find out 与答案句子中的 understand 为同义词。

(**17**) D。文中 "the worst mistake you can make is not keeping people up to speed with what you're doing at every single stage of the process" "不让别人知道你在每个阶段都做什么事并且跟上你的节奏是很糟糕的" 与题目中的 "let people know your plans" 相符合。

听力原文

(**13**) There are always people who don't like everything in a company, and if you've created an atmosphere in which they're encouraged to contribute ideas freely, you have to learn to deal with complaints. Revealing that you are, for example, upset by their comments is a crucial error — you will have shown a weakness in your character that others may try to exploit — and may lead to a general lack of support for you.

(**14**) Over the years, I've learnt same valuable management lessons in how to avoid the failure of a project. Whatever post you are holding, you always have to be prepared for opposition. And it's important to anticipate this by getting as many colleagues as possible on your side, so that if, in discussions, someone objects to your plans, you — and a number of others — are able to give an immediate response in order to silence your opponent.

(**15**) When I first started running my own company I made some serious mistakes in the way I dealt with my employees. The worst thing you can do is stick to one strategy and apply it to every situation. Sometimes you just need to show them who's boss; other times some gentle persuasion is more effective — in my opinion, anyway. I'm sure I was often opposed for my management style — not that I let it bother me, though.

(**16**) It's always important to know exactly who the individual is I'm communicating with. No matter what kind of business situation I'm in. The worst mistake you can make is to fail to find out what drives them — money, status or whatever. Once you've worked that out, you'll be able to ensure you communicate what's in it for them personally. This should essentially govern the way you respond to people, enabling you to stay in control of the situation and achieve the desired outcome.

(**17**) I've found if you want to stay in charge of a situation, the worst mistake you can make is not keeping people up to speed with what you're doing at every single stage of the process. Of course, that doesn't mean you need to be seeking universal agreement or approval for your actions and opinions — some people will always be critical — but at least adopting this approach will encourage an atmosphere in which everyone feels included.

小结

本题考查的是对录音内容的主旨进行概括的能力。这五段短文考查的是让考生判断出说话人的目的，考生在处理这类问题时应注意了解同一个大意的不同英文表达，平时在练习时多积累同义词和同义短语。在这类题中，在短文中找到同义表达是解题的重要方法。有时，同义短语出现在谓语动词上，例如本题第 16 项中的 find out 与 understand。有时同义表述出现在做宾语的名词上，如第 14 项中的 colleague 和 support。也有的时候同义表述是对短文整个大意的概括，就需要考生具备对文章概括的能力。

练习二

Section One

(Questions 13-17)

- You will hear five short recordings.
- You hear five different people who all work in the offices of a large company talking about letters they have just received.
- Write one letter (**A-H**) next to the number of the recording.
- Do not use any letter more than once.
- After you have listened once, replay the recordings.

(**13**) ________

(**14**) ________

(**15**) ________

(**16**) ________

(**17**) ________

A	An enquiry about future plans.
B	A complaint about a product.
C	Agreement with a recent decision.
D	A request for an appointment.
E	An order for a new product.
F	Thanks for assistance.
G	An invitation to attend a presentation.
H	An apology for delay.

原文大意

（13）展会做得很成功，都是得益于好的有效的广告宣传，因此特意感谢您。
（14）由于有人缺席，要推迟下周一的会议，安排好一切后再马上通知你。
（15）贵公司的产品花费了机械师很长时间才安装好，然而却不能灵活地转换速度，可能是因为找不到该型号的说明书，希望贵公司查看一下是否产品与说明书是一起的。
（16）收到了关于合并 HTO 公司的计划，同意买下那家公司，会有更多的机会把产品推向国际市场。
（17）想要订购最新的打印机 100 套，用所要求的支付方式，我们需要更好的产品质量和更低的价格，减少能源浪费。

答案解析

（13）F。从“So I really appreciate your help.”一句可知，此人是在感谢得到的帮助。其中，appreciate 与 thank 为同义词，表示“感谢”的意思。故选 F 选项。
（14）H。“I feel regret to say that we have to postpone the meeting”这句表明此人是在延迟会议，之后在文中又说到了“I'm so sorry for the trouble taken to you”，为抱歉之意，因此此信是为延迟会议表示道歉，与 H 选项中的 apology 相对应。
（15）B。此段表述中说到了机械工花费很长时间安装好了机器，并且发现速度转换不灵活，可以推测出这是在表达对产品的质量问题的抱怨。其中，“I have to say that it took our mechanic a long time to fix up the machine we bought from your company.”为关键信息句，故选 B。
（16）C。从“I can't agree more with your idea.”可知此人的目的是表示同意，注意此句的表达技巧是用否定句表达肯定意思，不要错误理解成“不同意”。
（17）E。这道问题的答案容易找到，在文中直接出现了题干中的主要动词 order，“So we decide to order 100 sets.”从这句可知此人想订购产品。之后的内容说明产品的优良特点是订购的主要原因。

听力原文

（13）Do you still remember the exhibition hold last week? I want to tell you that was really a success. So I really appreciate your help. Without your attractive advertisement, we shouldn't have achieved such a large sale.
（14）I feel regret to say that we have to postpone the meeting, which is supposed to be held next Monday due to someone's absence. I'm so sorry for the trouble taken to you, but we will inform you as soon as we have made the right schedule.
（15）I have to say that it took our mechanic a long time to fix up the machine we bought from your company. We found it impossible for us to make the speed change freely. We guess it is because we could not find the instruction for the right mode. So would you please check your record to make sure you gave us the instruction we wanted?
（16）I have received your letter about your intension to merge with the HTO Company. I can't agree more with your idea. If we bought that firm, we will have more chance to push our product to the international market.
（17）We are very interested in your latest printer. So we decide to order 100 sets. The payment will be the same in your offer last week. You told us that the machine was in better quality but lower price than that of the old model. And besides, It can reduce wasting of power. That is what we need.

小结

本题考查的是根据说话人的语境判断谈话内容的性质，或是请求，或是抱怨。考生仍然需要掌握常见的同义词或词组的表达，同时还可以在听录音的过程中去体会说话人的语气、语调，从而判断出谈话的内容。如果在平时的练习中多加体会，就会对这部分的题目有更好的了解。

商务背景知识扩展

招　聘

招聘是人力资源管理的工作，当中过程包括招聘广告、二次面试、雇佣轮选等。负责招聘工作的称为招聘专员（recruiter），他们是人力资源方面的专家，或者是人事部的职员。聘请的最后选择应该是用人单位，他们与合适的应征者签署雇佣合约。

招聘种类：

猎头公司招聘：Headhunting，是一种十分流行的人才招聘方式，网罗高级人才。高级人才委托招聘业务，又被称之为猎头服务或人才寻访服务。

网络招聘：网络招聘也被称为电子招聘，是指通过技术手段的运用，帮助企业人事经理完成招聘的过程。

报纸招聘：利用报纸版面或者专刊发布企业的招聘信息，现在的报纸招聘已经和人才网紧密结合起来。

招募渠道：

（1）报纸电视

（2）供需见面会

（3）网络招聘

（4）朋友介绍

周四　搭配题巧应试

一、实战应用

（一）方法总结

对于多项选择题，由于不需要写，听明白后选出选项即可，因此，在预读时，一定要读懂选项，并推测大意。在听力时，要避免语言陷阱，明辨选项。

1. 三步走不可缺：先预读，后初选，再听定结果，三步不可缺。
2. 看关键明大意：听关键词，初步判断选项，仔细听全文，明确大意，避免语言陷阱。

（二）实战心态

在做搭配题听力时，一定要会运用关键词，以达到事半功倍的效果。

调整好心态，考试时切忌不要让完形填空时的心态影响多项选择题的听力。往事已矣，前面的听力已经结束，无论结果怎样，不要影响后面的听力。

二、典型样题

练习一

Section Two
（Questions 18-22）

- You will hear five short recordings.
- For each recording, decide what the speaker's purpose is.
- Write one letter（**A-H**）next to the number of the recording.
- Do not use any letter more than once.
- After you have listened once, replay the recordings.
- You have 15 seconds to read the list **A-H**.

（**18**）________

（**19**）________

（**20**）________

（**21**）________

（**22**）________

A To ask for assistance.
B To change the partner.
C To have a further discussion.
D To reject a request.
E To reduce the business.
F To offer some advice.
G To get some information.
H To deny a contract.

原文大意

（18）打电话通知投诉者，他们已经尽力按照要求来采取措施，认真完成你们的委托，所以不能接受提议。
（19）由于四分之一的产品投诉来自我们合作多年的 Rimond 公司的产品，所以已经决定更换别的合作者，想要与 Daylong 公司合作，因为他们口碑很好。
（20）Robinson 电子公司打电话来寻问为何不能正常使用报警系统。如问题没有得到解决，可以提供帮助。
（21）Mark Williams 打电话深入讨论该项目。通过计算发现该项目并不完全合理。如添加附加成本，该项目还有潜力，请尽快回复关于此问题的看法。
（22）竞争变得更加激烈了，需要从辛苦工作中看到利润。这就意味着不做不盈利的工作，把精力放在如何分辨哪些合同是有利可图的。

答案解析

（18）D。本段是女士对客户提出的抱怨做出的回应，其中最后一句“but perhaps your recommendation wasn't exactly what's needed”表明他对客户提出的要求是不能接受的，故选 D。
（19）B。在与 Rimond 公司合作了几年后，发现好多客户反映的产品质量问题都是来自于他们，因此，从“Daylong's range is fine for us, and one of their customers who I spoke to recommended them highly, so that's why we've changed to using them.”可以得知，女士的目的是寻找新的合作伙伴。
（20）F。文中男士对于客户的回应是希望能够有人去客户的公司解决问题或者通过电话交流，之后他说到“Well perhaps you'd like to get back to me as soon as it's convenient and tell me exactly what the problem is, and I'll see what I can do.”可知他是在为客户提出建议。
（21）C。文中男士对于之前所讨论的项目做出了回应，他认为还有一些细节问题，比如没有考虑某些成本在内需要讨论。其中他说“Could you give me a ring so that we can talk about it a bit more?”这句与 C 选项中的 To have a further discussion（进一步讨论）意思符合。
（22）E。其中，“We need to see more benefit from the hard work we're putting in, and this means saying no to jobs which aren't profitable.”表明女士希望能够选择一些利润高的业务，减小那些不盈利的业务经营范围。故可知选 E 选项。

听力原文

（18）**Woman:** Hello, this is Julian, from DOM Company, returning your call. I feel great regret you aren't happy with the latest consignment you've had from us. It's rather strange, because following your complaint about the last delivery, we did in fact take action to change the specifications in the way you suggested. So it isn't quite fair to say that we ignored your advice. I know it's important to achieve the consistency that you require, <u>but perhaps your recommendation wasn't exactly what's needed.</u>

（19）**Woman:** Well, as you say, Rimond has been supplying us for years but, quite honestly, a quarter of the complaints we receive about our products are actually due to faults in components we've had from Rimond. So I talked to the Manager and he agreed that I should look at some alternatives. <u>Daylong's range is fine for us, and one of their customers who I spoke to recommended them highly, so that's why we've changed to using them.</u>

（20）**Man:** Hello. This is James from Robinson Electronics here. I believe you rang for some advice about your alarm system, which isn't functioning properly. The message I got said you weren't sure if you needed someone to come and sort it out, or if we could advise you over the phone. <u>Well, perhaps you'd like to get back to me as soon as it's convenient and tell me exactly what the problem is, and I'll see what I can do.</u>

（21）**Man:** Mark Williams here, calling about the project we discussed earlier. Could you give me a ring so that we can talk about it a bit more? I've done a few calculations and I'm beginning to wonder whether it's really a practical proposition. I still think the project's got potential, but there are significant additional costs which we hadn't taken into account. So could you get back to me as soon as you can, please?

（22）**Woman:** The competition's getting tougher, and you know we're facing serious problems. We need to see more benefit from the hard work we're putting in, and this means saying no to jobs which aren't profitable. It would be much more beneficial to put all our efforts into winning higher-margin contracts. So the way I feel you can help most is by identifying the types of contacts which will bring in the income we need in order to ensure our future.

练习二

Section One
（Questions 13-17）

- You will hear five short recordings.
- For each recording, decide what the speaker is.
- Write one letter（**A-H**）next to the number of the recording.
- Do not use any letter more than once.
- You will hear the five recordings twice.

（13）________

（14）________

（15）________

（16）________

（17）________

A	a new clerk
B	a change of management
C	a new computer system
D	the introduction of social programme
E	how to keep workforce
F	the distraction of the package
G	a new idea of the promotion
H	the service for the customers

原文大意

（13）我一见到经理就很紧张。大多数同事都认为她特别严厉，如果工作做得不够完美她就会发脾气。事实并不是如此，但是由于原来的一些坏印象，不知如何是好。

（14）第二段对话的大意是自己对包装很痴迷，通常总是因为奇怪的造型趋使自己买了很多本来没有用的东西。

（15）售后服务能提高顾客满意度与忠实度。好的服务可以提高公司形象并提高销售额。所以，大规模生产对公司是非常经济实惠的。

（16）内部提升有激励价值。这是对员工过去表现的肯定，并能鼓励他们继续努力，也能为其他员工树立榜样。这可以在组织内部提高士气。

（17）一个公司要保持员工稳定是很困难的，提供升职机会、好的工作关系、员工职业规划、免费培训、使命感，甚至是表扬员工等等此类方式有助于留住员工。

答案解析

（13）A。本题很好判断，从原文可直接判断出答案。由原文“Actually she is nice to me since I started my job last month”可以知道，这个人是从上个月才来公司工作的，推断应该是新员工。

（14）F。本题比较简单，由原文“attracted by the unusual shape”和“I'm easily influenced by the package”可以判断出，说话者购物时总是被包装吸引。
（15）H。此题非常简单，从第一句话就可以得到答案。
（16）G。从原文大意可以判断主要说的内容是给员工提升的作用与意义。
（17）E。细节题，从原文第一句话就可听出答案，保持员工稳定的重要性和方法。

听力原文

（13）I feel a little nervous whenever I see the manager appear. Most of my colleagues think that she is a very strict person and will fly into a rage if the job she requires was not accomplished perfectly. Actually she is nice to me since I started my job last month. I'm in a dilemma now. And I really don't know what I should do to change the terrible feelings in my heart after hearing the rumors from other people.
（14）I'm easily influenced by the package. Many times I find that I am attracted by the unusual shape, graphics of products without considering the quality of the products. So I have bought many useless things.
（15）Customer service can enhance customer satisfaction and loyalty. Good customer relationship helps to improve your company image and boost sales. As a result, large-scale production will be cost effective for your company.
（16）Promotion-from-within has some motivational value. It is a kind of reward for employees for their past performance and will encourage them to continue their efforts and also give other employees anticipations of promotion for similar efforts. This can improve morale within the organization.
（17）To keep workforce stable is a challenge for every company. Opportunities for growth in the company, a good working relationship, career plans for employees, providing or paying for training, a sense of empowerment, open communication and even praising employees can help retain employees.

商务背景知识扩展

品　牌

品牌是给拥有者带来溢价、产生增值的一种无形的资产，他的载体是用以和其他竞争者的产品或劳务相区分的名称、术语、象征、记号或者设计及其组合，增值的源泉来自于消费者心智中形成的关于其载体的印象。

品牌一般的定义

品牌是指消费者对产品及产品系列的认知程度。

品牌内涵

是指一个名称、名词、符号或设计，或者是它们的组合，其目的是识别某个销售者或某群销售者的产品或劳务，并使之同竞争对手的产品和劳务区别开来；品牌最持久的含义和实质是其价值、文化和个性；品牌是一种商业用语，品牌注册后形成商标，企业即获得法律保护而拥有其专用权；品牌是企业长期努力经营的结果，是企业的无形载体。

品牌的价值

品牌的价值包括用户价值和自我价值两部分。品牌的功能、质量和价值是品牌的用户价值要素，即品牌的内圣三要素；品牌的知名度、美誉度和普及度是品牌的自我价值要素，即品牌的外王三要素。品牌的用户价值大小取决于内圣三要素，品牌的自我价值大小取决于外王三要素。

品牌误区

现在社会各界都在谈品牌，企业希望把自己的品牌做起来，把品牌做好，国家在政策上也给予了很多支持，媒体也在传播各种品牌理念。但当前我们的品牌观念存在很多误区，很多人对品牌的认识并不清晰，造成其塑造品牌的行为模糊、随意，产生的品牌结果自然也是不如人意。

周五　三步攻破选择题

一、题型分析

（一）命题规律

在这部分会听到一段较长的正文，通常大约4分钟。典型的内容为访谈、谈话或有两个或更多人参与的讨论，也可能是一个人的讲述或报告。有8道三个选项的选择题，重点考查文章的细节和主旨。也可能问及意见或观点，但都相对浅显，并不要求考生记住长而复杂的信息。

（二）应试方法

1. 预读明方向：考生做这一题时首先仍然是先快速阅读选择题，从而了解录音中对话或独白的背景、大意，以便听录音时有一个大致的方向。

2. 一听初选择：考生听录音时要认真将主要内容抓住，决不能因为某一个问题没听懂就停下来，听录音的过程中可以针对每一个问题做些快速记录，记下录音中人的身份、讨论的问题，以及不同的观点；如果是独白，对独白的主题、涉及的人或物等则要尽可能弄清楚。对各题结果进行初步选择。

3. 再听定结果：再次听录音时要针对各题选项仔细辨别，确定最终答案，对依旧不能确定的也不能浪费时间，要继续往下听，决不能因一题之得失而影响后面更多的题。

二、典型样题

练习一

(**Questions 23-30**)

- You will hear Julie, the General Manager of Raymond Holiday Company, and Robinson Cooper, the Operations Manager, discussing problems at the Raymond Holiday Company.
- For each question (**23-30**), mark one letter (**A**, **B** or **C**) for the correct answer.
- After you have listened once, replay the recording.

23 What does Julie say about the Raymond Holiday Company's problems?

A She hadn't expected Raymond to have problems.

B She doesn't know what has caused them.

C She doesn't think they will last for long.

24 Robinson says the European division solved a similar problem by ________.

A investing in the company

B closing some company

C advertising the company

25 Julie proposes that the Raymond Company should ________.

A be sold to a company in a different sector

B continue to operate as a Raymond Holiday Company

C stop running and keep the asset cycling

26 Robinson believes that the main cause of the problem is ________.

A a change in consumer tastes

B the economic situation

C the design of the company

27 According to Julie, advertising would ________.

A improve the company's image

B produce only temporary results

C take time to improve the figures

28 Robinson suggests that part of the solution is to ________.

A employ staff on lower wages

B limit the promotional offers

C reduce opening hours

29 The Board wants to sell the Raymond Company because ________.

A the company's share price has been falling

B they need to compensate for losses

C it would fetch a good price

30 Julie finally agrees to propose to the Board that they ________.

A keep the company running as normal

B allocate money for extra promotions

C give the company a chance to reduce its costs

原文翻译

女： 你好，Robinson，请坐。你知道我们的 Raymond 公司在过去的几个月里营业额明显下降了。事实上比我们在英国的公司表现糟糕多了，我还没有能够找到原因。现在的处境令人担忧，并且即便是采取了及时的措施，我觉得公司今年也不能够回到盈利状态了。现在看起来我们面临着两个选择：第一是想办法继续经营，第二是完全地关闭，你认为如何？

男： 如果关闭将会是场灾难，你知道，在欧洲的机构曾经有这样的处境的时候，他们采取了特别的促销手段，并且很有效。你还记得去年的这个时候吗？那时我们认为我们应该卖掉一些法国的公司。现在，他们进展得很好，甚至我们不用花任何钱在那里了。

女： 嗯，对。但是 Raymond 已经在五个月内损失了将近两百万，我们不能再承担那样的损失了。我真的认为我们应该尽快地关掉，并且使我们的资产运转起来。我不认为值得把它卖给我们的竞争对手。

男： 那不是只顾眼前的利益吗？这样的事情到处都在发生。在你说我们的公司看起来过时和顾客的品位已经改变之前，我已经做了一些顾客调查，结果说明人们如果有钱的话还是会来的。

女： 那不是唯一的理由，Robinson，并且关键问题是董事会催促我改进现在的数据。我们在竞争中已经处于落后，如果我们继续让 Raymond 营业，我们需要在形象上改变一下。一个好的广告会吸引更多的顾客，但这仅仅是一个短期的办法。

男： 我不同意你的观点，我有另一个办法。为什么不用最少的员工来经营公司呢？没有更多的招聘，而且考虑在一些时候关门，直到处境好转。我们可以继续经营我们的特别的业务，因为它们可以吸引一些新顾客，并且不花费我们的任何成本。

女：是个办法，但是我不知道董事会是否会支持。他们很希望卖掉公司，这样就能弥补赤字并且让股东们满意。那是一个吸引人的办法。

男：即使他们决定了卖掉公司，也不会得到很多，现在资产的价值是很低的。我们不能尝试着继续经营吗？

女：好吧，可能不会像现在这样经营了，但是你的节约成本的想法可能会奏效。你认为你能够在五个月内使公司回复吗？要记得已经没有额外的钱进行促销了。

男：我想有机会能尝试一下。Julie，我认为我能够做到，以最小规模的促销。

女：那么给我为下周的董事会写一份书面提议，好吧？

答案解析

23 B。文中针对 Raymond Holiday Company 的收入额下降的问题后面提到“for reasons we haven't really been able to get to the bottom of”，即没能找到营业额下降的原因。

24 C。在“when there was a situation like this in the European division, they turned it around with a special promotion which worked very well”中找到关键词 promotion，与答案中的 advertising 意思一致，意为“广告促销”

25 C。题目问女士的建议是什么。文中说到“I really think we should close it dawn as soon as possible and cycle our assets.”，表明她的想法是关闭公司并且使资产运转起来。其中，close 与选项 C 中的 stop running“停止经营”意思一致。故选 C。

26 B。此题考查人物观点的判断，文中并没有直接出现答案。关于造成这种结果的原因男士说到“people would still came if they had the money”，说明了顾客没有足够的钱来 Raymond 公司，也就是在经济上的困难。故选 B。

27 B。此题考查对文中具体信息的准确理解的能力。题目问的是广告会有什么影响，A 选项“改变形象”是要采取的措施，并不是广告所产生的结果；C 选项的内容是董事会希望女士做的，故排除该选项。文中女士说：“but that would just be a short-term solution.”其中，short-term solution 与选项 B 中 temporary results 的意思符合，可以定位准确的信息。故选 B

28 C。在“Why don't we run the centre with minimum staff, no more expensive recruiting, and think about closing during the quiet times”中说到了在淡季的时候适当考虑关门，意思是减少营业时间。C 选项中的 reduce opening time 与男士的说法符合，故选 C。A 和 B 选项的内容在文章中没有提及，故排除。

29 B。“They're really keen to sell the Raymond Company. That way they could cover their deficit”说明了董事会卖掉 Raymond 的目的是为了弥补赤字，也就是减少损失。“cover their deficit”与选项中 compensate for losses 意思符合。

30 C。从“but your idea for snaking savings might work.”一句可知，Julie 同意 Ronbinson 的降低成本的观点，与选项 C 中的 reduce its costs 意思符合，故选 C。

听力原文

Woman: Hello, Robinson. Take a seat. As you know, our Raymond Holiday Company has had a significant drop in income over the last few months. In fact, it's doing much worse than our other British company, for reasons we haven't really been able to get to the bottom of. The situation is now pretty worrying, and even if immediate action is taken, I don't expect Raymond to return to profitability this year. Now, it seems to me we have two options facing us: the first is to see if we can create a strategy to keep the operation going, and the second is to close it down completely. How do you think of it?

Man: Closing it down would be a disaster. You know, when there was a situation like this in the European division, they turned it around with a special promotion which worked very well. Do you remember this time last year, when we thought we'd have to sell some of the French company? Well, now they're doing well and we didn't even have to spend any extra money on them, either.

Woman: Yes, that's true. But Raymond has lost nearly two million in the five months and we can't afford to keep absorbing that kind of loss. I really think we should close it down as soon as possible and cycle our assets. I don't even think it's worth trying to sell it as a going concern to one of our competitors.

Man: Isn't that rather short-sighted? The same thing's happening everywhere. And before you say that the company is looking outdated and that consumer tastes and fashions have changed. I've done my homework and the consumer surveys show that people would still come if they had the money.

Woman: That's not the only reason, Robinson. And the bottom line is, the Board are pushing me to improve figures now. We're falling behind the competition, and if we keep Raymond open, we'll need a major change in our image. A good advertising campaign might fire in more customers while we're running it, but that would just be a short-term solution.

Man: I don't agree with yon, However, I've got another idea. Why don't we run the company with minimum staff, no more expensive recruiting, and think about closing during the quiet times of day until the situation improves? We could go on with the special offers we're running, because they bring in a few new customers, and don't cost us anything.

Woman: It's a thought, but I'm not sure the Board will go for it. They're really keen to sell the Raymond Company. That way they could cover their deficit and make the shareholders happy at the same time. It's an attractive solution.

Man: Even if they decide to sell, they're not likely to get very much for it, are they? Not at the moment. Property values are low. Can't we at least try to keep the Raymond operational?

Woman: Well, it's not going to be possible to keep it running as it is now, but your idea for savings might work. Do you think you'd be able to get the company to recover even within five months? But remember, there's no extra money for major promotions.

Man: I'd like to have the chance to try, Julie. I think I can do it, with minimal promotions.

Woman: Then let me have a written proposal in time for next week's Board meeting, will you?

小结

这部分的听力题型考查的是对文章重点信息的理解、分析和判断能力。由于录音内容比较长，考生在遇到困难时容易失去信心，从而影响考试状态。因此保持一个冷静的心态是很重要的。同时要抓住这类题的解题规律。八个题目对应的问题答案往往在文中排布比较紧凑，经常是一个问题的答案对应句子出现后，隔两三个句子又会出现下个问题的答案。而且答案的顺序与文章的顺序是一致的。另外，还要注意答案经常会出现在文中人物提出问题之后的段落里。只要掌握了这类题的出题规律，就能做到胸有成竹。

练习二

(Questions 23-30)

- You will hear a conversation through a phone.
- For each question (**23-30**), mark one letter (**A**, **B** or **C**) for the correct answer.
- After you have listened once, replay the recording.

23 Why did the woman make the call?

A Make a complain. **B** Express thanks. **C** Ask for help.

24 When did the woman receive the bill?

A Today. **B** Yesterday. **C** Last week.

25 What's the problem with the bill?

A It was not her bill. **B** It was late. **C** It was overcharged.

26 Where is the wrong call from?

A New Zealand. **B** Shenzhen. **C** Guangzhou.

27 Where was the woman between 13th and the 24th of August?

A Shenzhen. **B** Guangzhou. **C** New Zealand.

28 What's the number of the woman?

A 862 8503. **B** 862 8603. **C** 862 8505.

29 How long would it take for technical department to check the problem?

A 24 hours. **B** 12 hours. **C** 48 hours.

30 What would the company do to solve this problem?

A Credit the over-charged amount.

B Make apologize for their mistake.

C Send her a new bill.

原文翻译

A：早上好，中国移动，王华为您服务。请问有什么可以帮助您的吗？

B：是的，早上好，我打来是投诉我的电话账单，简直太荒谬了！

A：好的，女士，您能告诉我是哪儿出了问题吗？

B：我昨天接到的账单，你们多收了我电话费，账单说我在八月 13 号和 24 号之间从深圳打了几个电话到新西兰，根本不可能，我那时正在新西兰度假！

A：我知道了。请问您的姓名和电话是？

B：我叫 Shirley Lee，我的电话号是 862 8503，可以了吗？

A：好的，女士，我已经看到了您的电话是在我们的系统中注册的，我要和我们的技术部门核查一下，当我们调查完您的投诉以后，客服部门会在最快时间给您致电的。

B：我得等多久？

A：通常来说，技术部是在 48 个小时之内完成调查的，客服部门会在调查完成后最快给您致电。

B：然后呢？

A：根据调查结果，多收取您的费用会打到您的账户或者给您支票。

B：所以，我只要等你们的电话就可以了是吗？

A：是的，女士，我们会在 48 个小时之内给您回复，感谢您的来电。

B：嗯……再见。

A：再见，女士。

答案解析

23 A。本题考查考生对信息的认知与判断能力。题目问打电话的目的，由“I would like to make a complaint about my bill. It's ridiculous”可知，打电话的目的并不是要表示感谢和寻求帮助。故选 A。

24 B。本题考查考生对细节的捕捉能力，一般情况下，这种细节问题往往容易被忽略，但由“I received my bill yesterday”可知，打电话者是昨天才收到的账单。

25 C。本题考查学生根据原文进行合理的推断能力，通常来说原文不会直接说出答案，需要学生合理推断。由原文“you have over-charged me”可知是多收了那位女士的钱，故答案选 C。

26 B。本题考查学生对信息的整合能力，在考试中需要根据原文来推断相应的答案。原文说“ it says I made several calls from Shenzhen to New Zealand”，可知是账单的问题，应该是错误的计算了那位女士所打的电话。故可知答案为 B。

27 C。本题考查学生对信息掌握的准确度。如果只出现一个时间或地点，学生可以很好掌握，但时间和信息一多，学生可能会混淆，故在听力过程中要特别注意时间与地点等是否与问题相符合。由原文“between the 13th and the 24th of August, but that's impossible, because I was in New Zealand on holiday at the time”即可知答案。

28 A。本题为细节题，考查学生在听力过程中的认真程度，很多情况下，这类语句非常容易被学生忽略。故由原文“I'm Shirley Lee and my number's 862 8503”可知答案为A。

29 C。本题考查学生的理解与推断能力。由原文“It usually takes about 48 hours to check all the technical details.”可知，通常出现这种相应问题，是要由技术部门先做好技术检查，然后再做出相应判断，故可知答案为C。

30 A。本题目考查学生的推断能力。由原文“depending on the results of the investigation, we credit the over-charged amount to your account or send you a cheque.”可知答案为A。

听力原文

A: Good morning, China Mobile. Wang Hua speaking. How may I help you?

B: Yes, good morning. I would like to make a complaint about my bill. It's ridiculous!

A: Certainly, madam. Can you tell me exactly what the problem is?

B: Well, I received my bill yesterday and you have over-charged me: it says I made several calls from Shenzhen to New Zealand between the 13th and the 24th of August, but that's impossible, because I was in New Zealand on holiday at the time!

A: I see. Could you give me your full name and phone number, please?

B: Yes, I'm Shirley Lee and my number's 862 8503, alright?

A: That's fine, madam. I can see the calls registered here on my screen. I will have to check this with my technical department. Our customer services department will call you as soon as we have fully investigated your complaint.

B: Well, how long do I have to wait?

A: It usually takes about 48 hours to check all the technical details. Our customer services department will call you as soon as we have fully investigated your complaint.

B: And then?

A: Well, depending on the results of the investigation, we credit the over-charged amount to your account or send you a cheque.

B: So I just wait for a call from your company?

A: Yes, madam. Someone will call you within 48 hours. Thank you for calling and bringing this matter to our attention.

B: Hmmm ... goodbye.

A: Goodbye, madam.

小结

本题为长对话，一般规律是每道题的先后顺序会根据文章的顺序来安排。原文放两遍，第一遍尽最大努力全部听出，如有个别题没有听到，不要徘徊，马上做下面的题，第二遍的时候再认真听没太听懂的题。

练习三

(Questions 23-30)

- You will hear a conversation on introducing new colleagues.
- For each question (**23-30**), mark one letter (**A**, **B** or **C**) for the correct answer.
- After you have listened once, replay the recording.

23 Who is Scottish?

A Andrea. **B** Nellie. **C** Andrea's husband.

24 Who is Head Accountant in this company?

A Andrea. **B** Lee Chung. **C** Nellie.

25 Where is Lee Chung hometown?

A London. **B** Australia. **C** Hong Kong.

26 How long has been since our previous Finance Officer left?

A Three years. **B** Four years. **C** Two years.

27 Who is Kevin?

A Head of Finance. **B** Head of Sales. **C** Head of Marketing.

28 What kind of job does Jane probably do?

A Do marketing research.

B Do publicity work.

C Work out budget of whole company.

29 When is the big meeting tomorrow?

A 10:00 . **B** 11:00 . **C** 11:30.

30 What are Nellie and Andrea going to do?

A Have a cup of coffee. **B** Have lunch. **C** Have a meeting.

原文翻译

Nellie： 所以，Andrea来自澳大利亚？

Malcolm： 是的，她丈夫是苏格兰人。噢，但不用担心，她的英语非常好，并且，她非常了解我们公司并和我们公司里的人很熟。我希望她能在公司给你很多帮助。

Nellie： 好的。

Malcolm： 有其他一些人你应该马上见见，像Lee Chung，我们的财务主管和首席会计师，他是香港人，自1995年就一直在咱们公司。和你一样，他也是从伦敦公司被派到这儿的——三年前，我们的前财务主管突然离开。我相信你一定会喜欢他的。他和你差不多年纪，非常热情，并富有想象力——并不像一般的财务人员！我相信他对你新产品的发表计划一定会很支持。除了Lee，你还要见见Kevin，他是我们的销售主管，另一个活宝。还有Jane，我们的公关经理，如果你的新计划有什么社会推广活动，应该就是和她联络……

Nellie： 好的。

Andrea： 你好，McKenzie先生，我能进来吗？

Malcolm： 当然，Andrea，来见一下Nellie Hamilton女士，从现在开始你就是他的下属了。

Nellie： 你好，Andrea，很高兴认识你。

Andrea： Hamilton女士，很高兴认识你。

Nellie： 噢，叫我Nellie，我们会一直在一起工作，我们不要这么客套了，Nellie，好吧？

Malcolm： 好了，你们一定还有好多话要说，Andrea，你能带Nellie到她的办公室并带她转转吗？她需要知道这里的每一件事——从停车工到洗手间！

Andrea： 当然可以。

Malcolm： 对了，你可以告诉她员工食堂的事吗？我们不会让员工缺少粮食，晕在岗位上，对吗?!

Andrea： 好的。

Malcolm： 好的，Nellie，你和Andrea安顿一下，我们明早11点还有个重要的会要开，你还有很多要在会上讲，我最好让你去工作！

Nellie： 好的，非常感谢，先生……，呃，Malcolm。那么明天见。

Malcolm： 好的，祝你们有个愉快的一天。

Both：谢谢，Malcolm/Mckenzie 先生。

Andrea：那么，呃，Nellie，我们到办公室去吧，就在前面拐角处。

Nellie：好的，Andrea，我们在路上买杯咖啡吧？我想今天会是忙碌的一天。

答案解析

23 C。考查学生信息收集与掌握能力。原文说秘书是来自澳大利亚，她丈夫是苏格兰人。由于原文中出现的地名很多，考生往往听到一个就以为是答案，故要特别注意，通常在商务英语听力考试中，最后听到的才是答案。故根据原文第一句与第二句话可知答案为 C。

24 B。考查学生准确抓取信息的能力。原文出现了很多人物，有账务主管、销售部主管、公关经理等人，学生要认真读题，看考查的是具体哪个人。由原文“Like Lee Chung, for one. He's our Finance Officer and Head Accountant”可知答案为 B。

25 C。考查考生对信息掌握的准确程度。原文出现很多地名，有加拿大、伦敦香港等、要认真读题，知道考查的是关于谁的、什么时间的以及什么地点。由原文“He's from Hong Kong originally”可知答案为 C。

26 A。考查推断能力，此类语句通常语速较快，尤其是插入句的时候考生听起来有困难，如在此处出题，大多数考生都会做错。根据原文“our previous Finance Officer left rather suddenly I'm afraid, and that was about three years ago”可知前财务主管应该离开三年了，可知选答案 A。

27 B。考查学生的信息掌握准确度。由原文“you'll need to meet up with Kevin. He's our Head of Sales and another live wire.”可知，Kevin 是销售部门的主管，要与公关经理和财务主管区分开。故答案为 B。

28 B。考查考生合理推理的能力。由原文“she's our Public Relations and Press officer”可以看出是在公关部门工作的，公关部门主要是做宣传工作。故选 B。

29 B。考查学生对时间的掌握能力。通常考生应该熟悉表达时间的各种说法，认真听数字进行判断。根据原文“As I said, there's the big meeting tomorrow at 11:00”可知，会议是在明天上午 11 点举行，故选答案 B。

30 A。考查学生的合理推断能力。原文“...could we pick up a cup of coffee?”虽没有直接说要去喝咖啡，通过说话者建议一起喝咖啡，我们可以推断出一会儿两人可能要在一起喝咖啡，故可知答案为 A。

听力原文

Nellie: So Andrea is from Austria?

Malcolm: Yes, her husband's Scottish, you see. Oh, don't worry, her English is perfect, and she really knows our business and all the people in the firm. I hope she'll be a big help in getting you started in the company.

Nellie: Right.

Malcolm: And there are some other people you'll need to meet pretty soon. Like Lee Chung, for one. He's our Finance Officer and Head Accountant. He's from Hong Kong originally but has been over here since 1995. Like you, he was sent up here from the London office　our previous Finance Officer left rather suddenly I'm afraid, and that was about three years ago. You'll like Lee, I'm sure. He's about the same age as you and is very enthusiastic and imaginative — not always the case with the finance boys! I'm sure he'll be very supportive in your plans for the new product launch. Apart from Lee, you'll need to meet up with Kevin. He's our Head of Sales and another live wire. And of course there's Jane, she's our Public Relations and Press Officer, so she's probably the person you'll be most in contact with when you're working out your wee schemes for the publicity of the new brand...

Nellie: OK.

Andrea: Hello, Mr. McKenzie. Can I come in?

Malcolm: Yes, of course, Andrea. I'd like you to meet Nellie Hamilton, who you are going to be reporting to from now on.

Nellie: Hello, Andrea. It's very nice to meet you.

Andrea: And to meet you, Ms. Hamilton.

Nellie: Oh, Nellie, please. We're going to be working together all the time, so let's drop the formalities right from the start. It's Nellie, OK?

Malcolm: Right you two, you've got a lot to talk about. Andrea, could you take Nellie to her office and show her around? She'll need to know where everything is — right from the staff car parking boys to where the loos are!

Andrea: Yes, of course, Mr. McKenzie.

Malcolm: Oh, and can you tell her about the staff restaurants as well? We don't want you fainting on the job from lack of sustenance, do we?

Andrea: Right.

Malcolm: So Nellie, I'll let you and Andrea settle in for today. As I said, there's the big meeting tomorrow at 11:00 so you've a lot to take on board before then. I'd better let you get on with it!

Nellie: Yes, well, thanks very much Mr..., er Malcolm. I'll see you tomorrow then.

Malcolm: Right you are. Have a good day, both of you.

Both: Thanks, Malcolm/Mr. McKenzie.

Andrea: So, er, Nellie, let's go through to our office. It's over there in the far corner.

Nellie: OK, Andrea. And on the way, could we pick up a cup of coffee? I think it's going to be a busy day.

练习四

(Questions 23-30)

- You will hear a dialogue between a new man and HR Manager.
- For each question (**23-30**), mark one letter (**A**, **B** or **C**) for the correct answer.
- After you have listened once, replay the recording.

23 Where does Nellie live now?

A In the office.

B Near the factory.

C Far from office.

24 What will Nellie do in this company?

A Help launch a new product range.

B Take place of general manager.

C Do market research for company.

25 How long has Nellie been in London?

A Over one year.

B Over half a year.

C Over one and a half year.

26 Where did Nellie do a MA in marketing?

A In London.

B In United States.

C In Toronto.

27 How long did Nellie work as a placement for Biscuit Barrel London office?

A One year.

B Half a year.

C One year and a half.

28 How long did Nellie work as a permanent for Biscuit Barrel London office?

A One year.

B Half a year.

C One year and a half.

29 What's Andrea Mueller's job?

A General Manager.

B PA of Nellie.

C HR of this company.

30 How long has Andrea Mueller been in this company?

A One year.

B Two years.

C Three years.

原文翻译

Malcolm：嗯，你一定是 Nellie Hamilton。欢迎来到 Biscuit Barrel 公司！

Nellie：非常感谢，Mckenzie 先生。

Malcolm：这是办公室，我的办公室就在这尽头。你认为这里怎么样？和伦敦与南部有点不同是吧？

Nellie：是的，不过我有几个亲属在这，所以我对这片比较熟。上学的时候我总是在这过假期，现在我也和他们在一起，直到我找到落脚的地方才搬出来，现在我住在离工厂很近的地方。

Malcolm：是的，正如你所知道的，你是由我们伦敦办公室派来帮助我们管理新产品系列发布工作的。你在伦敦有多久了？

Nellie：我想，超过 18 个月了。我在加拿大多伦多修了市场学的文学硕士，然后直接到伦敦公司实习了半年。一年前，很庆幸他们喜欢我，让我成了正式员工。自那以后我一直负责产品策略和人员配置。

Malcolm：好的，我希望这些经验在你和我们一起的时间里也发挥好的作用。你已经知道“Country Crumbles”系列了吗？

Nellie：在伦敦办公室有关于一些新产品的谈论。但是对“Country Crumbles”我不敢说全知道。

Malcolm：当然。好的，明天上午我们会有个大型会议，你能在会上把你不知道的全部跟上。当然也希望你见一些要在这一起工作的同事。

Nellie：好的！

Malcolm：但是有一个人你必须现在就见一下。Janet，你能叫 Andrea Mueller 进来一下吗？谢谢。Andrea Mueller 将是你的个人秘书和私人助理。她来自澳大利亚，两年前开始在本公司工作。

答案解析

23 B。考查考生对信息的掌握能力。原文出现很多时间、地点与人物，要认真读题，准确判断是问谁、什么时间、在哪个地点的事情。故根据原文“I find my feet and somewhere to live a bit nearer the factory”可知答案为 B。

24 A。考查考生的合理推断与逻辑分析能力。由原文“you've been sent up by our London office to help us on the project management of the launch of this new product range”可知，伦敦公司让此人来负责新产品的开发与发布工作，于此可以判断出答案为A。

25 C。考查学生区分时间与地点的能力。原文出现三个时间：十八个月，六个月与一年，本题考查的是在伦敦办公室一共待了多长时间，由原文“Well, a little over eighteen months, I think”可知答案为C。

26 C。考查学生准确掌握地点与事件的能力，要认真判断是谁什么时间在什么地点做的什么事，故由“I did an MA in marketing over in Canada, in Toronto”可知说话者在加拿大完成的市场文学硕士，故答案为C。

27 B。考查学生对时间的掌握。由原文“went straight from there to a work replacement in the Biscuit Barrel London Office for six months”可知，说话者是在伦敦首先实习了半年，然后才转为正式工人的，故答案为B。

28 A。考查学生区分时间与事件的能力。上一题说的是实习的时间为半年，如果上一题没有做对，那么此题也一定会做错，根据常识也可判断出答案，说话者总共在伦敦待了一年半，半年是当实习生，那么转正的日期也应该就是一年。如认真听原文“made me permanent about a year ago.”也可知答案为A。

29 B。考查学生对人物的判断能力，原文中提到“Andrea Mueller is going to be your own secretary and PA”，可知是要做Nellie的私人助理和秘书工作的，故答案为B。

30 B。考查学生对细节的注意程度。由原文“started with us here about two years ago.”可知秘书已经来公司两年了，所以答案为B。

听力原文

Malcolm: Ah, you must be Nellie Hamilton. Welcome to the Biscuit Barrel!

Nellie: Thank you very much, Mr. McKenzie.

Malcolm: So this is the general office, and my office is right at the end there. How are you finding things up here? A bit different from London and the south, isn't it?

Nellie: Yes, but I've got some family up here, so I know the area quite well. I used to come on holidays here all through my school days. And I'm staying with them now, just until I find my feet and somewhere to live a bit nearer the factory.

Malcolm: Now as you know, you've been sent up by our London office to help us on the project management of the launch of this new product range. You were in London for how long?

Nellie: Well, a little over eighteen months, I think. I did an MA in marketing over in Canada, in Toronto, and went straight from there to a work replacement in the Biscuit Barrel London Office for six months. Luckily they liked me and made me permanent about a year ago. And I've been helping them with product strategy and placement since then.

Malcolm: Well, we hope that's going to come in very useful in your time with us up here. You know about “Country Crumbles”, don't you?

Nellie: Well, there was quite a lot of talk going on in the London office about a new product range but I can't say I know any of the details of “Country Crumbles”, no.

Malcolm: No, of course not. Well, we've got a big meeting tomorrow morning and that should help you fill in some of the blanks, and also allow you to meet a lot of the colleagues you'll be working with.

Nellie: Great!

Malcolm: But there's one person you ought to meet straight away. Janet, can you ask Andrea Mueller to come in here please? Thanks. Andrea Mueller is going to be your own secretary and PA. She's from Austria, and started with us here about two years ago.

商务背景知识扩展

弹性工作制

弹性工作制是指在完成规定的工作任务或固定的工作时间长度的前提下，员工可以灵活地、自主地选择工作的具体时间，以代替统一、固定的上下班时间的制度。

弹性工作制的形式

1. 建立自主型组织结构
2. 工作分担方案
3. 临时性工作分担方案
4. 弹性工作地点方案
5. 选择弹性工作时间
6. 核心时间与弹性时间结合
7. 紧缩工作时间制

周六　本周技巧总结

在这部分内容中，我们对一周的学习内容进行了总结，把中级听力每个部分题型的考查重点归类，同时也从语法的角度归纳了考点在文中的位置。希望通过复习，大家对听力考试有更好的掌握。

一、内容分析

这部分我们对题目的内容进行归纳，希望考生通过对这部分的学习，对出题特点有所了解。同时在备考过程中注意积累一些分类的词汇，比如常见的职位名称、公共场所或办公室各个部门的英文表达等。

（一）职位

题目再现

Visitors are five European ________.

原文摘录

Woman: No problem. Who are the customer representatives from Paris again?

Man: Not this time. It's the tech-managers. There's about five.

题目浅析

此题目出现在周一中的第一道样题中，所填的空白处答案为人物从事的工作，也就是他的职位、头衔等。故此处填写 tech-managers。这部分内容经常出现在第一部分题型中。

（二）地点

题目再现

8:30am meet visitors at the ________.

原文摘录

Man: I thought you could meet them at eight thirty in the office. I would suggest meeting at reception, but it'll be busy then.

题目浅析

此题目出现在周一的第一道样题中，此处填写与参观者见面的地点。从文中可直接得到答案，填写 office。这类答案经常出现在第一段对话中。

（三）原因

题目再现

For the reason of (**2**) ________ given by an expert, the buyer has to (**3**) ________ a claim first.

原文摘录

The result shows that damage was caused by deficient packing. So we have no choice but to lodge a claim for losses.

题目浅析

此题目出现在周一第二道样题中，需要填写买方提出索赔的原因，从对话中可知是由于不恰当的包装造成的，故填写原文中出现的 deficient packing，之后填写 lodge。此类答案经常出现在听力考试第一部分第二段对话中。

（四）人名

题目再现

Frank is asking some information about a staff called (**5**) ________.

原文摘录

Woman: Sure, what's the name?
Man: The surname's Grate. First name Stephen.
Woman: How does he spell his surname?
Man: G-R-A-T-E. Got that?

题目浅析

答案可填写 Stephen Grate，此题目出现在周二的第一道练习中。文中男士向女士询问一名曾经在公司工作的员工的资料，首先问了他的姓名。填写人名的问题经常出现在第一部分听力的第一段对话中。

（五）部门

题目再现

The staff worked in (**6**) ________.

原文摘录

Woman: And you say he was working in Production?
Man: Uhm, Customer Services, actually.

题目浅析

此题目位置同上，需填写这名员工的工作部门。答案是 customer services。

（六）数字

题目再现

The number Enid asked for is (**11**) ________ for the marketing executives.

原文摘录

I'm sure I asked for four hundred for each of the marketing executives and six hundred and fifty for me but you've put everyone down for seven hundred and fifty.

题目浅析

填写400。本题来自周二的第三道练习，此处填写数字，这类题目经常出现在第一部分题型的对话中。从对话中可知，Enid 为市场执行部门订购的手册是400份，考生在听录音时要注意后面出现的干扰信息。

二、语法分析

在这部分我们将从语法的角度来分析题目特点，通过这部分的学习可以知道在考试中考查的重点往往是动词、代词、名词，极少出现形容词。而特别是动词，需要考生掌握一些表示反对、支持、接受、拒绝、感谢、抱怨等意义的词汇。同时也可以通过分析录音中说话人的语气，比如惊讶、愉快、怀疑、转折等来判断他的观点。我们将在以下部分进行简要的介绍。

（一）动词

题目再现

For the reason of (**2**) ________ given by an expert, the buyer has to (**3**) ________ a claim first.

原文摘录

The result shows that damage was caused by deficient packing. So we have no choice but to lodge a claim for losses.

题目浅析

此题出现在周一的第二道样题中。第一个空填写 deficient packing，而对第二个空白处在句子中的成分分析可知是做谓语，应该填写动词 lodge。因此，在听录音之前我们应该对题干进行猜测，是要对索赔进行如何处理，是“提出”，还是“拒绝”等类似的动词。当听录音时应对出现的谓语进行判断，往往直接就得到答案。

（二）名词

题目再现

Visit to the (**3**) ________ firstly.

原文摘录

Woman: Do you want me to show them around the product first?
Man: I think they've seen it before. Maybe you could take them around the produce line instead?
Woman: Good idea. What about after coffee?

题目浅析

此题出现在周一样题一，原文中女士问到参观的地点，应该填 produce line。我们可以根据题目分析所填写的答案在句子中的成分为宾语，可以判断出所填的应该是个表示地点的名词。在听录音的时候要集中注意力从名词上获取信息。

（三）纠正

题目再现

His monthly earning (**8**) ________ pounds.

原文摘录

Man: Right, got that. They also want to know about his monthly earnings.

Woman: Let's have a look... six hundred and thirty-five pounds a month... Oh, sorry, he was a new one, so that's five hundred and thirty pounds. Anything else?

题目浅析

此题出现在周二的第一道练习中，答案为530。女士说到员工的工资数字时，首先给出了一个干扰数字，之后她进行了纠正。在第一部分听力的对话中，经常是说话人说了错误的信息，然后进行纠正，比如人名的拼写、电话号码、数字的表达。因此考生在听到这类词的时候不要匆忙得出答案，要冷静分析，等待正确信息的出现。

（四）应答

题目再现

30 Julie finally agrees to propose to the Board that they ________.

A keep the company running as normal

B allocate money for extra promotions

C give the company a chance to reduce its costs

原文摘录

Man: Even if they decide to sell, they're not likely to get very much for it, are they? Not at the moment. Property values are low. Can't we at least try to keep the Raymond operational?

Woman: Well, it's not going to be possible to keep it running as it is now, but your idea for savings might work...

题目浅析

此题出现在周五的样题中，答案选择C。在这部分题型中，往往有的答案就出现在某人提出问题之后，对问题进行的应答会包含重要的信息。因此考生在听录音的时候，要仔细对文中人物所提出的问题后的回答进行分析。

（五）同义

题目再现

29 The Board wants to sell the Raymond Cmpany because ________.

A the company's share price has been falling

B they need to compensate for losses

C it would fetch a good price

原文摘录

Woman: It's a thought, but I'm not sure the Board will go for it. They're really keen to sell the Raymond Company. That way they could cover their deficit and make the shareholders happy at the same time. It's an attractive solution.

题目浅析

此题位置同上，答案选择B。在听力考试三个部分的题型中，最容易出现的就是同义表达，如果能够找到题目和听力原文中对应的同义词或词组，将会很容易判断出正确答案。本题说到卖掉公司的目的，文中说的是 cover their deficit（弥补赤字），而题目选项中的是 they need to compensate for losses（补偿损失），其中损失和赤字是同义对应的词，compensate 和 cover 也属同义，故可判断出正确选项。

（六）转折

题目再现

27 According to Julie, advertising would ________.

A improve the company's image

B produce only temporary results

C take time to improve the figures

原文摘录

A good advertising campaign might fire in more customers while we're running it, but that would just be a short -term solution.

题目浅析

此题位置同上，答案选B。文中根据女士的观点，广告策略可以解决短期的问题。根据录音中的表述，我们可以得出这样一个规律，很多重要的信息经常出现在转折词之后，例如but，however等词，可以根据转折句子的信息来分析答案。

（七）推断

原文摘录

Revealing that you are, for example, upset by their comments is a crucial error — you will have shown a weakness in your character that others may try to exploit — and may lead to a general lack of support for you.

题目浅析

此题目出现在周三中的样题一，这类题目一般给出五段对话，根据对话的内容判断说话人的目的或身份。这段对话考查的是推断能力。文中说到，如果容易被别人的评价所干扰，就会暴露性格上的弱点，这样容易失去别人的支持。因此可推断出避免在处理问题时感情用事，即为给定选项的 Don't appear to take things personally。

商务背景知识扩展

网上订货系统

网上订货系统（订货宝）是专为贸易型或生产型企业开发的新一代实时网上订货管理平台，该平台基于互联网，实现分销商（经销商/代理商）与下级零售商，或生产厂家与下级分销商之间实时高效的订货、收货、发货管理、清晰明了的收付款对账管理、便捷的物流信息查询、安全可靠的在线支付管理，以及方便快捷的订单短信通知等全方位、高效的订货流程管理，全面提升企业管理竞争力。

周日　本周测试

PART ONE

Conversation One
(**Questions 1-4**)

- Look at the note below.
- You will hear a message about a woman calling about a meeting.

Telephone Message
From: Linda　　　To: (**1**) ________
◇ She wants to (**2**) ________ the meeting on 16th, November.
◇ And she is available on (**3**) ________, November.
◇ She asks you to call back to (**4**) ________ the date.

Conversation Two
(**Questions 5-8**)

- Look at the note below.
- You will hear a message about a man calling about an order.

Message
To: Mary Smith
From: John Willington at New York Crisps
◇ The delivery date for our new (**5**) ________ has been delayed.
◇ He wondered if he will be (**6**) ________ on this occasion.
◇ He is offering free (**7**) ________.
◇ There is one thing which is not mentioned in the contract — who is responsible for (**8**) ________ during the transit?

Conversation Three
(**Questions 9-12**)

- Look at the note below.
- You will hear a man describing a problem with a woman who works in an advertisement company.
- You have 15 seconds to read through the note.

Call of Changing Information

Enid is calling Tony about the (**9**) ________ he has ordered.
Tony will be back (**10**) ________.
The number Enid asked for is (**11**) ________ for the marketing executives.
The position of (**12**) ________ has to change to the left.

PART TWO

Section One
(Questions 13-17)

- You will hear five short recordings.
- For each recording, decide what recommendation the speaker makes.
- Write one letter (**A-H**) next to the number of the recording.
- Do not use any letter more than once.
- After you have listened once, replay the recordings.

(**13**) ________

(**14**) ________

(**15**) ________

(**16**) ________

(**17**) ________

A Advertise posts within the company as well as outside.
B Include detailed information about vacancies.
C Make sure your website is kept up to date.
D Allocate suitable staff to maintain the website.
E Re-design your non-web-based recruitment advertising.
F Use a range of technologies for contact with applicants.
G Ask potential applicants the most important questions first.
H Maximize the opportunities offered by the internet.

Section Two
(Questions 18-22)

- You will hear five short recordings.
- For each recording, decide what the speaker's purpose is.
- Write one letter (**A-H**) next to the number of the recording.
- Do not use any letter more than once.
- After you have listened once, replay the recordings.
- You have 15 seconds to read the list **A-H**.

(**18**) ________

(**19**) ________

(**20**) ________

(**21**) ________

(**22**) ________

A Make more profit.
B Take some action to improve production
C Attract skilled workers.
D Cease the production.
E Propose some ideas.
F Close the factory.
G Get invest for the company.
H Send for more staff.

PART THREE

(Questions 23-30)

- You will hear the conversation between Emily, Sales Manager of a company and David Parker, a market expert. They are talking about what is going to influence the life style and how the life style will affect the purchasing process.
- You have to complete the sentences (**23-30**), mark one letter (**A**, **B** or **C**) for the correct answer.
- After you have listened once, replay the recording.

23 When we talk about AIC, it means ________.

A activities, interests and changes

B advertising, impact and opportunities

C activities, interests and choice

24 AIC measurement can also be called ________.

A psychographics **B** statistics **C** demographics

25 According to the author, the most important social factor in purchasing process is ________.

A culture **B** reference groups **C** social classes

26 If you are running an upper level fur store, you'd better attract your customers by ________.

A mass advertising

B lowering prices

C improving the product quality

27 According to the reference groups' influence on the purchase progress, a retailer must pay much attention to the reference groups composed by ________.

A suburbanites **B** city dwellers **C** family members

28 For the customer with much self-confidence, the purchasing process is ________.

A long **B** endless **C** short

29 When the consumer thinks of alternatives and makes a final decision, the most important individual factor will be ________.

A performance **B** motives **C** personalities

30 One of the individual dimensions of lifestyle mentioned by the expert is ________.

A interests

B performance

C class consciousness

答案解析

(**1**) David Smith。从题目可以判断出，此空应该填人名或公司名等名称。由听力原文“Could I speak to David Smith, please?”可知电话是要打给David Smith的，故此空应该填David Smith。

(**2**) Cancel。首先从题目判断本题应该填写动词，由原文“I want to cancel our meeting on the 16th, November.”可知答案应该为cancel。

(**3**) 19th。从题目判断，本题考查对信息的敏感度，由原文“I want to cancel our meeting on the 16th, November. But I'm available three days later.”来推断，答案应该是19^{th}。

(**4**) Confirm。本题只要认真听原文“I hope he can call me back to confirm the date.”即可知道答案。

(**5**) packaging machine。从原文中的第三句话“It's about your packaging machines which you ordered.”可以得知订单是关于packaging machine的，打电话的目的是通知订单延迟，此空应该填名词。

(6) fined。从原文“Under the contract I signed, I will be fined if I delay the delivery date. But I hope Mary will waive that, since I also provided a special discount.”可以得到答案，他怀疑是否会被罚款。
(7) installation。从题目可以得知此空应该填名词。从原文“I won't charge for installation.”可知答案。
(8) insurance。根据原文“I can't find anything in the contract about who's dealing with insurance while the goods are on the road.”可以得知，他不知道是谁负责保险事宜。
(9) brochures。本段录音主要是关于男士打电话要求广告公司更改宣传手册的数量，从“I was hoping to speak to Tony Wilson about the brochures you're designing for us.”一句可知男士打电话的目的。
(10) next Thursday。男士打电话找 Tony 时，女士说他不在，将在下个周四回来。
(11) 400。从对话中可知，Enid 为市场执行部门订购的手册是 400 份，考生在听录音时要注意后面出现的干扰信息。“I'm sure I asked for four hundred for each of the marketing executives.”为关键信息句。
(12) company logo。此处考查对细节信息的获取能力，从“Could you ask Tony to move the company logo further to the left?”一句中可得到答案。
(13) G。根据原文“Do you have hands-on experience of the latest technologies in this field? People who can't give the answers are immediately advised not to continue with their application.”可知道这道题的选项就应该是 G，会首先询问申请者最重要的问题。
(14) H。由原文大意可知道英国所有公司都在使用网络招人，目的应该就是把网络提供工作的机会最大化。
(15) F。由原文“for instance when inviting someone to interview: it shows that the firm has joined the twenty-first century. And although the phone is much more traditional, it's still a valuable form, because you can talk to applicants in person”可知，打电话与面试远远追不上 21 世纪的步伐，所以应该选 F。
(16) D。原文“abilities required for dealing with online recruitment”的意思是需要专业能力来经营在线招聘，所以要有专门的人来保证支持在线招聘。
(17) B。由原文“perhaps with a personal statement from them”可推断出在招聘时要有详细信息。
(18) D。本段文字主要介绍了过去两年所取得的效果，并对未来市场进行了预测，说到某种商品的需求已经不是很强烈了。其中，“so we should stop production as soon as current contracts expire”一句表明了应该停止生产这种产品，与选项 D 说法一致。
(19) E。文中女士说到了工厂的位置随着所在的城市的迅速发展，导致了在那里的成本将增加，因此决定考虑选择其他的地点，先后提出了两个建议，因此选择 E。
(20) B。此处考查考生对录音中人物谈话内容的把握和正确分析。男士说：“We think the company should consider introducing an evening shift to maintain seventy percent capacity on all the machines.”可知他的目的是增加夜班，以便能够保证百分之七十的机器连续生产，之后他又提出引进更多的机器，变成两条生产线，从中可以推测出他的目的是采取措施保证生产效率的提高，故选 B。
(21) G。录音中女士介绍了公司的经营状况，产品的市场需求增加，公司处于业务量提升的阶段，这就意味着不久以后会需要更多的资金。从“And that means we'll need additional funding before long. So, let's start approaching people who've expressed an interest in us in the past.”这两句所表达的内容来看，女士的目的是寻找对公司感兴趣的人，其中选项 G 中的说法与女士的目的符合。
(22) C。文中女士谈到了各公司最近对工人的需求在增加，特别是熟练工人，如果想要留住他们，就要给他们提供好的条件，不仅仅是提高工资，而且女士提出了几项奖励措施，她这样做的目的就是让有能力的工人留在公司，与选项 C 中的说法一致。
(23) C。男士向我们介绍了影响消费者购买行为的主要因素，从“The consumer's activities, interests, and choice or AIC can be used to analyze life styles and their impact on purchase behavior.”中我们可以知道，可以分析顾客的行为、兴趣爱好和选择。

（**24**）A。文中解释了AIC所代表的意义之后，介绍了它具体影响了消费者的哪些方面，之后又说到“The use of the AIC measurement has also been called psychographics; it is in the early stages of development.”，我们能知道AIC又可以被叫作psychographics（消费心理学）。其中B选项和C选项的意思都是“统计”，文中只是说到AIC对于统计是很有价值的，并不是说它就是指“统计”的意思，因此可以排除这两个选项。

（**25**）A。男士在文中提到除了AIC方法之外，还可以通过顾客的文化、社会阶层、偏好群体等了解他们的购买行为，主要介绍了culture，之后的句子“From a retailing perspective, the norms or standards of behavior that are influenced by culture are most important. Culture has an impact on all aspects of the purchasing process.”告诉我们文化影响购买行为的很多方面，故选择A选项。

（**26**）C。本题考查考生对信息的分析判断能力。题干的意思是：对于经营高档皮装店来说如何能够吸引消费者。短文中介绍了高层次消费者的消费特点，“higher-class consumers use media information and shop at prestige stores. For products or services that are conspicuous, reference groups have an important role in the purchasing process.”说明他们更喜欢去高档的商店，因为服务和产品质量都是很出色的，所以我们可以分析出，如果是高级商店，应该注重产品的质量和服务，来吸引那些高端消费者。

（**27**）A。文中男士说到偏好群体对购买行为有很大的影响，因此应该给予正确的理解。题目问的是：应该对由哪部分组成的偏好群体给予注意。“As an example, one's neighbors are a membership reference group. The suburbanite will follow his or her neighbors and know them much better.”说明影响购买行为的主要群体是那些居住在郊区的人们，而城市中的人大部分都独自生活，因此他们的购买行为很少受到别人的影响。故选A。

（**28**）C。此题考查的是逆向思维，题目的答案没有直接给出。文中说到“For someone with little self-confidence, the process is long.”，意思是：那些没有足够自信的人购买过程持续的时间会很长，因此可以推断出自信的人购买过程应该会是短暂的。故选C。

（**29**）B。文中男士说到了影响顾客购买行为的个人因素包括个性、行为和动机，其中，“Consumers have different motives when they buy products. Motives are critical when the consumer ranks alternatives and makes a final decision.”这句表明，三个因素当中最重要的是人的购买动机，它影响了顾客的选择和做出最后的决定。因此B选项符合题意。

（**30**）B。此题可以根据题文同序的规律来确定答案。题目问“影响购买行为的个人因素是什么”，文中最后说到了“A person's performance in various roles determines his or her social acceptance and influences the purchasing process.”，可以找到关键词performance，因此可得出答案为B。

对话大意

PART ONE

Conversation One

这是一个要更改会议时间的电话信息。由于Linda在11月16日这天要出差，所以要更改会议时间。考生要注意的是，她想把日期定在三天后，并希望David能够回电话确认一下。

Conversation Two

这是一个关于订单信息的对话。此题的关键部分在于考生对信息细节的捕捉。对话的主要内容是男子想延迟交货日期，由于他们的起重机出了问题；鉴于此种情况，询问是否会被罚款；愿意提供免费安装。最后提到了在合同当中遗漏的问题——保险。

Conversation Three

假日旅行公司的 Enid Stevens 打电话给阳光广告公司的 Sheila Dallas 找 Tony Wilson 谈谈关于宣传手册的问题，但 Tony Wilson 下周四才回来，要 Sheila Dallas 传达一下信息。假日旅行公司对设计方案很满意，但弄错了数量，市场部门定的是 400 份，Enid Steven 订的是 650 份，但阳光公司却给每个人 750 份。并希望能把公司的标语向左面移动一下，它离公司的地址太近了。

PART TWO

Section One

(**13**) 在第一段独白中，讲话人首先表明自己的工作是招聘专员，并且对网络的依赖性很大，通过网络，会首先排除掉没有机会的申请。

(**14**) 在第二段独白中，说英国几乎所有的商务都在使用网络，多数都用网站作为平台来找工作。

(**15**) 第三段独白是说很多公司认为自己是与时俱进的，能利用网络发电子邮件来招聘员工并给他们发邮件，但这远远不够。

(**16**) 第四段独白表明网络招聘也是需要有专项技能去运作的。

(**17**) 第五段独白建议在用网络招聘时，要列出这个职位的详细信息。

Section Two

(**18**) 两年前通过各种方法增加了销售额，并且通过引进新机器降低了成本，但仍没有达到增加销售的目标。由于没有需求，应该停止生产。

(**19**) 首先得到厂址，租金很合适，但因为多方面原因，成本会增加。在工业区重新选址可以节约大量的成本，改善产品分销渠道。第二个建议是由于员工不多了，应该把顶楼空出来。

(**20**) 引进夜班可以保证百分之七十的机器运转，并增加一个包装线，增加效率。并采取奖金制度来鼓励员工，但是最后我们觉得不会有太好的效果。

(**21**) 产品做得很好，但是市场需求不够高。如果要利用业绩上升的优势，应该发起促销活动，并提高机器的生产能力。这意味着额外的资金，因此要紧紧抓住对我们感兴趣的投资商。

(**22**) 两三年前，有很多的应聘者。但现在，失业率总体下降了，并且每个人都在找工人，特别是熟练工人。如果想得到好的人手，并留住他们，就得提供更好的待遇。不仅是提高工资，还有离职补贴、再就业补贴、忠诚奖金等。

PART THREE

女：一个人的生活习惯对购买过程有很大的影响。因此我要怎么做出决策并且理解我的目标市场呢？

男：顾客的活动、兴趣和选择可以被用来分析生活方式和它们对购买行为的影响，也可以叫作 AIC。活动、兴趣和选择用来分析人口统计数据的时候是很有价值的。根据这三个因素，消费群体在使用产品、购买时间、购物体验、商店位置等有很大的不同。典型的顾客调查包括会员的问题、兴趣爱好、旅行、购物、工作和娱乐活动，也包括家庭、团体对经济、政治和广告的感觉和兴趣程度。AIC 测量也可以叫作心理测量，这是研究的初步阶段。

女：因此，AIC 调查是不够的。我还要注意什么其他的问题吗？

男：文化、社会阶层、偏好群体和阶层意识是从社会的角度来分析生活方式对购买行为的影响。一个人的文化层次影响了家庭、宗教信仰、教育水平和其他因素。例如，一个国家北方的居民和南方的人的行为就很不一样，或者从销售的角度来看，有文化影响的行为标准是最重要的，文化对购买过程的各个方面都有影响。

女：社会阶层如何影响一个人的购买行为呢？

男：底层消费者的信息来源有限，中层消费者使用媒体信息，他们愿意到外面去购物。高层消费者们使用媒体信息，并且在有声誉的店购物。对于特色显著的产品和服务，偏好群体在购买过程中扮演了很重要的角色，因此应对他们的类型有很好的理解。例如，一个人的邻居属于偏好群体，那么他如果是住在郊区，就很容易在购买行为上去模仿他的邻居，而住在城市里的人们更加独立，对他们的邻居了解甚少。

女：你不认为人的动机对人的购买行为也很重要吗？

男：是的，个性、动机和表现是从个人生活方式的角度去理解它对购买行为的影响。一个顾客的个性特征影响其购买行为。对于一个没有耐心的顾客，购买过程是很短的。没有自信的顾客，购买过程是很长的。购买后的满意度对于顾客是很重要的。顾客在购买时具有不同的动机，它在购买时进行选择和做出最后决定至关重要。动机在不同的条件也会改变。一个人的不同的社会角色影响其购买过程。

女：非常感谢，我认为我了解到了生活方式的重要性。

听力原文

PART ONE

Conversation One

R = Receptionist **L** = Linda

R: Good morning. Can I help you?

L: Good morning. Could I speak to David Smith, please?

R: Hold on for a moment, please.

R: Hello?

L: Hello?

R: I'm afraid he's not in the office. Can I take a message?

L: Could you tell him that I'll have to go to India on business and I want to cancel our meeting on the 16th, November. But I'm available three days later. So I want to ask him if it is OK.

R: OK. May I ask who's calling?

L: Oh, sorry. I forgot to tell you that. This is Linda from Danish Telecommunications Trade Fair.

R: I got that. Anything else?

L: I hope he can call me back to confirm the date.

R: OK. I'll pass the message and he'll ring you back later.

L: Thank you.

R: Oh, does he have your number?

L: I think he does.

R: Thanks for your calling.

L: Thanks. Bye!

Conversation Two

Man: Hello. Could I speak to Mary Smith, please?

Woman: Oh, sorry. She's out for the moment. Could I take a message?

Man: Of course. It's John Willington from New York Crisps. It's about your packaging machines which you ordered.

Woman: Oh, dear. What's wrong?

Man: I want to postpone the delivery date. There's something wrong with the lifting machine.

Woman: I see.

Man: Under the contract I signed, I will be fined if I delay the delivery date. But I hope Mary will waive that, since I also provided a special discount.

Woman: I'll check for you.

Man: Thanks a lot. I've decided that, as we're busy with the maintenance, I won't charge for installation.

Woman: OK. I've got that.

Man: Oh, one more thing — I can't find anything in the contract about who's dealing with insurance while the goods are on the road.

Woman: I'll check that.

Conversation Three

Woman: Hello, Sunshine Advertisement Company. Sheila Dallas speaking. How can I help you?

Man: Hello. This is Enid Stevens from Holiday Travelling Company. I was hoping to speak to Tony Wilson about the brochures you're designing for us.

Woman: I'm afraid Tony's away until next Thursday.

Man: Oh — you see I'm not very happy with the brochures and I wanted to see if I could make a couple of changes to the paper, too.

Woman: Would you like me to pass on a message?

Man: Yes, please. The thing is I've just received your designs. The brochures themselves are good, but you seem to have misunderstood the quantities. I'm sure I asked for four hundred for each of the marketing executives and six hundred and fifty for me but you've put everyone down for seven hundred and fifty.

Woman: Right, I've made a note of that. Is there anything else?

Man: Yes, well this is my mistake really. Could you ask Tony to move the company logo further to the left? It's too close to the address at the moment. I think that's all for now. Thanks.

PART TWO

Section One

(**13**) I'm in charge of the recruitment in the company, and in most cases, we depend on the internet. It actually eliminated the kinds of applications that don't have a chance. We have an online application system that works well, because it elicits the vital information at the outset. For example, there will be something like, "Do you have hands-on experience of the latest technologies in this field?" People who can't give the answers are immediately advised not to continue with their application.

(**14**) It's astonishing that, while nearly all British businesses use the internet in one way or another, most of them just use their websites as shop windows for advertising jobs — then expect people to send in paper-based applications. They're simply not using the technology to its best advantage. There are so many refinements that the internet makes possible, so every recruitment officer ought to be looking at making optimal use of it and cutting out as much paper as they can.

(**15**) Many companies think they're up to date if they advertise vacancies on their website and send emails to applicants instead of letters. But that just isn't enough. These days, lots of people send text messages, so businesses should follow suit, for instance when inviting someone to interview: it shows that the firm has joined the twenty-first century. And although the phone is much more traditional, it's still a valuable form, because you can talk to applicants in person.

(**16**) Companies sometimes get the wrong idea about online recruitment. They focus on the fact that it can reduce administration, but forget that it takes specific skills to manage the online process. After all, the recruitment section of the website needs to be organized, applications dealt with quickly and effectively, and so on. People who are used to circulating details of vacancies internally, planning newspaper advertising, acknowledging applications, etc. may not have the abilities required for dealing with online recruitment.

(17) So often, people apply for jobs they know very little about, because positions with the same title can vary considerably in different organizations. So when you're recruiting, you should use your website to list projects and assignments of the post and give case histories of people in similar posts in the company, perhaps with a personal statement from them. It doesn't affect the procedure you follow, but it helps potential applicants to decide if it's a job they really want.

Section Two

(18) **Man:** As you know, we adopted various measures two years ago with the aim of boosting sales. We managed to increase output and cut costs by introducing new machines. We also cut our profit margins still further. But even though we were able to lower prices as a result, I'm afraid we still didn't meet targets. The demand for this particular commodity just isn't there any more, so we should stop production as soon as current contracts expire.

(19) **Woman:** When we first acquired the factory premises, the rent was well within our means. But because that area of the city has developed more quickly than others, it's now a prime site and the cost of retaining it has risen accordingly. In fact, we would make considerable savings by relocating to the industrial estate on the other side of town, which would improve product distribution, anyway. A second suggestion is to vacate the top floor of the building — we do have fewer staff now.

(20) **Man:** We've looked at various measures and we'll be making recommendations to senior management next week. We think the company should consider introducing an evening shift to maintain seventy percent capacity on all the machines. We're also aware of the hold-ups on the packaging line, and we'd like to bring in an additional machine and split the line in two. That'll speed things up. We did consider bonus schemes for certain categories of employee, but decided that this wouldn't have sufficient impact.

(21) **Woman:** I think your analysis of the situation is correct. The product is already doing very well, but demand hasn't peaked yet, by any means. And if we want to take full advantage of a boom, we've got to step up our promotion and have mechanisms in place to increase manufacturing capacity if necessary. And that means we'll need additional funding before long. So, let's start approaching people who've expressed an interest in us in the past.

(22) **Man:** Two or three years ago there were ten, or even twenty, applicants for every job we advertised, but things have changed. Unemployment in general is right down and everyone's competing for workers now, especially skilled workers. If we want to get good people, and retain them, we'll have to offer a better package. I'm not suggesting we put wages up yet; I think we ought to try other things first, like one-off welcome payments, relocation allowances, and, possibly, loyalty bonuses.

PART THREE

Woman: A person's life habit has a great impact on the purchasing process. So how do I make decision and understand my target market?

Man: The consumer's activities, interests, and choice or AIC can be used to analyze life styles and their impact on purchase behavior. Activities, interests, and choice are very valuable when they can be related to demographic data. Grouping people according to these three criteria will reveal substantial differences in product usage, time spent shopping, enjoyment of shopping experience, location and hours of the store, and so on. A typical consumer AIC survey would include questions on membership, hobbies, travel, shopping, work, and entertainment activities, involvement in the home, the family, and community interests and feelings about economics, politics, and advertising. The use of the AIC measurement has also been called psychographics; it is in the early stages of development.

Woman: So the AIC survey of consumers is not enough. What else should I pay attention to?

Man: Culture, social class, reference groups and class consciousness are social dimensions of life style that have an impact on purchasing behavior. A person's culture affects the importance of family, religion, education and other concerns. For example, North citizens of a country act differently from South ones. From a retailing perspective, the norms or standards of behavior that are influenced by culture are most important. Culture has an impact on all aspects of the purchasing process.

Woman: How does social classe influence a person's purchasing behavior?

Man: Lower-class consumers have limited information sources. Middle class consumers utilize media information and extensive search. They are willing to shop out of their houses. Higher-class consumers use media information and shop at prestige stores. For products or services that are conspicuous reference groups have an important role in the purchasing process. Those reference groups that are face-to-face have the most impact on the purchasing process. The different types and uses of reference groups need to be understood. As an example, one's neighbors are a membership reference group. The suburbanite will follow his or her neighbors and know them much better. City dwellers are more independent and know little about their neighbors.

Woman: Don't you think motives are very important in purchasing behavior?

Man: Yes. Personality, motives, and performance are individual dimensions of life style that affect purchasing behavior. A consumer's personality traits affect the purchase process. For an impatient person, the process is short. For someone with little self-confidence, the process is long. Post purchase satisfaction is very important to a customer. Consumers have different motives when they buy products. Motives are critical when the consumer ranks alternatives and makes a final decision. Motives do change in different situations. A person's performance in various roles determines his or her social acceptance and influences the purchasing process.

Woman: Thank you very much. I think I've learned about the importance of life style.

商务背景知识扩展

信用证

信用证（Letter of Credit，L/C）是指开证银行应申请人的要求并按其指示向第三方开立的载有一定金额的、在一定的期限内凭符合规定的单据付款的书面保证文件。信用证是国际贸易中最主要、最常用的支付方式。

信用证种类：

跟单信用证：是凭跟单汇票或仅凭单据付款的信用证。

光票信用证：凭不随附货运单据的光票付款的信用证。

不可撤销信用证：指信用证一经开出，在有效期内，未经受益人及有关当事人的同意，开证行不能片面修改和撤销。

可撤销信用证：开证行不必征得受益人或有关当事人同意就有权随时撤销的信用证。

即期信用证：指开证行或付款行收到符合信用证条款的跟单汇票或装运单据后，立即履行付款义务的信用证。

此外还有可转让信用证与不可转让的信用证等等各种各样的信用证。

第四周

口 语 部 分

一、题型介绍

BEC中级口试与其他两个级别的口试一样，采用两人一组的面试方式（在考生人数出现奇数时，最后三位考生一组进行）。两名考生一组的口试时间约为14分钟；三名考生一组的口试时间约为20分钟。由两位考官主考，一位为提问考官（interlocutor），负责与考生对话交谈并打出总体表现分（Global Achievement）；另一位为评分考官（assessor），旁听并从语法与词汇（Grammar and Vocabulary）、话语组织（Discourse Management）、语音（Pronunciation）及互动交际（Interactive Communication）四个方面分项评分。口试具体分为三个部分：

第一部分：对话

这部分内容为考官向每个考生轮流提问。分两个阶段：第一阶段，询问有关考生个人的一些情况；第二阶段，提问一般商务问题。考生必须能够做自我介绍，提供有关姓名、籍贯、学习、工作、兴趣、过去经历以及将来打算的信息，能就与商务有关的常识性问题发表简短的看法，并给出简要理由。第一阶段两个考生通常为相同问题，前后作答；第二阶段通常有四个问题，前两个问题两个考生相同，后两个问题内容不同，两个考生分别作答。考生直接应答提问，没有准备时间。这部分口试时间为：两个考生一组大约3分钟，三个考生一组大约为5分钟。

第二部分：简短发言

这部分内容为一分钟简短发言。考官会分别给每个考生一张题卡，上面各有三道不同的题目（一道为日常话题，一道为一般性商务话题，另一道为专业商务话题），由考生在自己的三道题目中任选一题作答。每道题目下面提供两个代表论点的提示词，外加一个空白圆点符号。考生有一分钟准备时间，两位考生同时准备。允许利用这段时间记下一些发言要点。按照要求，一位考生作答完毕后，另一位考生要提1~2个问题，因此在搭档发言时要注意听并在头脑中想好要提问的问题。该部分内容虽然为一分钟简短发言，但要求内容完整，有开头，有结尾；能将所提供的两点提示词扩展为论点，并加以论证，同时能围绕题目，自己再提出一个论点并简短论证。要求考生使用词语得体，条理清晰地构思、组织、表达自己的观点。这部分口试时间为：两个考生一组大约为6分钟，三个考生一组大约为8分钟。

第三部分：讨论

这部分内容为考生与考生之间讨论商务语境中的工作话题。由考官发给考生一张讨论题卡，上面有几行提示词，简单描述一个商务情景，以及用圆点符号标出需要讨论和做出决定的要点。考生有30秒钟时间共同阅读提示词并各自打腹稿进行准备，然后根据文字提示，进行3分钟讨论。考生需首先共同构建一个语境（例如，他们所在的公司），自然地将讨论引入决策，而不仅仅是讨论各种选择方案。讨论结束后，考官会根据时间和考生表现情况，酌情加问一至数个问题。这部分口试时间为：两个考生一组大约为5分钟，三个考生一组的大约为7分钟。要求考生无须考官介入就能主动发言、得体应答并自然转换话题。

二、评分标准

除总体表现分外，四个单项分根据以下详细标准给分：

Grammar and Vocabulary（语法和词汇）

主要测试考生在口头表达中语法和词汇运用是否正确、得体并丰富多样，能否避免词汇和句型单一或不断重复相同的词句。

Discourse Management（话语组织）

主要测试考生运用句子以上语言单位进行口头交际的能力。包括能否恰当地展开话题，话语是否连贯、流畅、切题（例如，在提出观点的同时，能进行有条理的论证，善于使用衔接词语等）。在口语第一部分问答中，考生需尽量完整地回答考官的提问；在口试第二部分个人简短发言中，考生可充分利用机会扩展话语；在口试第三部分讨论题中，要求考生围绕规定题目，表达、论证自己的观点。

Pronunciation（语音）

主要测试考生清晰发音的能力。根据各个单音、单词及句子重音、语调节奏的正确性打分。考生要特别避免母语口音给交际带来的困难，恰当使用重读、节奏、语调，清晰发音。

Interactive Communication（互动交际）

主要测试考生在两人或三人小组中积极参与、相互合作、有效交际的能力。打分依据主要看考生是否有能力恰当得体地主动引入话题、应答自如，轻松转化话题，充分参与讨论，最终圆满完成题目要求。需要注意的是，考生要避免在口试中表现得咄咄逼人，不给对方留说话的机会；有效地交际应该注意在说话的产出和接受之间能够轻松转换。

总结

本周的学习内容是通过对中级口语的命题规律、评分标准、解题技巧等的分析、总结，配以经典范例、实战习题等内容，加以详细解析、深入研究 BEC 考试中级的规律、特点，利用一周的时间，帮助考生认清自身水平，树立应对信心；使考生熟悉考试题型，掌握应对方法；从而在 BEC 中级口试的学习和备考过程中抓住重点、难点，制定科学可行的复习计划，提高复习效率，以期在考试中取得最理想的成绩。

周一　四步解决对话透析

一、命题规律

这部分内容为考官向每个考生轮流提问。分两个阶段：第一阶段，询问有关考生个人的一些情况；第二阶段，提问一般商务问题。考生必须能够做自我介绍，提供有关姓名、籍贯、学习、工作、兴趣、过去经历以及将来打算的信息，能就与商务有关的常识性问题发表简短的看法，并给出简要理由。第一阶段两个考生通常为相同问题，前后作答；第二阶段通常有四个问题，前两个问题两个考生相同，后两个问题内容不同，两个考生分别作答。考生直接应答提问，没有准备时间。这部分口试时间为：两个考生一组大约3分钟，三个考生一组大约为5分钟。

二、解题技巧

1. 口试前，充分考虑如何回答一些可能被问到的问题，如，工作或学习情况，所在国家的商务概况，以及内容广泛的商务话题。
2. 在口试过程中，要集中精力，听清考官的问题，回答要切题。必要时可以请求考官重复一遍，说话时要面对考官和另一位考生，另一位考生发言时要注意听。
3. 回答要尽量全面、有深度，并简单举例说明。
4. 切记，口试考查的是考生的英语会话能力，而不是某个商务领域的专业知识。因此，如果不清楚某个答案，尽管直说，并力图陈述理由来加以弥补。

三、经典范例

我们先来看一组范例，希望能让考生对该题型有一个基本的理解。

PART ONE

In this part, the interviewer asks questions to each of the candidates in turn. You have to give information about yourself and express personal opinions.

Possible Questions	Suggested Answers
Could we have your name, please? How do spell your name?	**Version 1:** Yes, It's my pleasure. I'm ... You can call me ... for short. It spells ... **Version 2:** Yes, my name is Wang Qiang. It's W-A-N-G, Wang, my surname; and Q-I-A-N-G, Qiang. Chinese people put their surnames before the given names. So you can call me Wang Qiang, or Qiang Wang in the English way.

续表

Possible Questions	Suggested Answers
Where are you from? How do you come here?	**Version 1:** I'm from ... where it is famous for it's local delicacies. I just arrived yesterday afternoon by air, which is about 2 hours' flight from here. **Version 2:** My home is quite near from this city. It's about 1 hour's ride by high-speed train which is safe and convenient.
Could you tell us something about your family?	**Version 1:** OK. I come from a medium-sized family where I have my mother, father and one younger brother. Well, I'm fortunate to get a brother in my family because most of the people at my age are the "only child" in their family. **Version 2:** Yes. I'm from a Nuclear Family, which means there are just 3 members in my family: my mother, my father and I. My mother is a teacher who teaches English in a middle school. And my father works as a pediatrician.
Do you work or are you a student?	**Version 1:** I'm a third-year student in ... university. I major in Marketing and Commercial. **Version 2:** I just got my B. A Degree this July, but I'm going to take further study as a postgraduate student in another famous university of ...
What do you like most about your study?	**Version 1:** My major lies in Auto Engineering in which I have the chance to study and design all kinks of cars. It's amazing because I've been fond of cars since a boy. **Version 2:** I took International Financial Management as my major, English as my minor because my favor lies in Finance and English is so useful for me.
Do you think taking a part-time job in university is a waste of time?	**Version 1:** You mean working while studying. I think it's a waste of time. Because I think I have so much to do in university besides reading and attending classes like socializing, sporting. By the way, studying is the most important thing for a student. **Version 2:** I don't think taking a part-time job is a waste of time. Instead every college student should take a part-time job for some while at least. Because a part-time job can give us the chance to learn about the society. **Notes:** auto engineering 汽车工程 socialize 社会交往

四、经典实战

根据BEC口试第一部分对话的特点，我们设计了一些模拟问题，供考生进行实战演练。

Possible Questions	Suggested Answers and Brain Storms
1) What's your name? How do you spell your name? How do you spell your family name / surname / last name?	• My last name is … • My given name is …, but my friends always call me …, and my English name is …. • You can call me …, if you like / wish. • L-V pronounced ly …
2) Where are you from? Would you say it's a good place to live in? (Why?) Do you like living in…? Where would you like to live… or…? (Why?) Do you think it would be better to live in… or…? (Why?)	• I come from the capital city of Changchun, Jilin Province… / I was born in a little town called … However I grew up in … • Yes, I think so. /No, I can't say that. Because I like the weather there. It's pretty cool in summer, though a little bit cold in winter. But it snows a lot in winter, and I like snow. /I have too many reasons why I'm going to live in a big city like … : first, I don't like the weather there. It's so hot and scorching in summer that I have to stay under air-conditioning the whole day; second, I'm fed up with the traffic jam; third, there's so much pollution in a big city like …; the list can go on and on. **Brain Storms** • Weather • Transportation • Environment • Housing • Night life (exciting, dynamic) • Local people • Job opportunities **Notes:** traffic jam 交通拥堵 dynamic 有动感的，充满活力的
3) Do you come from a large family or a small family? Can you tell me a bit about… in your family?	• I'm the only child of my family. / A big family, I might say it. I have one elder sister and a younger brother. • Yes, I'd like to. Both my parents are workers. They are honest, kind and trustworthy. They work hard and never complain about their own gain or loss. They are my life models. /My

续表

Possible Questions	Suggested Answers and Brain Storms
	father migrated from his hometown to this city when he was only 20 years old. And he set up his own business, almost scratched from nothing. He does well with industrious and enterprising spirit in his life and career. I'm very proud of him. **Brain Storms** • intelligent family • public servants • farmers **Notes:** extended family 大家庭（如数代同堂的家庭） nuclear family 三口之家（只有父母和独生子女的家庭） scratch from nothing 白手起家
4) Do you work or are you a student in...? What do you do? What do you study? What's your major? What do you like most about your job? (Why?) What do you like most about your studies? (Why?)	• I work as a sales rep at a joint venture in IT industry for three years after graduation from ... university. I majored in Computer Science and minored in Financing. My job is to develop new customers and keep follow-ups with existed customers. We have our own production base in ... • Well, what interests me most about my job is the challenge and satisfaction I get after weeks' and even months' of hard work. /I like my job very much because it's both challenging and rewarding. And I can travel frequently to different places. • I'm particularly fond of solving problem, which I can make it in computer programming. Ever since I was a child, I found my deep interest in figures. Later, I got fascinated with computer programs. The combination of figures and computer is a perfect match through which we can do almost anything beyond imagination. **Brain Storms** • job satisfaction • travel opportunities • training/career development • financial benefits • vacations

续表

Possible Questions	Suggested Answers and Brain Storms
	Notes: joint venture（中外）合资公司 major in 主修…… minor in 辅修…… combination 组合

周二　三点注意发言总括（上）

一、命题规律

这部分内容为一分钟简短发言。考官会分别给每个考生一张题卡，上面各有三道不同的题目（一道为日常话题，一道为一般性商务话题，另一道为专业商务话题），由考生在自己的三道题目中任选一题作答。每道题目下面提供两个代表论点的提示词，外加一个空白圆点符号。考生有一分钟准备时间，两位考生同时准备。允许利用这段时间记下一些发言要点。按照要求，一位考生作答完毕后，另一位考生要提 1 ~2 个问题，因此在搭档发言时要注意听，并在头脑中想好要提问的问题。该部分内容虽然为一分钟简短发言，但要求内容完整，有开头，有结尾；能将所提供的两点提示词扩展为论点，并加以论证，同时能围绕题目，自己再提出一个论点并简短论证。要求考生使用词语得体，条理清晰地构思、组织、表达自己的观点。这部分口试时间为：两个考生一组大约为 6 分钟，三个考生一组大约为 8 分钟。

二、解题技巧

1. 在三个题目中任选一题做一分钟发言。三道题目形式相同，都是以“What’s important when…?”开头。每道题下都有两个提示词或短语帮助考生阐述论点。
2. 充分利用一分钟准备时间。写下要点和关键词，使发言结构紧密，层次清晰，并能借助关键词扩展成句。
3. 注意使发言条理清晰。例如，开头和结尾要简明扼要，能用连接词衔接各个部分内容。说话时要面对考官和另一位考生，注意眼神和肢体语言交流，同时注意聆听另一考生的发言。另一位考生作答完毕后，要就其发言内容进行提问。

三、经典范例

下面我们还是先来看一组范例，希望能让考生对该题型有一个基本的理解。

PART TWO

In this part of the test, you are asked to give a short talk on a business topic. You have to choose one of the topics from the three below and then talk for about one minute. You have one miute to prepare your ideas.

A: What is important when…?
Planning a presentation
- Audience
- Equipment needed

B: What is important when…?
Selecting an interpreter for a meeting with foreign customers
- Experience
- Reliability

C: What is important when…?
Introducing a new product range onto the market
- Timing
- Advance publicity

Possible answers:

Topic A

I choose Topic A. In my opinion, the audience we are going to address, the necessary equipment and the way how to deliver a presentation are all important factors in planning a presentation.

Before a presentation, we have to make sure what kinds of audience we are going to face. Then we will decide what language we are going to use in the presentation accordingly.

Second, we need the necessary equipment for our presentation like a projector, audio equipment, etc., so that we can get the best result out of our presentation.

Third, it is of the same importance that we should use the proper way in delivering a presentation. We need to think over the best way to attract our audience and make our presentation better understood.

In addition, if time allowed, we'd better have a rehearsal at spot to make sure that everything would go smooth in our presentation.

Topic B

I choose Topic B. I think good knowledge to our business, enough experience of interpreting and virtue of reliability are important in selecting an interpreter for a meeting with foreign customers.

Here are my reasons:

Firstly, good knowledge to our business is necessary for a smooth interpretation in a meeting. The interpreter should be familiar with some of the basic terms in our business, and if possible some basic ideas of how our businesses are going.

Secondly, enough interpreting experience is alway better for an interpreter. Enough experience can make the interpreter look more confident and is helpful in the critical time.

Thirdly, reliability is also important for a good interpreter. Because in a business meeting, some business secrets are going to be mentioned, a good interpreter should focus on his/her job of interpretation and keep the secrets from outside. Therefore, we need to find the interpreter we trust.

▶ **Useful words & expressions:**

- rehearsal *n.* 演练，彩排
- reliability *n.* 可靠，可信

四、经典实战

根据发言部分试题的特点，我们设计了一些模拟问题，供考生进行实战演练。

Topic 1. What is important when…?
choosing people to work in teams
- Variety of experience
- Personal qualities
- Disciplines

What is important when…?
Topic 2. Attending a job interview
- Information about the company
- Personal appearance
- Good communication skills

参考答案

Topic 1

I'll choose Topic 1. When choosing people to work in teams, there are many factors to consider. The first one is their various experience in one or more fields like different majors, education backgrounds as well as work experience, which are important to team work.

The second to consider is their own abilities and capacities. In a team, there should be a leader in general to make decisions. Also, the team members should be able to work closely to the leader and take their own responsibilities and make their contributions to the team work creatively in one way or another.

The third but of the same importance is the good cooperation in team work. Team members should have the basic disciplines to work together and get along with each other in an efficient way. While people are encouraged to develop their own individual talents, they need to respect some rules and regulations in a team.

▶ **Useful words & expressions:**

- capacity *n.* 才能，能力
- contribution *n.* 贡献

Topic 2

In attending a job interview, interviewees need to get full prepared in getting information about the company, a good personal appearance, and efficient communication with the interviewers.

Basic ideas of the company such as what kind of business the company is doing, the business prospect, the business scope, even the corporate cultures will help us better understand the company.

A decent dress is regarded as a kind of politeness showing our respect to others. It can also build up interviewee's confidence.

Good communication skills are necessary for tough questions and leave an impressive print to the interviewer, which can lay a good foundation to the success of an interview.

▶ **Useful words & expressions:**

- interviewee *n.* 面试者
- interviewer *n.* 面试官

周三　四步攻破发言要点（下）

一、命题规律

BEC 考试一个较为合理和公正的方面是它给考生提供一定选择空间。考生的知识领域、兴趣特点各有不同，对一些商业领域问题的认知和理解也会因人而异。因此，选择一个最熟悉的、最有感而发的话题是解题的前提条件。一旦选择了话题，可以参考所给的思路线索加以细化、深入。如果你对这一话题有过思考或感悟，就可以不借用提示思路，而加以自己认识上的补充，即使不一定会为你赢得更多的亮点，也可以确保你不用无话可说或人云亦云。

我们将以考生最熟悉的话题为讲解重点，为考生开辟一条攻克发言题的思路。

二、解题技巧

熟悉话题的四个选择及四步走：

1. 对阅读所给的三个话题及相应的提示语，根据自身掌握的知识结构特点，选择自己最熟悉的话题。
2. 根据话题自己选择另一个最关联的讨论点，使分论点增加为三个。然后围绕三个分论点展开论述。
3. 选择不同的展开方式展开分论点，如解释、举例、对比等。
4. 论述时，选择有变化、有新意的连接词。比如段与段之间的连接词、总结时所用的短语等。

三、经典范例

PART TWO

In this part of the test, you are asked to give a short talk on a business topic. You have to choose one of the topics from the three below and then talk for about one minute. You have one minute to prepare your ideas.

A: What is important when…?

Planning a presentation

- Audience
- Equipment needed

B: What is important when …?

Motivating the staff

- Financial benefits
- Career development opportunities

> **C:** What is important when …?
> Dealing with complaints of the consumers
> - Offering an apology
> - Suggesting a solution to the problem

Possible answers

Topic B

I choose Topic B— what is important when motivating staff. Concerning this topic, as far as I can see, three items are listed.

For the first place, financial benefits is a particular encouragement to the staff. As the employees, staff are always eager for reward for their contribution to the company and what they are worth. Such factors are just like market forces. The fundamental reason of looking for a job is to get pay. Staff do the job what they are paid for. However, quite often, the staff work overtime under their managers' demand. If the company fails to give proper financial benefits, staff might subsequently feel not being fairly treated, and therefore frustrate their enthusiasm for their work.

Second, career development opportunities is a tempt for the staff. Nowadays, very few people would like to go for that kind of job-for-life posts. They all wish to have their jobs better and better. If an employee is able to get the opportunities to obtain some sort of professional training during the course of employment, this experience will definitely enhance his value in the employment market and therefore benefits his future job-hunting.

Third, the friendly attitude of the boss can be useful to absorb the staff. Under different kinds of stress and trouble, the good atmosphere can make them pleasant. In all, financial benefits as well as career development opportunities and the friendly attitude of the boss is important when motivating staff.

Topic C

I choose Topic C — what is important when deal with complains from clients. With regard to this topic, I have the following ideas:

First of all, apology is a way to show your respect to your wlients when the clients think that they have received unfair treatments, the first thing that the company should do is to calm them down and try to keep the client. Besides, offering an apology is an important gesture to show that the hosting company is fully aware of the situation and would like to take the potential responsibility for its mistakes.

In the second place, suggesting a solution to the problem is necessary as well. The clients want to enter into the transaction in a good mood and with a reliable and trustworthy business partner. Apart from an apology, the client would want to have the problems and misunderstanding solved before their communication moves to the next level.

The last but not least, the promise of after-sales services is an indispensable part. It can provide a assurance for the consumption of the complaint clients. So what they worried about is of no sense. Certainly, their complaints fly away soon. In a conclusion, the apology, solution and promise of after-sales services are very important when dealing with complaints form clients.

▶ Useful words & expressions:

- trustworthy *adj.* 值得信赖的
- transaction *n.* 交易，业务

四、经典实战

Topic 1. What's important when ...?
Aiming to slash business overheads
- Budget and management
- Long-term effects

Topic 2. What's important when ...?
Coping with a heavy workload
- Benefits system
- Time management

参考答案

Topic 1

First of all, business overhead expenditure needs to be budgeted and appointed as fairly as possible to different departments of the business. Once we have set a clear budget plan, we'll be able to manage the overheads costs by limiting budget spending and improving work productivity.

Secondly, long-term effects should also be taken into consideration. In reducing overheads costs, we should not aim to seek the short-term interests only, instead, we should think and re-evaluate our business in a long-term mentality. Sometimes reduced budget may affect some instant loss or success, but in the long, it is good for the company's future development.

In addition, all the employees should be involved in the overheads reduction campaign. After all, if everyone can make some contribution to the cost reduction, it will make real difference.

▶ Useful words & expressions:

- overhead expenditure 工作预算支出
- mentality *n.* 心态

Topic 2

I think companies can introduce more benefits programmes to the staff in stimulating employees to deal with a heavy workload like childcare and nursing care for working parents so that they can balance their work and family better.

Second, time management is important. Companies can provide related training programmes to help employees better manage their time, improve their work efficiency. In this way, employees can become more organised and feel more at ease with their everyday work.

Third, companies can also help reduce employees' work pressure through psychological advice. And another good practise is some vacations for the employees to get refreshed after a period of heavy work, so that they can better deal with their work after they return.

▶ Useful words & expressions:

- stimulate *v.* 刺激，激励
- psychological *adj.* 心理上的

周四　五点注意讨论总括（上）

一、命题规律

这部分内容为考生与考生之间讨论商务语境中的工作话题。由考官发给考生一张讨论题卡，上面有几行提示词，简单描述一个商务情景，以及用圆点符号标出需要讨论和做出决定的要点。考生有 30 秒钟的时间共同阅读提示词并各自打腹稿进行准备，然后根据文字提示，进行 3 分钟讨论。考生需首先共同构建一个语境（例如，他们所在的公司），自然地将讨论引入决策，而不仅仅是讨论各种选择方案。讨论结束后，考官会根据时间和考生表现情况，酌情加问一至数个问题。这部分口试时间为：两个考生一组大约为 5 分钟，三个考生一组大约为 7 分钟。要求考生无须考官介入就能主动发言、得体应答并自然转换话题。

二、解题技巧

1. 讨论必须严肃认真，相互交换意见的方式应符合实际工作情况。
2. 两位考生应努力通过想象，将自己置身于真实的工作环境中。讨论提示卡上提示的某个实际工作问题应尽量达成某项决策，而不是简单列举提示的观点。
3. 考生有 30 秒时间进行准备、整理思路。要充分利用这段时间，看清题目要求。有不明白之处可请考官给予解释。
4. 尽量详细、深入地陈述自己的论点。
5. 讨论结束后，考官会就同样话题追加一些问题（follow-on questions）。回答时要以论据加以说明。同时注意听另一位考生的发言。

三、经典范例

我们先来看一组范例，希望从中能帮助考生对该题型有一个基本的理解。

PART THREE

In this part of the test, you are given a discussion topic. You have 30 seconds to look at the task prompt, an example of which is below, and then about three minutes to discuss the topic with your partner. After that, the examiner will ask you more questions related to the topic.

For two candidates

Selling Old Stock

The manufacturing company you work for needs to make space in its warehouse to stock its new products. The company would like to sell off end-of-range products at discounted prices.

You have been asked to make recommendations.

Discuss the situation together and decide:
- whether to offer the same discount on all products
- how customers could be informed of the discounts

Follow-on questions

- Do you think discounts are a good way of selling old stock? (Why? /Why not?)
- In what other ways do you think companies can get rid of unwanted stock? (Why?)
- What do you think is the main disadvantage for a company of having too much stock in its warehouse?
- How do you think companies could plan their stock requirements more accurately?
- Why do you think it can be difficult to sell stock sometimes?
- How do you think discounting could affect a company's image? (Why?)

Possible answers

For two candidates

A: I suggest we offer the same discount on all our products. We could average the costs and benefits to all our in-stock products, and offer the same discount for sale. In this way, we can send out a signal that we are launching a sales campaign through giving some of our profits back to our customers, instead of just trying to get rid of the stock.

B: I'm afraid it may not an idea as good as it sounds, as we have so many products in stock, and the costs and profits of these products are varied. If we simply offer the same discount on all the in-stock products, some are going to be much cheaper to buy and are selling out quickly, while others may comparatively more expensive and are going to remain unsold. Therefore, my suggestion is we could sell our products at different discounts in accordance to the costs and profits. Thus we will sell the in-stock products more quickly.

A: Your concern is understandable. But what I'm trying to express is as a reliable company, this is another sales campaign by returning some profits to our customers. We do this just because these products are end-of-range, and we are going to maintain steady prices at any time. One more thing I'm going to say is the same discount can avoid some unnecessary trouble of bargaining from the customers if otherwise.

B: OK. You said the point. We should not let our customers feel that we are in a hurry to sell off the in-stock products. It's just another sales campaign. A uniform discount has its advantages, but it seems to be lack of flexibiltiy. I think we can make an average discount to see how the market responds. If it doesn't work well, we can make some changes later. One more thing we have to think about is how customers could be informed of the discounts.

A: Well, I think advertising is the first way that occurs to my mind. The question is how. I don't think advertising openly on newspaper or TV is a good idea as our products always sell well in the market and it is also costly to do so.

B: Yes, I agree. I think we need some strategy. We could make a sales promotion event and we can telephone some of the most regular customers first. Those who receive our phone calls are entitled to a ticket to this event and any customers by the ticket are in priority to certain amount of our products on sale.

A: That's a good idea.

Follow-on questions

- Do you think discounts are a good way of selling old stock? (Why? /Why not?)
  Yes, I think discounts are a good way of selling old stock. Since a product is more attractive to customers, and often sells at a good price, thus make more profits. As for the old stock, it may get out of the fashion as time goes by, selling at discounts may be attractive to some customers.
  No, I don't think discounts are a good way of selling old stock. Because to some customers, discounts mean something less attractive or in inferior quality, they would rather pay more for better products, instead of discounted ones.
- In what other ways do you think companies can get rid of unwanted stock? (Why?)
  I think re-educate the customers is a good way of getting rid of unwanted stock. As the fashion cycles, some previously out-of-date fashion may become popular again.
  Another way of getting rid of unwanted stock is to add the value of old stock to the new product and sell them in bind.
- What do you think is the main disadvantage for a company of having too much stock in its warehouse?
  Having too much stock in the warehouse means more risk in the market, because some of stocks are going to out of fashion soon, and won't sell good.
  Furthermore, too much stock in the warehouse makes too much of a company's liquid capital, and thus slow down the circulation of capital inflow, which inevitably cut down the gross profits of a company.
- How do you think companies could plan their stock requirements more accurately?
  One way of planning the stock is produce by orders: a company produces according to orders from customers, thus no more stock is left.
  Another way of controlling the stock is keep a close eye to the market. By following the market, a company will produce only what are best needed in the market. In this way, it can reduce its stock as much as possible.
- Why do you think it can be difficult to sell stock sometimes?
  Stock can be difficult to sell sometimes because it is out of date, or it is no long needed in the market.
  Another problem is some stock are in bad condition for lack of good maintenance or just for the long-time storage.
- How do you think discounting could affect a company's image? (Why?)
  To some customers, steady price means something as good reputation, good quality. If a customer bought a product earlier and found it sells at a discounted price later, he/she would feel deceived and betrayed. Next time, he/she will not trust the company any more.

▶ **Useful words & expressions:**

- bargain *v.* 讨价还价
- gross profit 毛利润

四、经典实战

Some managers are leaving your company in recent years, and your company is worried about the situation. You have been asked to make recommendations about the situation. Discuss the situation together, and decide:

- why some managers are leaving your company
- how to improve the situation

Follow-on questions

- Is career planning important for people? (Why? /Why not?)
- Is further study or training important to managerial staff for career development? (Why? / Why not?)
- How important is flexible working management for you when considering a career change? (Why?)
- How important is first impression when taking a new career chance? (Why?)
- How important is it for a new manager to have good relationships within the team? (Why?)

参考答案

A: You see, more and more managers are quitting our company. It's high time for us to face the problem. Otherwise we will lose more talents and will suffer greater loss.

B: Yes, it's really disastrous. So many managers resigned in the past years, and there must be some reasons behind. What do you think are responsible for it?

A: I think the reasons are various. Perhaps some quit just for personal reasons, such as their own career growth. That's normal nowadays.

B: Yes, that's understandable. However, something must go wrong in our company for so many leavers recently.

A: You said it. Actually, there have been some managers who were quite unsatisfied with their benefits from work. I've heard some complaints about the poor work conditions. Some felt ove-stressed in their work.

A: I think that's something we should pay more attentionto. I think we need to show more concern to our managers.

B: I can't agree more. Relieve them some of the work pressure may keep them from quitting in the future.

A: Yes, in fact, we can do a lot to win them back.

Follow-on questions

- Is career planning important for people? (Why? /Why not?)
  Yes. Career planning is important. A successful career planning can lead people to a satisfying and rewarding life.
- Is further study or training important to managerial staff for career development? (Why? /Why not?)
  Yes. Further study and training will improve skills, knowledge and strengths which are important for career development.
- How important is flexible working management for you when considering a career change? (Why?)
  Flexible working management is important to me, because it allows me a certain degree of freedom.
- How important is first impression when taking a new career chance? (Why?)
  First impression counts. The impact you make in the first days and weeks in a new job can have a lasting effect. A positive impact is necessary for your salary increase, promotion and career development in your company.
- How important is it for a new manager to have good relationships within the team? (Why?)
  Building good relationships within the team is invaluable for a new manager to carry out work successfully and to move up the career ladder smoothly, since colleagues can offer the necessary support and cooperation.

周五　三点注意讨论要点（下）

一、命题规律

大家都知道讨论需要你来我往，一家言不能称之为讨论；然而，另一方面，各执己见、各自为政似乎也不是本部分讨论所要达到的效果。尤其是商业领域，效率永远都是一种美德。考生在考试中随机组合，在讨论中没有提前的预演和彩排，如何才能做到默契的配合？

二、解题技巧

要做到配合默契，至少有以下三点值得考生思考借鉴：

1. 要有大局观，讨论的话题通常是要求考生围绕两点或三点展开，考生切不可长时间就一点争执不下，因小失大。
2. 尊重自己的搭档，口试中你与搭档的关系更多是配合，而远非竞争关系，考生切不可存有刻意自我表现、抢话，甚至有意压着搭档等心理。
3. 讨论中尽量找到一个或几个共同点，达成一致。虽然讨论就是要各抒己见，但考生应尽量向一点靠拢，达成一致后进入下一个论点，或者说可以围绕一点从不同方面加以论述，补充要比反对效果好。

三、经典范例

PART THREE

In this part of the test, you are given a discussion topic. You have 30 seconds to look at the task prompt, an example of which is below, and then about three minutes to discuss the topic with your partner. After that, the examiner will ask you more questions related to the topic.

English Language Training

Your company is planning to offer 30 hours of English language training to employees.

You have been asked to help with the planning and organization of the training. Discuss the situation together, and decide:

- how to encourage employees to take part in the training
- what kind of schedule would be suitable for the training

Follow-on Questions

- What practical preparations would be necessary before running a foreign language course for employees? (Why?)
- What are the advantages of learning a foreign language with work colleagues?
- Are there any other foreign languages you would like to learn? (Why/Why not?)
- What ways of learning English are most helpful for people working in business? (Why?)
- What kind of help with language would you give to a foreign colleague who has just arrived to start a job in your company? (Why?).
- Do you think foreign language skills will continue to be useful for business in the future? (Why/Why not?)

参考答案

A You know, due to the enlargement of our business, many new staff have be recruited. And the company will plan an English Candidate Language Training recently. Do you think the new staff will actively attend?

B Maybe. But you can make some measures to encourage them to attend.

A It is a good idea. But what kind of method should I adopt? Give me some advice.

B For my part, you can organize a contest along with the English language training, and give prizes to the excellent new staff. For them it is not only training, but also a chance to express them. They will not miss this valuable opportunity.

A I agree with you. But at the beginning we should give a specific introduction on this English language training to every department. During the introduction, the importance of English should be focused.

B It's true. Then how many parts is the English language training divided into?

A It may compose of reading, listening and writing, especially focusing on the business dialogue and the writing about business. Since these skills are practical in our regular work, they are the basis for good communication with clients.

B Exactly. I suggest, you should plan more practice in real situations, which contributes to applying their theoretical knowledge to regular work.

A That is right. This training will center on the practice in real situation. It is always the trouble that we even don't know what to say in real business situation. And that is the focus of this training.

A OK. It sounds very good. I will actively mobilize the participation of the English language training.

B Thanks a lot. You are so nice.

Follow-on Questions

- What practical preparations would be necessary before running a foreign language course for employees? (Why?)
  First, the place for training should be considered. And the time should be determined. Because for the new staff, they should work as well as attend the training. So you should find a balance point for them.
- What are the advantages of learning a foreign language with work colleagues?

With their colleagues, they can imitate the real situation on business. They can exchange their views between each other. And they could form a tacit understanding on work.

- Are there any other foreign languages you would like to learn? (Why/Why not?)
  Yes, I want to learn French. It sounds very nice.
- What ways of learning English are most helpful for people working in business? (Why?)
  In my opinion, the imitation of real situation can be most helpful for people working in business. Because what this kind of people need is the real ability of communication face to face, such as dialogue, not only the theoretical knowledge.
- What kind of help with language would you give to a foreign colleague who has just arrived to start a job in your company? (Why?)
  They can learn in the real situation of business with guidance of the experienced colleagues. They can learn things from small tasks.
- Do you think foreign language skills will continue to be useful for business in the future? (Why/Why not?)
  Yes, it's definitely true. With the development of technology and science, the world becomes closer and closer. Different countries become neighbors. So the rate of business between different countries becomes higher. So the learning of foreign language will do great help on our business.

▶ **Useful words & expressions:**

- mobilize *v.* 动员，调动起来

四、经典实战

Your company are discussing about a formal orientation programme for new staff. You have been asked to make recommendations about the orientation programme. Discuss the situation together, and decide:

- whether it's necessary to organise a formal orientation
- what should be covered in the orientation programme

Follow-on questions:

- What training would you hope to have in the future? (Why?)
- Is it better to attend a full-time or a part-time training course? (Why?)
- Do you think companies should provide training for all their staff? (Why? / Why not?)
- Do you think companies will use external agencies to run their staff training programme more in the future? (Why/ Why not?)
- Are there any disadvantages of turning to an external agency to run staff training programme? (Why? / Why not?)

参考答案

A You see, our company are currently discussing about a formal orientation programme for new staff. There're various opinions toward it. Some are quite enthusiastic about it, others dislike the idea. What's your opinion?

B In my opinion, it is necessary to provide the new staff formal orientation. Since formal orientation can make them familiar with the organisation, their work units and their jobs.

A I agree with you on that point. I think the more time and efforts we spent in helping new employees, the more likely they are to identify with our company and become a part of our company as quickly as possible.

B Besides, a well-planned orientation programme is always effective in helping to retain and motivate employees.

A And I think orentation programme can also help the new employees reduce their anxiety at work, and improve their work efficiency.

B So it's worthy to put effort and time on the planning of the orientation programme.

A Sure. First, let's figure out the topics to be covered in the orientation programmme.

B Yes. I think we should introduce our company's history, purpose and strategic goals, a framework of job-related tasks, specific job expectations and descriptions, appraisal criteria, etc.

A And job duties and responsibilities. Disscussing responsibility can give these new comers a clear idea of their future job and obligations, and can help them on the right track in no time.

B Yes. Besides topics, what else do you think of like methods of organising and presenting?

A We cannot ignore that either. Effective methods can ensure an effective orientation. I think it would be a good idea if the supervisors or other managerial personnel can arrange co-workers to welcom the newcomers and show them around the premises.

B Good idea indeed. Showing the new hires around the premises will give them a concrete map of our company, and get them familiar with the layout of the organisation, which will undoubtedly contributes to the efficiency of their future work.

Follow-on questions

- What training would you hope to have in the future? (Why?)
  I hope to have the training of foreign languages, such as English. Because the globalisation and the wide-spread international cooperation all need the bridge of a common language, and English is one of the most widely-used languages.
- Is it better to attend a full-time or a part-time training course? (Why?)
  I prefer a full-time training. Because it allows the employees a complete rang of time to focus on learning. With no interruption of work, they can concentrate on acquiring new knowledge and skills, thus ensuring an effective training.
  A part-time training is preferable. Since I can not only improve my skills and knowledge, but also take care of my job and my family at the same time.
- Do you think companies should provide training for all their staff? (Why? / Why not?)
  Yes. I think all the staff in a company should be treated equal. They should have equal opportunities to receive training programmes.
  No, I don't think it necessary, because not all the training are suitable for all the staff. They have different backgrounds, knowledge and skills. Furthermore, companies should provide training programmes to their best need.
- Do you think companies will use external agencies to run their staff training programme more in the future? (Why/ Why not?)

It's difficult to predict. It depends on the development and reputation of the external agency, on people's attitudes towards the training agency, as well as on the financial condition of the companies, etc.

- Are there any disadvantages of turning to an external agency to run staff training programme? (Why? / Why not?)

  Yes, there are. Using external agency to train staff involves a great deal of investigation and can be risky. An inexperienced external agency will not only cost time but also waste money.

▶ **Useful words & expressions:**

- orientation programme 入职指导/培训计划
- premise *n.* 场所，场地

周六　商务拓展

经过前五天对 BEC 中级口试题型的分析和了解，相信考生对口试已经有了基本的了解。口语虽然随机性强，没有一定之规，但熟练掌握一些固定句式和套语在口试中是极为必要的。我们都有过心中知道怎么去说，却找不到合适语言、词汇的尴尬。下面我们就针对中级口试的特点，介绍一些实用的口语表达句式。

一、开始某个话题的表达

Let's start with…　让我们以……开始。
Shall we begin with…?　以……开始可以吗？
So, the first item on the agenda is…　那么，第一项是……
Linda, would you like to kick off?　Linda，由你来开始好吗？

二、结束某个话题的表达

Right, I think that covers the first item. 好的，我觉得这一点概括了第一条。
Shall we leave that item?　我们先将这个话题谈到这吧？
If you don't have anything else to add, …　如果你没有什么要补充的，……

三、转移话题的表达

Let's move on to the next item.　我们进入下一个话题吧。
The next question on the agenda is…　下一个问题是……
Now let's come to the question of…　下面我们看一下……的问题。

四、打断对方的表达

Excuse me, may I interrupt?　对不起，我可以打断一下吗？
Just a moment, but…　稍等片刻……
Can I say something here?　我能说两句吗？
Sorry, …　对不起……
Sorry to interrupt, but…　抱歉打断一下……

五、评价的表达

a）同意

That's a good point. 好主意。
I agree with you. 我同意你。

I can't agree with you more. 我非常同意你说的。
I see what you mean. 我明白你的意思。
Yes, …是的, ……
That's quite a good idea. 那是一个十分好的主意。
That's absolutely true. 绝对正确。

b）反对

I totally disagree with you. 我完全不同意你。
I couldn't agree less. 我不同意。
You must be joking! 你一定在开玩笑!

六、询问对方意见

What do you think about this? 你对……的看法如何呢?
What's your opinion on this? 你的意见如何?
Have you considered…? 你考虑过……吗?
I haven't heard your opinion about…我想听听你对……的意见。

七、表达自己观点

I think/feel/believe that…我认为/感觉/相信……
You mentioned that…, but, in my view… 你的意思……, 但是我认为……
In my opinion, we should…我认为, 我们应该……
I'd like to point out…我想指出的是……
Let me emphasize…我想强调……
My view is that…我的观点是……
Just let me finish. 请允许我把话说完。

八、评论

That's a good idea/an excellent idea. 好主意。
That's very interesting. 这个主意很有趣。
I'm sure we'd all agree with that. 我相信大家会同意我的观点。
That's a very good point/an important point. 这一点很重要。

九、要求对方澄清观点

I don't see what you're getting at. 你的意思我不太明白。
I'm not sure what you mean. 你说的我不太懂。
I'm not sure what you are saying. 我没明白你的话。
It's not clear what you mean. 我没明白你的意思。

十、避免跑题

We're missing the point. 我们没有抓住主题。
We're getting off the point. 我们跑题了。

Let's get back to the main point. 让我们回到主要问题上吧。
It's not on the agenda, but…这点没有要求，但……

十一、回应

That's marvelous. 太棒了。
That's great. 非常好。
That's fine. 很好。
OK. 没问题。
All right. 好吧。
I see your point. 我明白你的意思。
I understand your concern. 我理解你的考虑。

一些更加口语化的表达方式

1. 口语化表达简单同意
a. Yeah!
b. How true!
c. Exactly!
d. Absolutely!
e. Well said!
f. You got it!
g. You bet!
h. That's for sure.
i. My opinion exactly!

2. 表同意
a. I share your view on that!
b. Oh, yes, I couldn't agree with you more. You are genius!
c. Okey, you are the doctor.
d. I don't think anyone would disagree.
e. I have no problem with that.
f. I couldn't have said it better.
g. I wish I had said that.
h. I am with you there.
i. I think I will go along with your proposal.

3. 部分同意
a. Could be!
b. Yes, you've point there.
c. So it seems! (似乎有点道理!)
d. So to speak!
e. In the manner of speaking.
f. I agree with much of what you said.
g. That's one way of looking at it, I admit.

4. 口语化表达不同意
a. Not really.

b. Not at all.
c. Of course not.
d. No way.
e. Not a chance.

5. 不同意

a. Do you really think so?
b. I am not convinced.
c. Don't speak too soon.
d. I will believe it when I see it.
e. I'm afraid we don't see eye to eye on this.
f. That was not the case.

6. 强烈不同意

a. No, I don't agree. Don't waste your breath.
b. You must be joking / kidding.
c. You can't be serious.
d. You are way off base.（棒不在垒上。）
e. You don't know up from down.
f. Over my dead body.
g. I wasn't born yesterday.
h. That's ridiculous.
i. It's pure fiction.
j. Non-sense!
k. Bullshit!
l. That's out of the question!

周日　本周测试

我们将通过两套实战模拟题来检验我们这一周的理论和技巧的学习效果，考生可以在教师的主持下进行，或者以小组搭配的形式进行演练。

Test 1

PART ONE

In this part, the interlocutor asks questions to each of the candidates in turn. You have to give information about yourself and express personal opinions.

1. What do you think is the basic objective underlying all promotion?
2. What do you think are the most commonly used advertising media?
3. Do you think advertising cost-effective? (Why? / Why not?)
4. Why do you think companies use sales promotion?

PART TWO

In this part of the test, you are asked to give a short talk on a business topic. You have to choose one of the topics from the three below and then talk for about one minute. You have one minute to prepare your ideas.

A: What is important when...?
Promoting a product
- Advertising
- Sales promotion

PART THREE

In this part of the test, you are given a discussion topic. You have 30 seconds to look at the task prompt, an example of which is below, and then about three minutes to discuss the topic with your partner. After that, the examiner will ask you more questions related to the topic.

For two candidates

Promoting a Product

Your company has launched a new medicine into market and now decides to increase sales.
You have been asked for your views about how to promote the product.
Discuss the situation together, and decide:

- what are the promotional strategies
- what promotional gifts can be offered and what are the cost and quality of promotional gifts

Follow-on Questions

1 What do you think is an effective strategy for image building?
2 Are you willing to be a salesperson? (Why? / Why not?)
3 Do you think the give of free-gifts is effective in promotion sales?
4 What do you think are the most common promotion methods?
5 What are the advantages of positive publicity?

Test 2

PART ONE

In this part, the interlocutor asks questions to each of the candidates in turn. You have to give information about yourself and express personal opinions.

1. Would you promote a competent but self-centered candidate to the position of a sales manager? (Why? / Why not?)
2. Are there any disadvantages of internal recruitment? (Why? / Why not?)
3. Do you wish to be promoted? / Will you accept a promotion? (Why? / Why not?)
4. What is the most important factor when you accept a promotion? (Why?)

PART TWO

In this part of the test, you are asked to give a short talk on a business topic. You have to choose one of the topics from the three below and then talk for about one minute. You have one minute to prepare your ideas.

A: What is important when...?

Thinking about going for a promotion

- Work-related qualities
- Personal qualities

PART THREE

In this part of the test, you are given a discussion topic. You have 30 seconds to look at the task prompt, an example of which is below, and then about three minutes to discuss the topic with your partner. After that, the examiner will ask you more questions related to the topic.

For two candidates

Making a Good and Sound Promotion Policy

There is a job opening for sales manager in your company. And it is decided that the opening should be filled within the company.

You have been asked for make recommendations about the promotion policy.
Discuss the situation together, and decide:
- why to have promotion from within the company instead of external recruitment
- how to make a good and sound promotion decision

Follow-on Questions

1 Is the leadership quality important for a sales manager? (Why? / Why not?)

2 Is satisfying performance important when selecting a sales manager from the sales staff? (Why? / Why not?)

3 Would you consider a well-educated candidate when promoting a sales manager? (Why?)

4 Is it important for a sales manager to be ambitious? (Why? / Why not?)

5 Would you consider a competent candidate who is a stranger in sales when filling the vacancy of sales manager?

参考答案

Test 1

Part One

1 What do you think is the basic objective underlying all promotion?
I think it's to provide information. Firms want to tell customers about themselves as well as what products are available, where they can be purchased, and for what prices.

2 What do you think are the most commonly used advertising media?
There are many advertising media like newspapers, television, direct mail, radio, magazines, and outdoor displays.

3 Do you think advertising is cost-effective? (Why? / Why not?)
I don't think so, because advertising especially using national media with immense audiences is very expensive.
Yes, although advertising can be quite expensive, many firms still find it cost-effective because it can reach vast numbers of potential customers at a low cost relatively per person.

4 Why do you think companies use sales promotion?
Sales promotion can provide direct incentives to customers, motivate sales people, and stimulate dealers to be interested and involved in distributing a product.

Part Two

I think advertising is very important when promoting a product. It can reach millions of people at a low cost per person. By placing an ad with a mass medium, such as television, radio, newspaper, and magazines, etc., a company can aim at its target market and promote a product effectively.

In addition to advertising, sales promotion is also important. Companies can use free samples, premiums, trading stamps, loyalty schemes, contests, trade shows and so on to attract existing and potential customers and boost the sales of a product.

Apart from those, I think direct marketing is also very important in promoting sales of a product. Direct mail, telephone, and Internet links are now used by many companies to promote a product.

Part Three

A I think the most effective promotional strategy is advertising, since advertising can reach large audiences in a wide area.

B I agree with you on that point. Our product is a new product. We should tell customers that we have launched a new medicine and what kinds of diseases it can cure. Therefore, we need enough advertising to send the information to customers.

A That's right. We could have ads on television or in influential newspapers, through which many people can get to know our product.

B That's true. We can also put up posters and arrange point-of-sale displays to attract potential customers.

A Apart from advertising, we can also promote our medicine by person-to-person selling and even door-step selling. We could have a presentation and invite persons from hospitals and drug stores.

B Yes, person-to-person selling would be very effective for promoting our product. In addition, we can also use sales promotion to boost our sales.

A I think we can offer promotions gifts to customers who buy our new medicine. Any idea for what gifts to offer?

B Well, we can't afford too expensive gifts. I think we may give some small gifts like umbrellas or T-shirts, which are not very expensive and easy to be loged on.

A That's a good idea. And also raincoats with our logo. You see, in rainy days, the logo on the back of a raincoat will be quite eye-catching.

B What about the quality of these promotional gifts? Do you think they should be of high quality?

A Yes. I think high quality would be good. Gifts with low qualtiy would leave a bad image of our company to customers.

B I'm quite with you on that. If these gifts are of durable materials, then they may bear our product logo longer and I think it is worthy to make high-quality gifts.

Follow-on Questions

1 What do you think is an effective strategy for image building?
Publicity is an effective strategy for image building like an image ambassador.

2 Are you willing to be a salesperson? (Why? / Why not?)
Yes, because being a sales person is both challenging and rewarding.
No, I think salesmen are bad reputed. I think a lot of people just don't trust a sales person and it's hard for them to talk people into buying.

3 Do you think the give of freegifts is effective in promotion sales?
Yes, free gifts can attract customers to try the new products, or have a better memory about the product.

4 What do you think are the most common promotion methods?
I think there are many ways like handing samples, free gifts, trading stamps, contests, etc.

5 What are the advantages of positive publicity?
A newspaper or magazine article or television or radio broadcast can reach and influence a lot of potential customers but at relatively low cost to the company.

Test 2

Part One

1 Would you promote a competent but self-centered candidate to the position of a sales manager? (Why? / Why not?)
No. Because in the position of a manager, it is more essential for he/she to understand the importance of experience-sharing, cooperation and team spirit. A competent but self-centered candidate may make a

good salesman, but will never make a good sales manager.

2 Are there any disadvantages of internal recruitment? (Why? / Why not?)
Yes, I believe so. For some small companies or newly-set-up corporations, they may get very limited internal human resources. Thus, internal recruitment would lead to the risk of "employee cloning". Even for the big organisations, excessive reliance on internal sources will also lead to inbreeding of ideas and attitudes, thus run the risk of "employee cloning".

3 Do you wish to be promoted? / Will you accept a promotion? (Why? / Why not?)
Of course. A solider who doesn't wish to become a marshal isn't a good soldier. Similarly, promotion can bring one a sense of fulfillment, more opportunities, and more rewarding.

4 What is the most important factor when you accept a promotion? (Why?)
The type of the job. Whether the job or position interests me or whether I am confident about the job are important to consider, because they will affect my future performance and career development.

Part Two

When aiming for promotion, developing work-related qualities are important. These qualities include qualifications, training, skills and abilities. Qualifications and training prepare us the necessary knowledge and skills for our job, which are essential for our further development. Professional skills and abilities guarantee excellent work performance, while managerial skills and abilities contribute to an effective team performance.

In addition to work-related qualities, relevant personal qualities are of the equal importance, such as loyalty to the company, responsibility and so on, since these qualities can establish one's credibility and integrity among his colleagues.

Of course, it's also important for one to know and accept his own strengths and weaknesses so as to promote the strengths while making up for the weaknesses. Showing the sustained pattern of your achievements and giving a sense of how you will continue to achieve and develop in the future cannot be ignored, either.

Part Three

A As you know, there is a job opening for sales manager in our company and it is decided that the opening should be filled from within the company.

B It is a sound decision, isn't it? You see, our company is a big and well-established corporation. There are abundant human resources we can make full use of.

A Yes, I agree with you, since external recruitment is both costly and time-consuming.

B Furthermore, recruiting from outside may also disappoint some employees who are aiming high. As far as I can see, there are more disadvantages than good points by doing so.

A Yes, you said it. I think promotion-from-within can serve as a reward for the sales staff with ability and good performance, and encourage them to continue their efforts.

B Yes, it is.

A Undoubtedly, promotion from within benefits both the individual career development and the overall growth of our company. However, don't you think doing this can also lead to some internal conflict among employees?

B That's common. I think as a mature company we can manage to minimize the effect.

A I'd like to hear your suggestion to this problem.

B The answer I believe is just and fair. Through an effective, just and fair promotion policy, all the employees who can meet the qualifications, experience, and whoever acquire the abilities can compete for the manager position openly and fairly.

A Besides, we should also make sure that our promotion decisions are based only on the qualifications, performances, and skills of the candidates, and not on something else irrelevant.

B You said it. It's really crucial to avoid all forms of discrimination in promotion.

Follow-on Questions

1 Is the leadership quality important for a sales manager? (Why? / Why not?)
Sure, it is. A large part of a manager's job is to make sure everybody under his leading can dig up his best potential and contribute something to the team, which requires a good command of the art of leadership.

2 Is satisfying performance important when selecting a sales manager from the sales staff? (Why? / Why not?)
Yes. A satisfying performance is a best way to display the candidate's ability, and it is quite convincing to others.

3 Would you consider a well-educated candidate when promoting a sales manager? (Why?)
Yes, A well-educated person means he/she acquires some basic qualities like good learning habits, rich theoretical knowledge, and such person can adapt himself/herself more quickly and easily to a leading position, where he/she can make better use of his/her talents.

4 Is it important for a sales manager to be ambitious? (Why? / Why not?)
Yes, I think so. Because an ambitious person normally is more anxious for success. They are more persevering and work harder to fulfill their goals.

5 Would you consider a competent candidate who is a stranger in sales when filling the vacancy of sales manager?
No. Because being a sales manager needs to know some selling strategies besides a good leadership, which can only come from real sales experience. It's no game for amateurs.

附　录

附录 I　模拟题及答案解析

Test 1

READING　　1 hour

PART ONE

Questions 1-7

- Look at the statements below and the article about Plumper on the opposite page.
- Which section of the article (A, B, C or D) does each statement (1-7) refer to?
- For each statement (1-7), mark one letter (A, B, C or D) on your Answer Sheet.
- You will need to use some of these letters more than once.

Example:

0 Rodrigo Rato, help Turkey... reduce inflation

	A	B	C	D
0	▭	▬	▭	▭

1 Turkey's economy grows faster than any EU member now.

2 Foreign investors will enjoy a good economic prospect in Turkey.

3 Resilience is not always one advantage of Turkey.

4 Inflation rate in Turkey used to be very high.

5 The economy of Turkey used to be unsteady in the past.

6 There are three members in all that the EU could identify their position of full members at that time.

7 Steady GDP growth will help Turkey attract more foreign direct investment.

Plumper

A

How does the country's economy compare with those of the EU? Some of the concerns surrounding Turkey's application to join the European Union, to be voted on by the EU's Council of Ministers on December 17th, are economic-in particular, the country's relative poverty. Its GDP per head is less than a third of the average for the 15 pre-2004 members of the EU. But it is not far off that of one of the ten new members which joined on May 1st 2004 (Latvia), and it is much the same as those of two countries, Bulgaria and Romania, which this week concluded accession talks with the EU that could make them full members on January 1st, 2007.

B

Furthermore, the country's recent economic progress has been, according to Donald Johnston, the secretary-general of the OECD, stunning. GDP in the second quarter of the year was 13.4% higher than a year earlier, a rate of growth that no EU country comes close to matching. Turkey's inflation rate has just fallen into single figures for the first time since 1972, and this week the country reached agreement with the IMF on a new three-year, $10 billion economic programme that will, according to the IMF's managing director, (0) Rodrigo Rato, help Turkey... reduce inflation toward European levels, and enhance the economy's resilience.

C

Resilience has not historically been the country's economic strong point. As recently as 2001, GDP fell by over 7%. It fell by more than 5% in 1994, and by just under 5% in 1999. Indeed, throughout the 1990s growth oscillated like an electrocardiogram recording a violent heart attack. This irregularity has been one of the main reasons (along with red tape and corruption) why the country has failed dismally to attract much-needed foreign direct investment. Its stock of such investment (as a percentage of GDP) is lower now than it was in the 1980s, and annual inflows have scarcely ever reached $1 billion (whereas Ireland attracted over $25 billion in 2003, as did Brazil in every year from 1998 to 2000).

D

One deterrent to foreign investors is due to disappear on January 1st 2005. On that day, Turkey will take away the right of virtually every one of its citizens to call themselves a millionaire. Six noughts will be removed from the face value of the lira; one unit of the local currency will henceforth be worth what 1m are now-ie, about 0.53 ($0.70). Goods will have to be priced in both the new and old lira for the whole of the year, but foreign bankers and investors can begin to look forward to a time in Turkey when they will no longer have to juggle mentally with indeterminate strings of zeros.

PART TWO

Questions 8-12

- Read the extract below from an article about The Crisis of Credit.
- Choose the best sentence from the list on the opposite page to fill each of the gaps.
- For each gap 8-12, mark one letter (A-G) on your Answer Sheet.
- Do not use any letter more than once.
- There is an example at the beginning (0)

0	A	B	C	D	E	F	G
	▭	▭	▭	▭	▭	▭	▬

The Crisis of Credit

Here's the scary thing about the identity-theft ring that the feds cracked last week: there was nothing any of its estimated 40,000 victims could have done to prevent it from happening. (0) __G__. A lowly help-desk worker at Teledata Communications, a software firm that helps banks access credit reports online, allegedly stole passwords for those reports and sold them to a group of 20 thieves at $60 a pop. (8) ________. Cost to the victims: $3 million and rising.

Even scarier is that this, the largest identity-theft bust to date, is just a drop in the bit bucket. More than 700,000 Americans have their credit hijacked every year. It's one of crime's biggest growth markets. A name, address and Social Security number—which can often be found on the Web-is all anybody needs to apply for a bogus line of credit. Credit companies make $1.3 trillion annually and lose less than 2% of that revenue to fraud. (9) ________. As it stands now, it's up to you to protect your identity.

The good news is that there are plenty of steps you can take. Most credit thieves are opportunists, not well-organized gangs. (10) ________. Others steal wallets and return them, taking only a Social Security number. Shredding your junk mail and leaving your Social Security card at home can save a lot of agony later.

But the most effective way to keep your identity clean is to check your credit reports once or twice a year. There are three major credit-report outfits: Equifax (at equifax. com), Trans-Union (www. transunion. com) and Experian (experian. com). (11) ________. Of the three, I found TransUnion's website to be the cheapest and most comprehensive—laying out state-by-state prices, rights and tips for consumers in easy-to-read fashion.

If you're lucky enough to live in Colorado, Georgia, Maryland, Massachusetts, New Jersey or Vermont, you are entitled to one free report a year by law. (12) ________. Avoid services that offer to monitor your reports year-round for about $70; that's $10 more than the going rate among thieves. If you think you're a victim of identity theft, you can ask for fraud alerts to be put on file at each of the three credit-report companies. You can also download a theft-report form at www. consumer. gov/idtheft, which, along with a local police report, should help when irate creditors come knocking. Just don't expect justice. That audacious help-desk worker was one of the fewer than 2% of identity thieves who are ever caught.

A A lot of them go Dumpster diving for those millions of "pre-approved" credit-card mailings that go out every day.

B It used to get quite interesting around the dinner table.

C That allowed the gang to cherry-pick consumers with good credit and applies for all kinds of accounts in their names.

D So there's little financial incentive for them to make the application process more secure.

E All allow you to order reports online, which is a lot better than wading through voice-mail hell on their 800 lines.

F Otherwise it's going to cost $8 to $14 each time.

G This was an inside job, according to court documents.

PART THREE

Questions 13-18

- Read the following article about On a Roll, and the questions on the opposite page.
- For each question (13-18), mark one letter (A, B, C or D) on your Answer Sheet.

On a Roll

From The Economist print edition, Ford seems likely to sell its last luxury brand to a Chinese upstart.

DESPITE lingering misgivings, Ford Motor Company announced on October 28th that it had picked China's Geely as the preferred bidder for its Volvo subsidiary. If Geely, China's largest and brashest privately owned carmaker, succeeds in acquiring such a respected brand, it would be a testament to the extraordinary ambition of its chairman and founder, Li Shufu, the self-styled Henry Ford of China. Mr Li is thought to be prepared to pay around $2 billion for Volvo, about a third as much as Ford spent to acquire it in 1999.

A deal is unlikely to be signed before the end of the year, but negotiations would not have got this far if Ford had not satisfied itself that its biggest concern, the transfer of intellectual property to the Chinese firm, could be resolved. Because Ford and Volvo are joined at the hip in engineering terms, Geely has been forced to go to considerable lengths to reassure Ford that it will not simply purloin the pair's advanced platforms and powertrains for its existing car business. If the deal is done, Volvo's new owner will be a consortium led by Zhejiang Geely Holding Group, a privately held firm. It says Volvo will be run as an autonomous entity, headquartered in Sweden, at arm's length from Geely's manufacturing operations in China. Ford insists that Volvo and its technology will be protected by "internationally binding and enforceable agreements". There is no reason, however, why Volvo and Geely should not co-operate on future research and development projects if Volvo's "independent" management is willing.

Ford is keen to sell Volvo, its last premium unit after the sales of Aston Martin and Jaguar Land Rover, to focus on its "One Ford" strategy. But it is adamant that it would not do the deal if it did not believe that Geely would be a "responsible future owner". It could keep Volvo if necessary: although Volvo lost $231m in the second quarter, sales have since improved and losses have narrowed.

Apart from the prestige and perhaps an enhanced reputation for safety, what is Geely hoping to get from the deal? It claims that it will be able to enhance Volvo's sales and assemble more of its models in China, now the world's biggest and fastest-growing vehicle market. But that hardly seems enough. Whatever Ford and Geely are saying, Volvo's technology will not stay ring-fenced for ever.

13 To enhance the deal, Geely has to make one measurement about ________.

A the improvement of the service

B the cooperation between them

C more investment

D the guarantee on the reservation on technology

14 To achieve "One Ford" strategy, what action would Ford take?

A Developing new technology.

B Selling Volvo.

C Enlarging the market.

D Cooperating with other companies.

15 The position of Geely in the field of vehicle market in China is ________.

A the quality of Geely is the highest

B Geely occupies the first place of privately owned carmaker

C the price of Geely is the lowest

D the service of Geely is better than the others

16 According to the article, Ford show great attention to the condition that ________.

A more money should be paid in this business

B intellectual property should be maintained

C Ford can gain larger vehicle market

D Ford can have cooperation with Geely

17 The deal will fail, if Geely ________.

A can not be responsible for the future of Volvo

B can not give good attitude

C can not cooperate with Ford in the future

D can not provide a wider market

18 The main benefit Geely can obtain from this deal is ________.

A more money

B good service

C higher fame

D more good employees

PART FOUR

Questions 19-33

- Read the article below about Assets and Processes.
- Choose the best word or phrase to fill each gap from A, B, C or D on the opposite page.
- For each question (19-33), mark one letter (A, B, C or D) on your Answer Sheet.
- There is an example at the beginning (0).

Example:

A that **B** which **C** how **D** what

0	A	B	C	D
	▭	▭	▬	▭

Assets and Processes

World competitiveness also analyzes (0) ___C___ nations combine assets and processes in the management of competitiveness. Some nations can be rich (19) ________ assets — land, population, natural resources, etc. — (20) ________ not necessarily competitive, e. g., Brazil, India and Russia. On the other hand, there are nations such as Singapore, Japan and Switzerland which are (21) ________ in traditional assets (22) ________ they are very competitive. They have (23) ________ what economists call "the transformation process".

Japan's performance illustrates this situation well. Since 1950, the nation has (24) ________ only four Nobel Prizes in exact science and economics, (25) ________ to 164 awarded to the US and 44 to Britain. In fact, none of the fundamental technological (26) ________ which have changed our business lives have been discovered in Japan. The transistor, the robot, the video recorder, the computer, the fax, the compact disk, the color TV — all have been invented by companies in the US and Europe. The Japanese, however, have been extremely successful in (27) ________ these products: they have (28) ________ in the ability to transform an idea (29) ________ a product or service more cheaply, more quickly and more effectively than their competitors. In other words, Japan's competitiveness is process based.

The 1996 World Competitiveness Yearbook carefully distinguishes between competitiveness which (30) ________ from a nation's assets and that which is achieved through process. This crucial distinction is important, (31) ________ the future seems to belong those nations that master the transformation process (indeed, some economists refer to "the spell of natural resources" to describe the fate of asset-rich nations that become complacent). Companies usually use a similar strategy, (32) ________ they focus on the value added that is generated by (33) ________ processes as quality, speed, order fulfillment, mass customization, and customer satisfaction, etc.

19	**A** in	**B** out	**C** on	**D** about
20	**A** and	**B** then	**C** but	**D** therefore
21	**A** rich	**B** poor	**C** famous	**D** good
22	**A** however	**B** so	**C** and	**D** but
23	**A** known	**B** learned	**C** assured	**D** mastered
24	**A** had	**B** created	**C** received	**D** given
25	**A** response	**B** connecting	**C** come	**D** compared
26	**A** breakthroughs	**B** success	**C** failure	**D** change
27	**A** selling	**B** marketing	**C** producing	**D** changing

28	**A**	important	**B**	good	**C**	bad	**D**	excelled
29	**A**	in	**B**	on	**C**	into	**D**	from
30	**A**	stems	**B**	far	**C**	prevents	**D**	benefits
31	**A**	so	**B**	therefore	**C**	since	**D**	otherwise
32	**A**	despite	**B**	therefore	**C**	so	**D**	whereby
33	**A**	such	**B**	so	**C**	that	**D**	this

PART FIVE

Questions 34-45

- Read the extract below from Accounting Business Outsource Process.
- In most of the lines (34-45), there is one extra word. It is either grammatically incorrect or does not fit in with the meaning of the text. Some lines, however, are correct.
- If a line is correct, write CORRECT on your Answer Sheet.
- If there is an extra word in the line, write the extra word in CAPITAL LETTERS on your Answer Sheet.
- The exercise begins with two examples (0 and 00).

Example:

0	C	O	R	R	E	C	T
00	O	U	T				

Accounting Business Outsource Process

0 Maintaining accounts is one of the crucial aspects of the business.

00 In order to survive longer it is important to bring out perfection in every work. A professional accountant in accounting business outsources

34 One needs to have been professionals in this field to work for.

35 Everything is the sole responsibility out of the firm, right from dealing the financial tasks to the estimation of the profit. For every

36 business firm, whether operating on small scale or not large scale needs to maintain books of accounts. Accounting is constantly

37 changing field and one has to keep up on with the changes. It needs special care of for its maintenance. The business firm has to manage

38 the bookkeeping records till it finishes to paying up the taxes and again keep it safely for future reference. Accounting business

39 outsource process is ready to take care of all sorts of account related projects.

40 process company works towards the profits of the clients whom

41 they are serving. False entries in the accounts can lead up to wrong calculation in estimating the financial growth rate of the year.

42 Whether the company is bearing fruitful profits or going in

43 loss can be decided on only through the maintenance of proper records. Treasury, back -office services, bookkeeping, general ledger, tax computation and filing, data entry, spreadsheet and many

44 others are important accounting tasks to be performed. One which should be careful and also update himself with every change in the tax structure. It has been surveyed that accounting business outsource process is expected to have a yearly growth rate of 8% by 2008. In house employees for the accounting task can prove costly to the firm. Accounting business outsource process saves a lot of precious time of the company and the company can meanwhile gain expertise in from other areas and reap profits. The money saved can be utilized properly by investing in growth plans. When the company is outsourcing its accounting work then much time is left with the company to take care of marketing division, production, sales that one deals with.

WRITING 45 minutes

PART ONE

You are a manager of sale's department of a toy company and you want to buy a storefront at the trade fair. Write a note to your secretary Ann:

- Giving her the basic information of the fair.
- Asking her to fax the organizer for some enquiries.
- Suggesting when you want to get the result.

Write 40-50 words.

Notepad
To: Ann From: Mike

PART TWO

You are in charge of the technical department in your company. You have just received a letter from the Customer Serviced Manager at Yiren Communications, who are installing a new Fax at your office.

Look at the information below, on which you have already made some handwritten notes.

Then, using all your handwritten notes, write your proposal.

Write 120-140 words.

How many days' work

Date no good–explain why

We would like to begin installing your new fax on Friday 20 May. We hope to finish the work as soon as possible.

Please note that extension numbers beginning with 5 will now start with 3 and that all others will start with 8.

System too complicated

If you have any technical queries, please contact our technical representative at our main office.

A copy of our invoice is attached.

Name and number

Will pay when job finished–explain

LISTENING 40minutes (including 10 minutes' transfer time)

PART ONE

Questions 1-12

- You will hear three telephone conversations or messages.

- Write one or two words or a number in the numbered spaces on the notes or forms below.
- After you have listened once, replay each recording.

Conversation One (**Questions 1-4**)

- Look at the note below.
- You will hear a woman calling Scandinavian Conferences to book tickets.
- You have is seconds to read through the form.

Massages
Frida wanted to (1) give the _______ of tickets.
Frida need (2) _______ tickets.
Frida wanted the tickets on (3) _______ November.
Frida can give only two names, one is herself, the other is (4) _______.

Conversation Two (**Questions 5-8**)

- Look at the note below.
- You will hear a woman calling to put off the meeting.
- You have 15 seconds to read through the form.

Massages
Alice Green is calling from (5) _______.
Alice has cancelled our meeting on (6) _______.
Alice Green suggested the meeting on (7) _______.
Her number is (8) _______.

Conversation Three (**Questions 9-12**)

- Look at the note below.
- You will hear a woman calling to check the expense.
- You have 15 seconds to read through the form.

Massages
Roger wanted to check the expense for (9) _______.
Expenses is for (10) _______ in stead of a business trip.
The expense on the drinks cost (11) _______ pounds.
The client's name is (12) _______.

PART TWO

Section One (**Questions 13-17**)

- You will hear five short recordings.
- For each recording, decide which type of document the speaker is talking about.
- Write one letter (A-H) next to the number of the recording.
- Do not use any letter more than once.

- After you have listened once, replay the recordings.
- You have 15 seconds to read the list A-H.

(13) ____________

(14) ____________

(15) ____________

(16) ____________

(17) ____________

A to put the meeting off
B to issue another one straight away to pay
C to analyze the economic situation
D to make instruction on the behavior
E to get help to bring in the income to ensure the future
F to ask them to send a copy
G to discuss more detail
H to book a better hotel

Section Two (Question 18-22)

- You will hear five short recordings.
- For each recording, decide what the speaker's purpose is.
- Write one letter (A-H) next to the number of the recording.
- Do not use any letter more than once.
- After you have listened once, replay the recordings.
- You have 15 seconds to read the list A-H.

(18) ____________

(19) ____________

(20) ____________

(21) ____________

(22) ____________

A to offer complimentary tickets
B to know the data of the report
C to talk about that contract
D to get some advice
E to change arrangement for sale plan
F to know the time of the visit
G to understand what his mother wants to get
H to put off the sports meeting

PART THREE (Questions 23 to 30)

- You will hear a long dialogue on staff training and recruiting extra staff.
- For each question (23-30), mark one letter (A, B or C) for the correct answer.
- After you have listened once, replay the recording.

23 What is Roberto worried about?
A The menus for the conference.
B The level of training for new staff members.
C His budget for the conference dinner.

24 Who does Marina think needs refresher training?
A New staff only.
B New and old staff.
C Temporary staff.

25 According to Marina, what will happen if they hire student staff?
A It will push costs up.
B It will keep costs down.
C It will mean less kitchen accidents.

26 According to Steve, what will happen if they hire experienced catering staff?

A It will push costs up.

B It will keep costs down.

C It will mean more kitchen accidents.

27 What is Roberto worrying about the extra staff?

A High costs.

B Less catering experience.

C Causing troubles.

28 What is happening later in the week?

A A staff party. **B** A staff outing. **C** A staff meeting.

29 On which day will they be hiring extra housekeeper staff?

A Friday. **B** Saturday. **C** Sunday.

30 How many extra waiting staff will they hire?

A 10. **B** 15. **C** 20.

SPEAKING 14 minutes

PART ONE

In this part, the interlocutor asks questions to each of the candidates in turn. You have to give information about yourself and express personal opinions.

PART TWO

In this part of the test, you are asked to give a short talk on a business topic. You have to choose one of the topics from the three below and then talk for about one minute. You have one minute to prepare your ideas.

A What is important when...?
Maintaining customer loyalty to a brand
- Offering discounts to regular customers
- Provide high-quality products to customers

B What is important when...?
Selecting the type of marketing channel
- Geographic concentration of the market
- Services provided by agencies

C What is important when...?
Choosing transport for a business trip
- Comfort
- Cost

PART THREE

In this part of the test, you are given a discussion topic. You have 30 seconds to look at the task prompt, an example of which is below, and then about three minutes to discuss the topic with your partner. After that, the examiner will ask you more questions related to the topic.

For two or three candidates

Opening a Supermarket

You company decides to open a supermarket in your city.
You have been asked for make recommendations about it.
Discuss the situation together, and decide:

- what factors the company should consider for high sales volumes
- how the company can recruit employees

Follow-on questions

- What services do wholesalers perform?
- What do you think nonstore retailing includes?
- What do you think are the advantages and disadvantages of vending machines?
- What are the types of wholesalers?
- Do you think the location of a retail store important? (Why? / Why not?)

Test 2

READING 1 hour

PART ONE

Questions 1-7

- Look at the statements below and the article about A Risky Try on the opposite page.
- Which section of the article (A, B, C or D) does each statement (1-7) refer to?
- For each statement (1-7), mark one letter (A, B, C or D) on your Answer Sheet.
- You will need to use some of these letters more than once.

Example:

0 RealNetworks' move is another sign that the software industry is going hybrid.

0	A	B	C	D
	▭	▭	▭	▬

1 In 1998, Netscape made a dangerous copy.
2 Releasing the free source-code is the RealNetworks' new way of stopping Microsoft.
3 RealNetworks expects to make its own software into an industry standard.
4 RealNetworks suggest Software market is becoming a mixed market.
5 Releasing the source-code can bring about self-created competition.
6 RealNetworks wants to make profits by releasing the free source-code.
7 RealNetworks shows great focus on the strategy of doing your best.

Risky Try

A

Focus on what you do best. This age-old strategy has worked well for Real Networks, Microsoft's main competitor in multimedia software for the Internet. Now, the smaller Seattle-based firm is trying a novel way to contain the software giant. On October 29th, it released the underlying recipe, or source-code, of its RealPlayer software and will soon do the same for its other programs-giving away a big chunk of its intellectual property.

B

This may sound like a desperate echo of 1998, when Netscape, struggling in Microsoft's chokehold, published the source-code of its web browser (an initiative that yielded few real results until this June, when the first serious new version of the open-source browser, Mozilla, was released). Yet RealNetworks is not playing defence. It is trying to encourage the creation of a common multimedia software infrastructure for every kind of file format and device, thus thwarting Microsoft's ambitions in this promising market. The firm hopes that others in the industry (volunteer programmers, media firms and hardware makers) will take the code, called Helix DNA, improve it and make it run on new devices, such as mobile phones and home stereos, turning RealNetworks' software into an industry standard. Clever licensing terms are supposed to ensure that this standard does not splinter and that the firm still makes money.

C

Individual developers, universities and other non-profit organisations can modify the software as they please, and even redistribute it for free, so long as they also publish the source-code for their changes. This is a sort of payment in kind, for RealNetworks is then allowed to use these contributions. Firms, on the other hand, must pay royalty fees if they distribute more than 1m copies of the code. They also have to make sure that their software works with other Helix DNA products. The software's development community already has 2, 000 members. And several hardware makers back the effort. But there are risks. Afraid of piracy, media groups are suspicious of anything that might be related to hackers (although they also do not want to depend on, and pay for, technology controlled by Microsoft). The self-created competition could also hurt RealNetworks if customers decide its commercial products, which will be based on the open source-code but with extra features, are not worth paying extra for.

D

(0) RealNetworks' move is another sign that the software industry is going hybrid. Mixing elements of proprietary software, where the source-code is tightly controlled, with open-source programs enables firms to expand a market, harvest the ideas of others and, they hope, still make money. Even Microsoft is edging this way: it recently announced that partners can now look at—but not modify or re-use—the source-code for Passport, its controversial digital-identity service.

PART TWO

Questions 8-12

- Read the extract below from an article about Reliance on Intuition
- Choose the best sentence from the list on the opposite page to fill each of the gaps.
- For each gap 8-12, mark one letter (A-G) on your Answer Sheet.
- Do not use any letter more than once.
- There is an example at the beginning (0).

Example (**0**): G

0	A	B	C	D	E	F	G
	▭	▭	▭	▭	▭	▭	▬

Reliance on Intuition

The majority of successful senior managers do not closely follow the classical rational model of first clarifying goals, assessing the problem, formulating options, estimating likelihoods of success, making a decision, and only then taking action to implement the decision. (0) ___G___.

That problems require them to deal with ambiguity, inconsistency, novelty, and surprise; and to integrate action into the process of thinking.

Generations of writers on management have recognized that some practicing managers rely heavily on intuition. In general, however, such writers display a poor grasp of what intuition is. Some see it as the opposite of rationality; (8) ________.

Isenberg's recent research on the cognitive processes of senior managers reveals that managers' intuition is neither of these. (9) ________. First, they intuitively sense when a problem exists. Second, managers rely on intuition to perform well-learned behavior patterns rapidly. This intuition is not arbitrary or irrational, but is based on years of painstaking practice and hands-on experience that build skills. A third function of intuition is to synthesize isolated bits of data and practice into an integrated picture, often in an Aha! experience. Fourth, some managers use intuition as a check on the results of more rational analysis. Most senior executives are familiar with the formal decision analysis models and tools, and those who use such systematic methods for reaching decisions are occasionally leery of solutions suggested by these methods which run counter to their sense of the correct course of action. Finally, managers can use intuition to bypass in-depth analysis and move rapidly to engender a plausible solution. (10) ________.

One of the implications of the intuitive style of executive management is that thinking is inseparable from acting. Since managers often know what is right before they can analyze and explain it, they frequently act first and explain later. (11) ________. And in that managers develop thoughts about their companies and organizations not by analyzing a problematic situation and then acting, but by acting and analyzing in close concert.

Given the great uncertainty of many of the management issues that they face, senior managers often instigate a course of action simply to learn more about an issue. (12) ________. One implication of thinking/acting cycles is that action is often part of defining the problem, not just of implementing the solution.

A Used in this way, intuition is an almost instantaneous cognitive process in which a manager recognizes familiar patterns.

B Rather, senior managers use intuition in at least five distinct ways.

C They then use the results of the action to develop a more complete understanding of the issue.

D Others view it as an excuse for capriciousness.

E Sales had been expected to fall modestly again this month to a level of 4.85m.

F Analysis is inextricably tied to action in thinking/acting cycles.

G Rather, in their day-by-day tactical maneuvers, these senior executives rely on what is vaguely termed intuition to manage a network of interrelated problems.

PART THREE

Questions 13-18

- Read the following article about Video Games Move Online, and the questions on the opposite page.
- For each question (13-18), mark one letter (A, B, C or D) on your Answer Sheet.

Video Games Move Online

In the eyes of media executives, the internet is a malevolent vacuum-cleaner, sucking in one business after another. Music, software and videos are all increasingly obtained online — often free of charge. Now it is the turn of video games. A combination of new technology and compelling economics means that many, if not most, of them will be played online soon.

Online gaming is not new. Since the early days of the internet, netizens have indulged in "massively multiplayer role-playing online games", a genre that, now complete with fancy graphics, is still very popular, particularly in Asia. Some console games can be played online.

There are several reasons to think, however, that video games have begun the transition from an industry primarily based on consoles and shrink-wrapped software to one in which online services dominate. Conventional gaming has not proved as resistant to the recession as many had expected.

Meanwhile alternatives are emerging quickly. Many personal computers are powerful enough to run fast-moving, graphics-heavy games just as well as consoles. As a result, firms are offering online games that can be played either through "client" software, which users download, or via a web browser.

These trends are dwarfed, however, by the explosion of "social" games, which have become all the rage on social networks such as Facebook. These are more about interaction than action: players either join their friends for an online game of poker or Scrabble, or to create and show off virtual pets, farms and mob families.

As gaming moves online, the economics of the industry are changing. Conventional games take years to develop and cost millions to market, and rely on big sales in their first few weeks of release to recoup the investment, making the launch of a new game a gamble akin to a Hollywood studio's decision to produce a big-budget film. As a result, like Hollywood, big gamemakers focus on successful franchises with fancy effects and plenty of action — and have moved online only hesitantly.

Online games, in particular the social kind, are hard for firms steeped in this model to make, argues Kristian Segerstrale, the boss of Playfish, the number two in social gaming. Developing a new game takes only a few months and costs a few hundred thousand dollars. It can still be improved after its launch. Virtual distribution is far cheaper, and marketing tends to be too, since games often spread "virally" among friends on social networks.

The most important change will be in the way publishers earn money. Although some are charging subscription fees to players of online games or selling advertising, many of them make most of their money by managing an online economy, complete with virtual goods and a digital currency. Playing is free, but users can get ahead by buying extra bits and bobs.

13 In Asia, what make the online game remain so popular?

A Good service.

B More users.

C High speed movement.

D Perfect graphics.

14 The main reason why the video game will be played online is that ________.

A the unition of new technology and current economics

B the increase of the users

C the change on living styles

D the need of video game itself

15 For the online game, the most important change is ________.

A diversity of the use

B the way publisher earn money
C the improvement of the speed
D the increase of the types of video game

16 The way of managing online games is changing from selling software oriented to ________.
A selling the procedure oriented
B click rate oriented
C online services oriented
D fancy graphics oriented

17 The reason why the trend of playing the social games is not good enough is that ________.
A users seldom interact with one another
B the tech ology of this kind of game is not fancy enough
C the element of action not give much attention
D the condition on the game market is not good enough

18 Compared with the conventional games, the main difference of the online game is that ________.
A it takes so long time to develop
B it costs so much money
C it can easily get back the cost
D virtual distribution is much cheaper

PART FOUR

Questions 19-33

- Read the article below about Planning a Share Portfolio.
- Choose the best word or phrase to fill each gap from A, B, C or D on the opposite page.
- For each question (19-33), mark one letter (A, B, C or D) on your Answer Sheet.
- There is an example at the beginning (0).

Example:

A supply **B** shortage **C** change **D** improvement

0	A	B	C	D
	▭	■	▭	▭

Planning a Share Portfolio

There is no (0) __B__ of tipsters around offering "get-rich-quick" opportunities. But if you are a serious private investor, leave the Las Vegas mentality (19) ________ those with money to fritter. The serious investor needs a proper "portfolio" — a well-planned selection of investments, (20) ________ a definite structure and a clear aim. (21) ________ exactly how does a newcomer to the stock market go about achieving that?

Well, if you go to five reputable stock brokers and ask them what you should (22) ________ your money, you're likely to get five different answers — even if you give all the relevant information about your age, family, finances and what you want from your investments. Moral? There is no one "right" way to structure a portfolio. (23) ________, there are undoubtedly some wrong ways, and you can be sure that (24) ________ of our five advisers would have suggested (25) ________ all (or perhaps any) of your money into Periwigs.

So what should you do? We'll assume that you have (26) ________ out the basics — like mortgages, pensions, insurance and (27) ________ to sufficient cash reserves. You should then establish your own individual aims. These are partly a matter of personal circumstances, partly a matter of psychology.

For instance, if you are older you have less time to recover from any major losses, and you may well wish to (28) ________ your pension income. So preserving your capital and generating extra income are your main priorities. In this ease, you'd probably construct a portfolio with some shares (but not high risk ones), along with gilts, cash deposits, and perhaps convertibles (29) ________ the income shares of split capital investment trusts.

If you are younger, and in a solid financial position, you may decide to take an (30) ________ approach — but only if you're blessed with a sanguine disposition and won't (31) ________ sleepless nights over share prices. If you recognize yourself in this description, you might include a couple of heady growth stocks in your portfolio, alongside your more pedestrian investments. Once you have decided (32) ________ your investment aims, you can't then decide (33) ________ to put your money. The golden rule here is spread your risk — if you put all of your money into Periwigs International, you're setting yourself up as a hostage to fortune. "Periwigs" is the name of a fictitious company.

19	**A** in	**B** on	**C** to	**D** upon
20	**A** on	**B** with	**C** upon	**D** in
21	**A** but	**B** and	**C** therefore	**D** however
22	**A** change with	**B** rely on	**C** do with	**D** deal with
23	**A** however	**B** therefore	**C** although	**D** so
24	**A** certain	**B** some	**C** all	**D** none
25	**A** sink	**B** sinking	**C** sank	**D** sinked
26	**A** gave	**B** drew	**C** went	**D** sorted
27	**A** means	**B** mode	**C** kind	**D** assess
28	**A** change	**B** slow	**C** boost	**D** go up
29	**A** or	**B** and	**C** but	**D** except
30	**A** important	**B** aggressive	**C** regular	**D** common
31	**A** do	**B** want	**C** suffer	**D** enjoy
32	**A** up	**B** to	**C** in	**D** on
33	**A** where	**B** what	**C** which	**D** when

PART FIVE

Questions 34-45

- Read the extract below from Silicon Valley "Seeing Revival".
- In most of the lines (34-45), there is one extra word. It is either grammatically incorrect or does not fit in with the meaning of the text. Some lines, however, are correct.
- If a line is correct, write CORRECT on your Answer Sheet.
- If there is an extra word in the line, write the extra word in CAPITAL LETTERS on your Answer Sheet.
- The exercise begins with two examples (0 and 00).

Example:

0	C	O	R	R	E	C	T
00	I	N					

Silicon Valley "Seeing Revival"

0 Silicon Valley is stirring back to life, following a bruising economic downturn,

00 in according to industry insiders and start-up entrepreneurs.

34 The view seems to underscore Federal Reserve chairman Ben Bernanke's belief that the US recession has been ended.

35 He told a Washington think-tank that "from a technical perspective the recession is very like over".

36 Wall Street shares that pessimism — with the Dow Jones having been on a steady rise for the last six months.

37 "In the Valley we are seeing real signs of life," said Satish Dharmaraj,

38 a partner with Redpoint Ventures, and a firm specialising in internet start-ups.

39 "We are seeing an enormous amount really good company coming up and good people leaving their jobs and joining start-ups,

40 that is always a sign of confidence," Mr Dharmaraj told BBC News.

41 Recently acquisitions in the hi-tech field include the purchase of Mint. com by Intuit for $170m (£102m),

42 Adobe buys Omniture for $1. 8bn (£1. 08bn), the sale of Skype to a private equity syndicate

43 for $2bn (£1. 2bn) and the purchase of SpringSource by VMware for $420m (£254m).

44 "Looks like the economy, and with the urge to splurge, is back — especially in Silicon Valley," said Om Malik of tech blog Gigaom. com.

45 "What's even more encouraging is that none of these deals are the small micro — transactions that Silicon Valley got used over the past few years," he added.

WRITING 45 minutes

PART ONE

You are a marketing manager and going to market a new perfume product.

Write an email to team members:

- Saying who the target customers are.
- Telling them the amount of budget.
- Suggesting a meeting to collect ideas.

Write 40-50 words.

To...	Marketing team
Cc...	
Subject:	Marketing a new perfume

PART TWO

Your company plans to launch a new phone series in the local market. You have been asked to write a report recommending the possibility of success.

Look at the information below, on which you have already made some handwritten notes.
Then, using all your handwritten notes, write your proposal.
Write 120-140 words.

Year	City Size Increase	Sales Agents Increase
2008	11%	6%
2009	16%	9%
2010	24%	5%

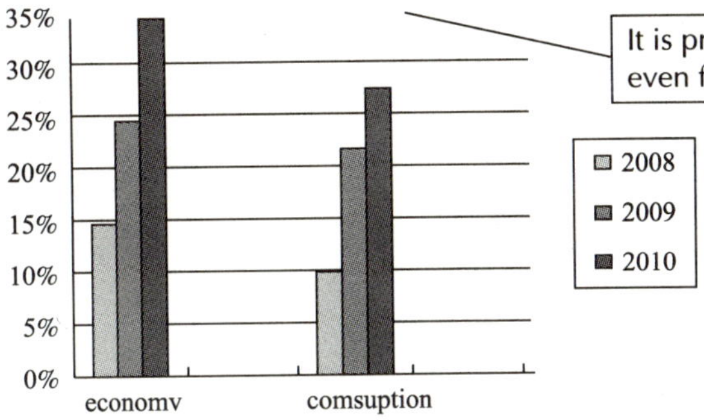

It is predicted to increase even further in city size

Sunday Times
The economic development well pushes up the confidence of consumption

Survey Company Data: 20% want a personal car
32% work or live in far places
56% believe car is affordable

These would add up to ready market

LISTENING 40 minutes (including 10 minutes' transfer time)

PART ONE

Questions 1-12

- You will hear three telephone conversations or messages.
- Write one or two words or a number in the numbered spaces on the notes or forms below.
- After you have listened once, replay each recording.

Conversation One (Questions 1-4)

- Look at the note below.
- You will hear Lacey calling to place an order.

An Account

Lacey's address is (1) ________ Hailsham Industrial Estate.
Lacey'd like (2) ________ boxes of printer paper.
She can get printer paper at the time of (3) ________.
Initial Business usually sends (4) ________ on payment.

Conversation Two (Questions 5-8)

- Look at the note below.
- You will hear a woman calling to talk about recruiting advertisement.
- You have 15 seconds to read through the form.

Information of the Interview

The job title should be (5) ________.
Salary that Sarah should put depends on (6) ________ of the candidate.
It should be bit about applicants including their CVs and (7) ________.
The interview will be held on (8) ________.

Conversation Three (Questions 9-12)

- Look at the note below.
- You will hear a woman calling to ask her schedule.
- You have 15 seconds to read through the form.

Notes

Roger left (9) ________ in the office.
The person Roger will see tomorrow is (10) ________.
The position of the woman's company is new (11) ________.
At 3:30 Roger should meet Raymond (12) at ________.

PART TWO

Section One (Questions 13-17)

- You will hear five short recordings.
- For each recording, decide what the speaker's post is.
- Write one letter (A-H) next to the number of the recording.
- Do not use any letter more than once.
- After you have listened once, replay the recordings
- You have 15 seconds to read the list A-H.

(13) ________________

(14) ________________

(15) ________________

(16) ________________

(17) ________________

A a dentist
B a customer
C a policeman
D a mechanic
E a salesman
F a plumber
G a doctor
H a manager

Section Two (Question 18-22)

- You will hear five short recordings.
- For each recording, decide where the speaker is.
- Write one letter (A-H) next to the number of the recording.

- Do not use any letter more than once.
- After you have listened once, replay the recordings.
- You have 15 seconds to read the list A-H.

(18) ________	**A** at the dentist's
(19) ________	**B** at the drugstore
(20) ________	**C** at the grocery store
(21) ________	**D** at the oil station
(22) ________	**E** at the parking lot
	F at the restaurant
	G at the pub
	H at the supermarket

PART THREE

Questions 23 to 30

- You will hear a long dialogue through a telephone.
- For each question (23-30), mark one letter (A, B or C) for the correct answer.
- After you have listened once, replay the recording.

23 Which room is Mr. Taylor in?

A 418. **B** 208. **C** 480.

24 Why does Mr. Taylor phone Luck?

A Want something to eat.

B Want something to drink.

C All the lights gone out.

25 How many glasses does Mr. Taylor want?

A 1. **B** 2. **C** 3.

26 Why does the female guest unable to check in?

A A temporary problem with our electricity.

B Computers are broken down.

C Too many people to check in and she should wait.

27 What is the female going to do?

A Check the room card.

B Relax in the main bar.

C Hang around waiting for your computers to come back on.

28 Who will pay for the female guest's drink?

A Female guest herself.

B Luck.

C The hotel.

29 Why does the male guest in room 208 come down for?

A No towels.

B No electricity.

C Want sandwiches.

30 What is the male guest in room 208 want to do?

A Take a shower.

B Want a bottle of Chablis.

C Have a look around the town.

SPEAKING 14 minutes

PART ONE

In this part, the interlocutor asks questions to each of the candidates in turn. You have to give information about yourself and express personal opinions.

PART TWO

In this part of the test, you are asked to give a short talk on a business topic. You have to choose one of the topics from the three below and then talk for about one minute. You have one minute to prepare your ideas.

A What is important when...?

Choosing a hotel for people on a business trip

- Location
- Facilities provided
-

B What is important when...?

Planning business trips

- Purpose
- Travel arrangement
-

C What is important when...?

Selecting an travel agency for business trips

- Reputation
- Speed of service
-

PART THREE

In this part of the test, you are given a discussion topic. You have 30 seconds to look at the task prompt, an example of which is below, and then about three minutes to discuss the topic with your partner. After that, the examiner will ask you more questions related to the topic.

For two or three candidates

Cutting Travel Costs

You company is planning to reduce the budget it spends on business trips.

You have been asked for make recommendations about it.

Discuss the situation together, and decide:

- how the total number of business trips can be reduced
- how the costs of some trips might be reduced

Follow-on questions

- Do you think there will be any negative effect on a company's performance if there is a reduction in business travel (Why? / Why not)?
- How to prevent employees spending more than they are supposed to during business travel?
- Do you think companies are willing to pay extra for business class travel (Why? / Why not)?
- How important is it to plan the itinerary before starting a business trip? (Why?)
- What's the most cost-effective way to reduce costs for business travellers?

Test 1 参考答案与解析

READING

PART ONE

Questions 1-7

参考答案

1 B **2** D **3** C **4** B **5** C **6** A **7** C

参考译文

经济缓解

土耳其加入欧盟的申请将于12月17日在欧盟部长会议上进行表决，围绕该申请的一些顾虑就是经济问题，尤其是该国的相对贫困问题。其人均GDP还不足2004年之前欧盟15国人均GDP的三分之一。但是和2004年5月1日加入欧盟的十个新成员国之一（拉脱维亚）相比，土耳其差得并不算太远，而和本周刚刚完成加入欧盟的谈判，并将在2007年1月获得完全成员地位的两个国家保加利亚和罗马尼亚相比，则相差无几。

不但如此，用经济合作和发展组织秘书长唐纳德·约翰斯顿的话来说，该国最近的经济发展“十分惊人”。本年度第二季度的GDP比去年增长了13.4%，这样的增长速度是任何欧盟成员国都无法匹敌的。土耳其的通货膨胀率最近刚从1972年以来首次跌进个位数，本周该国刚刚同国际货币基金组织达成一项新的为期三年总额100亿美元的经济项目协议。按照国际货币基金执行总裁罗德里戈·莱托的说法，这一项目将会“帮助土耳其……把通货膨胀率降到欧盟水平，并且增加其经济弹性”。

历史上该国经济并没有很强的韧性。近期如2001年，它的GDP下降超过7%。而1994年，下降超过5%，1999年仅比5%略低。的确，在整个20世纪90年代，该国的经济就好像一次猛烈的心脏病发作的心电图记录那样来回摆动。这种不规律性是导致该国很难吸引其急需的外国直接投资的主要原因之一（另外还有烦琐的公事程序和腐败）。现在这类投资总额（作为GDP的一个百分点）比20世纪80年代的时候还要低，而每年的外资流入量很少能够达到10亿美元（爱尔兰仅2003年一年就吸引外资超过250亿美元，而巴西从1998年到2000年每年的外资流入量都达到了这个数字。）

从2005年1月1日起，一个妨碍外国投资者的因素将会消失。到那一天，土耳其将取消其公民自称为百万富翁的权利。里拉的面值里将减少六个零；这样，当地货币的每个货币单位将和现在的1百万里拉等值——也就是0.53欧元（0.70美元）左右。商品将在一整年内用新旧里拉同时定价，但外国银行家和投资人现在可以期待今后在土耳其再不用快速心算一串串数不清的零了。

答案解析

本篇文章主要介绍了土耳其的经济状况。第一段主要是从经济情况方面将土耳其和其他几个欧盟新成员国进行了一下对比，强调土耳其的经济状况并非如人们担心的那么糟糕；第二段对土耳其这几年的经济增长情况进行了简要介绍；第三段说明土耳其的经济缺乏弹性以及由此带来的影响；最后一段说明妨碍投资者的一个因素即将消失。

第一题，所给句子的意思是现在土耳其的经济增长速度比欧盟任何成员国都要快，与B段中的"GDP in the second quarter of the year was 13.4% higher than a year earlier, a rate of growth that no EU country comes close to matching."这句话相对应。其中的"no EU country comes close to matching"与句子中的"grows faster than any EU member"意思如出一辙。所以正确答案是B。

第二题，外国投资者在土耳其将有一个很好的发展前景。与D段中的"but foreign bankers and investors can begin to look forward to a time in Turkey when they will no longer have to juggle mentally with indeterminate strings of zeros"相符。其中提到的开始期望有这么个时刻和享受好的商业前景相符。所以选择D。

第三题，经济上的弹性并不一直是土耳其的优势。与C段的第一句话"Resilience has not historically been the country's economic strong point."相对应。"Resilience"是关键词，也是线索词。而原文中的strong point被所给句子中的one advantage所替代。所以答案是C。

第四题，在土耳其，通货膨胀率曾经很高。其中"Inflation rate"是线索词，与之相关的内容在B段中出现。"Turkey's inflation rate has just fallen into single figures for the first time since 1972"，也就是说，1972年前，土耳其的通货膨胀率都是两位数，一直很高。所以与原题意思相符的是B段。

第五题，土耳其的经济在过去曾经不稳定。与之相对应的是C段中的这么一句话："Indeed, throughout the 1990s growth oscillated like an electrocardiogram recording a violent heart attack."这句中的关键词是oscillate，是"震荡"的意思。所以"used to be unsteady in the past"与"震荡"相对应。

第六题，当时共有三个成员国被欧盟确定他们的成员地位。与之相符的是A段中的"it is much the same as those of two countries, Bulgaria and Romania, which this week concluded accession talks with the EU that could make them full members on January 1st 2007"，所以答案是A。

第七题，稳定的国内生产总值将有助于土耳其吸引更多的外国投资。根据文章C段，GDP的不规律性是导致土耳其难以吸引外国直接投资的主要原因，可见稳定的GDP增长有助于土耳其吸引更多的外国直接投资。

PART TWO

Questions 8-12

参考答案

8 C　**9** D　**10** A　**11** E　**12** F

参考译文

信用卡危机

下面是有关上周已被联邦特工粉碎的盗窃团伙偷盗个人信息的令人惊慌的事例：估计受害人有4万人之众，而他们中间的任何人根本无法采取任何防范措施来阻止这种盗窃行为的发生。据法院档案记载，这是一种监守自盗行为。据说，一家帮助银行在线访问客户信誉报告的软件公司——远程数据通信公司——

的一个低级 help-desk 服务系统工作人员盗取了这些报告的密码，以每个 60 美元的价格卖给一个由 20 个小偷组成的团伙。这样，该盗窃团伙就从那些消费者的名单中精心挑选出信用好的人，然后以他们的名义申请各种账户。受害人付出的代价是：300 百万美元，而且仍在继续攀升。

甚至更令人震惊的是，迄今为止最大的个人信息窃盗案的告破仅仅是冰山之一角。每年有 70 多万美国人的银行存款被疯狂盗取，这是最大的成长性犯罪市场之一。一个名字、一个地址和一个社会保险号——这些东西在网上很容易找到——是想申请假信贷限额的任何人所需的全部东西。信贷公司每年赚 1.3 万亿，其中 2% 的收入被骗子诈取，因此，几乎没有任何金钱的刺激来促使他们把申请过程做得更安全一些。按现在情况看，保护自己的信用安全完全是你自己的事。

好消息是，有许多可采取的步骤供你选择。多数信用卡窃贼是投机取巧者，而非组织严密的团伙。他们当中的许多人常去翻垃圾桶，去寻找数百万件事先批准且已过时的信用卡邮件，而其他人则去偷钱包。到手后他们只留下社会保险号，把钱包返还给失主。粉碎垃圾邮件、把社会保险卡留在家里可减少你许多事后后悔莫及的痛苦。

但保护你的信用卡不被盗取的最有效的方法是检查你的信用报告，每年一至两次。有三个主要的信用报告查询网址：Equifax（atequifax. com），Trans-Union（www. transunion. com）和 Experian（experian. com）。你可在这些网址上在线订购信用报告，这比通过他们提供的 800 条专线进行令人痛苦的语音邮件炼狱式查询好得多。在这三个网站中，我发现 TransUnion 的网站收费最低，且内容包罗万象——以一种便于阅读的方式为消费者列出了各项价格、权利和提示。

如果你有幸住在科罗拉多州、佐治亚州、马里兰州、马萨诸塞州、新泽西州或佛蒙特州，那么，依照法律，你就有权每年享受一次免费报告，否则，这样的报告每次都要花去你 8 到 14 美元。要尽量避免使用要价 70 美元的全年信用报告监控服务；这笔费用比窃贼之间目前实行的价码还要高 10 美元。如果你认为你是信用卡被盗案的受害人，你就可要求将欺诈警报在这三家信用报告公司存档待查。你也可从 www. consumer. gov/idtheft 网站上下载一种窃盗报告表格。这张表格与地方警察局的报告一起，在怒气冲冲的债权人来找碴儿时，能派得上用场。别指望有什么公正。那位胆大妄为的 help-desk 服务系统工作人员就是不到个人信用信息窃贼 2% 的很少几个被捉的盗贼之一。

答案解析

A 他们当中的许多人常去翻垃圾桶，去寻找数百万件事先批准且已过时的信用卡邮件。

B 过去围坐餐桌就餐是相当有趣的。

C 这样，该盗窃团伙就从那些消费者的名单中精心挑选出信用好的人，然后以他们的名义申请各种账户。

D 因此，几乎没有任何金钱的刺激来促使他们把申请过程做得更安全一些。

E 你可在这些网址上在线订购信用报告，这比通过他们提供的 800 条专线进行令人痛苦的语音邮件炼狱式查询好得多。

F 否则，这样的报告每次都要花去你 8 到 14 美元。

G 据法院档案记载，这是一种监守自盗行为。

第八题，空的前一句说到“allegedly stole passwords for those reports and sold them to a group of 20 thieves at ＄60 a pop”，把偷来的密码卖给犯罪团伙。空的后一句“Cost to the victims: ＄3 million and rising”说的是顾客的损失。所以说，空应该表达的是犯罪团伙在得到密码以后对顾客实施的相关操作。C 中的“the gang to cherry-pick consumers with good credit and applies for all kinds of accounts in their names”说的就是相关内容。所以选择 C。

第九题，空的前一句“Credit companies make ＄1.3 trillion annually and lose less than 2% of that revenue to fraud”，信贷公司每年赚 1.3 万亿，其中 2% 的收入被骗子诈取，表示被诈骗的份额比较小。而后一句说，如此看来只有靠自己来保护自己了。所以空所说的内容应该是否定及消极的，而且是因为诈骗额小而引起的。

第十题，空的前一句提到“Most credit thieves are opportunists, not well-organized gangs”，多数信用卡

窃贼是投机取巧者，而非组织严密的团伙。后一句说的是“Others steal wallets and return them, taking only a Social Security number”，列举了另一些具体的信用卡犯罪的方式。其中的 others 表明，前空所讲的内容也是对方式上的列举。所以 A 符合。

第十一题，E 中提到“All allow you to order reports online”，所有这些都使你可以在网上订阅信用报告，与空前一句列举的三中方式相呼应。

第十二题，空的前一句提到“you are entitled to one free report a year by law”，依照法律，你就有权每年享受一次免费报告。而空的后面提到的却是要花费多少钱去干什么。所以说空格处应该是对前面免费的否定。F 符合要求。

PART THREE

Questions 13-18

参考答案

13 D　**14** B　**15** B　**16** B　**17** A　**18** C

参考译文

摇摆不定

福特可能将其唯一保留的奢侈品牌转让给一家新兴的中国企业。尽管还存在着顾虑和怀疑，但福特汽车公司已于 10 月 28 日正式宣布中国吉利汽车公司将成为其待拍卖子品牌——沃尔沃的优先竞拍者。吉利汽车公司是中国最大的私营本土汽车生产商，如果这次吉利公司成功中标，并将沃尔沃这一世界知名的汽车品牌纳入旗下，这将成为雄心勃勃的吉利创始人兼总裁——李书福成就的又一见证。外界推测，李书福将斥资 20 亿美元用去沃尔沃并购案，这个数目是福特公司于 1999 年购买沃尔沃品牌花费数目的三分之一。

这笔交易在今年年末之前签署的可能性不大，但是如果福特公司极力关注的知识产权转移到中国公司的问题得不到解决的话，谈判将不会有太大进展。因为福特和沃尔沃的合并是包括技术方面的，吉利被迫加大保证力度，以确保其不会盗用福特和沃尔沃先进的生产平台和动力系统，用于自己现有的轿车品牌。如果此次收购案成功，沃尔沃的新东家将成为浙江吉利股份集团——一家私营公司——下属的一家集团公司。据报道，沃尔沃在并入吉利公司之后，还将以独立形式存在，总部设在瑞士，生产线设在在中国。福特公司坚持认为沃尔沃和其技术应该受到“国际上强有约束力的协议”的保护。但是没有理由表明，如果沃尔沃的“自治”是其所乐见的，沃尔沃和吉利公司在未来就不可以协同开发新的产品项目。

为了达成“一个福特”的战略，福特是急于出售沃尔沃的，沃尔沃是作为其卖出阿斯顿—马丁、捷豹和路虎之后最后一个多余（非福特）品牌。但是福特公司坚持认为，如果吉利公司不能成为一个“未来称职的所有者”，他们将拒绝同吉利签订协议。如果有必要，福特公司将继续持有沃尔沃：尽管沃尔沃在第二季度损失了 23.1 亿美元，但在后来的表现有所好转。

吉利除了提高自己的声誉和其品牌的安全性名声之外，还可以从这桩并购中得到什么呢？这家公司宣称，中国现在已经成为世界上增长最快的汽车市场，这次并购将使得沃尔沃的车型更适合中国市场，以及增加这个品牌在中国的销量。但那还远远不够。不管福特和吉利的说法如何，沃尔沃的技术不会成为永远的秘密。

答案解析

第十三题说的是为了使交易更好地进行，吉利不得不实施的措施是什么。根据原文的第三段，有这么一句话：“Because Ford and Volvo are joined at the hip in engineering terms, Geely has been forced to go to considerable lengths to reassure Ford that it will not simply purloin the pair's advanced platforms and powertrains for its existing car business.”，因为福特和沃尔沃的合并是包括技术方面的，吉利被迫加大保证力度，以确保其不会盗用福特和沃尔沃先进的生产平台和动力系统，用于自己现有的轿车品牌。所以说选择 D“吉利不得不保证相应技术的保留”。

第十四题问的是为了成就“一个福特”的战略，福特公司采取了什么行动？根据原文的第四段第一句所说，“Ford is keen to sell Volvo, its last premium unit after the sales of Aston Martin and Jaguar Land Rover, to focus on its “One Ford” strategy,”也就是说为了达成“一个福特”的战略，福特是急于出售沃尔沃的。所以与之相匹配的答案是 B，卖掉沃尔沃。

第十五题问的是吉利在中国汽车行业的地位如何。根据原文的第一段中所提到的“China’s largest and brashest privately owned carmaker”，吉利汽车公司是中国最大的本土汽车生产商。所以 B 选项符合原文意思，即正确答案。

第十六题的意思是，根据文章可以推断出，福特更注重什么条件？根据文章的第三段中提到的，“Ford had not satisfied itself that its biggest concern, the transfer of intellectual property to the Chinese firm, could be resolved”，福特公司极力关注的知识产权转移到中国公司的问题得不到解决的话，谈判将不会有太大进展。所以说选项 B 为最佳答案。

第十七题是如果发生什么事，交易就会失败。根据原文第四段提到的“But it is adamant that it would not do the deal if it did not believe that Geely would be a “responsible future owner”，如果吉利公司不能成为一个“未来称职的所有者”，他们将拒绝同吉利签订协议。所以说答案为选项 A：如果吉利不能对沃尔沃的未来负责的话，交易必然会失败。

第十八题是说从这次并购中，吉利得到的最主要的益处是什么。根据原文第五段，“the prestige and perhaps an enhanced reputation for safety，prestige 与 C 选项中的 fame 为同义词。所以正确答案为 C。

PART FOUR

Questions 19-33

参考答案

19 A	**20** C	**21** B	**22** D	**23** D	**24** C	**25** D	**26** A	**27** B
28 D	**29** C	**30** A	**31** C	**32** D	**33** A			

参考译文

资源禀赋与加工经济

在竞争力管理中，世界竞争力组织同样分析了国家怎样将资源禀赋与加工经济相结合。一些国家如巴西、印度和俄罗斯，他们富有资源——如土地、人口、自然资源等——却并不一定有竞争力。另一方面，也有如新加坡、日本、瑞士这样的国家，其传统资源很贫乏，但却非常有竞争力。他们掌握了被经济学家称之为“转型加工经济”的经济形态。

日本的表现很好地说明了这种情况。从 1950 年以来，相较于美国 164 次、英国 44 次获得诺贝尔奖，日本仅在精密科学和经济学领域共四次得到该奖项。事实上，日本并没有什么能从根本上改变我们经济生活的科技突破。晶体管、机器人、录像机、电脑、传真机、磁盘、彩色电视机——所有这些都是美国和欧洲公司所发明的。日本的非凡成功在于其产品营销上：他们在将一个创意转化成更便宜、更快捷和更有效率的产品或服务方面的能力上，远超其竞争对手。换句话说，日本的竞争力是以加工经济为基础的。

1996 年世界竞争力年度报告将基于一国资源禀赋的竞争力与通过加工经济实现的竞争力，做了详细区分。这个关键性区分是重要的，因为未来似乎更倾斜于那些掌握了“加工经济”的国家（事实上，一些经济学家使用“自然资源魔咒”来描述那些因富有资源而洋洋得意的国家的命运）。通常，公司也采用相同的策略，他们关注在如质量、速度、订单执行、规模用户和顾客满意度等进程管理中所产生的附加价值。

答案解析

第十九题，此题考查的是固定短语，be ＋ *adj.* ＋in 表示“在某一方面怎么样”。此题中 be rich in 是“在某方面很富有”的意思，所以选择 A 选项。

第二十题，此题考查的是句子间的连接词的应用。空的前一句所说，Some nations can be rich in assets，后面却提到 not necessarily competitive。所以两个分句之间是转折的关系，应该用表转折的连词 but，因此正确答案是 C。

第二十一题，此题考查的是前后文的照应关系。前文中已经提到 some nations can be rich in，后面的 on the other hand 提示我们后面一部分是与前面一部分相对应的。所以，正确答案应该是 be poor in，选择 B。

第二十二题，此句考查的也是连接词。根据句意，poor in traditional assets，可是却 they are very competitive，所以前后是转折关系。B 和 C 排除。A 选项的 however 后面应加逗号。所以正确答案是 D。

第二十三题，此句考查的是考生对单词的掌握能力。四个选项分别是“知道”、“了解”“确认”和“掌握”。根据原文的意思，选项 D 更适合，即掌握经济学家所说的转换过程。

第二十四题，此题考查的是动词辨析。根据原文的意思，选择的应该是 C，received only four Nobel Prizes 的意思是指只得到过 4 次诺贝尔奖。

第二十五题，此题考查的是固定短语，compare something to something，“把……和……相比”。

第二十六题，此题考查的是词汇搭配。四个选项的意思分别是：突破、成功、失败和改变。根据原文意思应该是“技术上的突破”，所以选择 A。

第二十七题，此题考查的是词汇辨析。四个选项的意思分别是：买、营销、制造和改变。根据原文，应该选择 B，意思是“营销产品”。

第二十八题，考查的是固定短语。be excelled in 表示“在某方面很擅长”。而选项 B 中的 good 的搭配应该是 be good at。

第二十九题，考查的是动词的固定用法，transfer something into something，“把……转化为……”。所以答案是 C。

第三十题，考查的是固定短语，stem from…，表示“追溯到……或由……造成的”。

第三十一题，考查的是连接词。根据前后文的意思，我们可以推断出前后句是因果关系。所以选择 C，since 表示“因为，由于”。

第三十二题，考查的是 whereby 的用法：做副词时后可接句子，表示“凭借”。

第三十三题，考查的是固定短语 such… as…，表示“如……这样的”，所以选择的是 A。

PART FIVE

Questions 34-45

参考答案

34	been	**35**	out	**36**	not	**37**	on	**38**	to	**39**	Correct
40	Correct	**41**	up	**42**	Correct	**43**	on	**44**	which	**45**	from

答案解析

第三十四题，根据上下文可以看出，此句中的 have 是实义动词，表示“有”的意思，所以后面不应该接 been；再根据题意可以看出，have professionals 所在句子的意思是完整的，been 是多余的，所以说应该去掉。

第三十五题，此句中的 out of 是“在什么之外”的意思，是不包含的意思。而根据原文的意思，责任是属于公司的，所以，应该用介词 of。所以，out 是“多余的，应该去”掉。

第三十六题，此句主要是对短语的考查。whether 有两个比较重要的短语，whether…or… 和 whether …or not。显然在这一题中，两个短语被混淆了。根据原文意思也可以看出是两个并列的选项，而不是选择其一。所以，not 是多余的。

第三十七题，这句考查的是短语 keep up with，表示“紧跟……”的意思。所以说 keep up on with 中的 on 是多余的。

第三十八题，这道题考查的是短语 finish doing something，是“完成某事”的意思。所以，to 是多余的，应该去掉。

第三十九题，是正确的。

第四十题，是正确的。

第四十一题，考查的是短语 lead to something，是“导致某事”的意思。所以原文中的 up 是多余的。

第四十二题，是正确的。

第四十三题，这一题也是对短语的考查。decide on something 是“决定某事”的意思。后面直接接决定的事物。而原文中，on 后面并没有某物。所以，应该直接用 decide，on 是多余的，应该去掉。

第四十四题，此题考查的是定语从句。原句中很明显可以看出只有一套主位结构，而却出现了用于引导定语从句的 which，所以说，which 是多余的。

第四十五题，考查的是介词方面的语法知识。In... areas 在这里表示“在……方面、领域”。显然 from 是多余的，应该去掉。

WRITING 45 minutes

PART ONE

范 文

I'm interested in having a storefront at the International Furniture Exhibition in Paris on 15th March. Please fax the organizer and get some information as to the price, size, location and discount. I expect to have the feedback by Thursday next week.

范文解析

在本文写作中，首先要注意，本文文体类型是 note。不过在实际考试中，考生直接写邮件正文即可，字数限制是 40 ~ 50 词，然后根据 email 的格式要求以及常用句式布置安排全文。

由于家具展览会将于 3 月 15 日在巴黎举办，公司想要借此机会参展，因而决定购买一个展览摊位。

这封邮件正文的重点在于要求秘书询问展览组织方有关展位的价格、规模、位置以及有无折扣等相关信息，并且要求在下周二得到回复。

PART TWO

范 文

Dear Sir or Madam,

We are writing in connection with the installment of a new fax in our office.

I am sorry to inform you that the date you suggested is not convenient for us, as we'll have an international conference on the 12th of March. Could you please start on the 15th of March? In addition, we would like to know how long the work will last.

The system of extension numbers you mentioned seems to be complicated. Is there an easier way to handle this problem? And we would be grateful if you could give us the name and the direct telephone number of the technical representative.

We would like to pay as soon as the work is successfully finished so that there is no worry about any disputes.

We are looking forward to hearing from you.

Yours sincerely,
Peter Smith

范文解析

在本文写作中，首先要注意，本文文体类型是 Email，字数限制是 40 ~ 50 词，然后根据 email 的格式要求以及常用句式布置安排全文。

公司要安装新的传真机，联系电信公司过来安装，而得知对方的各项安排之后，对有些细节存有疑问和疑虑，因而写信再次确认并说明。

信函根据文中所给的信息进行加工整合，一一解答标注中的问题，指明所安排的安装日期与公司的大型会议相冲突，希望对方更改日期至会议结束后进行上门安装。并且要进一步了解整个安装过程需要的时间，而对于对方提到的数字扩展系统也感觉太复杂，希望换一种简单的方式进行处理。标注中的第四项问题是询问对方代理人的姓名和电话，方便有问题时直接联系，最后提到付款的问题。

可以说全文基本是回答并且解释说明了题目中标注的内容，考生在写作此类文章时，注意题目的要求和给出的信息，并且将信息用合理的方式恰当地衔接，进行整理成文。

LISTENING 40 minutes（including 10 minutes' transfer time）

PART ONE

Conversation One

参考答案

1 number **2** three **3** Tuesday 23 **4** Gersel

听力原文

T = Tom F = Frida

T: Good afternoon. Scandinavian Conferences.

F: Good afternoon. Could I speak to Frank Larsen, Please?

T: I'm afraid he's not here today. Can I help you?

F: I'm ringing about the Danish Telecommunications Trade Fair. Mr. Larsenphoned to offer me some tickets and he asked me to let him know how many I'd need.

T: Well, I can send you the tickets. That's no problem. I'll just need your name and address.

F: Right. It's Frida Andersson from Sanderlin. The address is Torshamnsgatan, S-126 25 Stockholm.

T: So, that's Frida Andersson at Torhamnsgatan, S-126 25. OK. How many tickets do you need?

F: Three, please.

T: And which days would you like them for?

F: Just for Tuesday 23 November, please.

T: And could I have the other names for the tickets?

F: I'm afraid I can only confirm two names at the moment. Kati Gersel and myself.

T: Could you spell Gersel, please?

F: Yes, that's G-E-R-S-E-L.

T: Right. I'll put the tickets in the post today.

F: Thanks very much. Bye.

T: Thank you for calling. Goodbye.

答案解析

1 文中女士说到有人给她提供了会议的入场门票，她打电话的目的是通知一下票的数量。

2 从文中对话可知女士需要三张票。

3　从文中“T: And which days would you like them for? F: Just for Tuesday 23 November, please.”这两句对话可以得出答案。

4　女士说到她只能确定参加会议的人是 Gersel 和她自己，后面的拼写可以知道人物的名字。

Conversation Two

参考答案

5　Head Office　　6　13th　　7　27th　　8　8969005

听力原文

R = Receptionist　　A = Alice

R: Good afternoon. Can I help you?

A: Good afternoon. Could I speak to Mellor, please?

R: May I ask who's calling?

A: It's Alice Green from Head Office.

R: One moment, please. I'll put you through.

R: Hello?

A: Hello?

R: I'm afraid she's not in her office at the moment. Can I take a message?

A: Yes. Could you tell her that I got her message and I've cancelled our meeting on the 13th. But I'm not available the following week, so I suggest meeting on 27 November. And could she call me to confirm the date?

R: OK. I'll give her the message and she'll get back to you as soon as possible.

A: Thank you.

R: Oh, does she have your number?

A: No. That is 8969005. And the fax number is 5842500.

R: OK. Thanks for calling.

答案解析

5　文中女士打电话找 Mellor，从下文可知女士来自总部。

6　从“Could you tell her that I got her message and I've cancelled our meeting on the 13th.”可以得知会议的时间原计划是在 13 日。

7　之后女士说到“But I'm not available the following week, so I suggest meeting on 27th November.”可以得知她把时间改在了十一月 27 日。

8　之后女士留下了她的电话号码，注意干扰信息，之后那个号码是传真号码。

Conversation Three

参考答案

9　business　　10　marketing conference　　11　56.70　　12　Limbert

听力原文

D = David Hopes　　R = Roger Harry

R: Hello, Mr. Hopes. This is Roger Harry from Accounts. I am just ringing about your expenses for the business last week. There are a couple of things I need to check.

D: Okay, what would you need to know?
R: Well, you think it was a business trip, but do you think you could be a bit more specific?
D: Yes...Sorry, it was actually a marketing conference.
R: OK. And stayed in the conference hotel, but you didn't know how much it cost.
D: It was 80 pounds, it was for one night. If you stay for more than three days, it will be 60 for each night.
R: I see. Now under client entertaining, you put 56. 70 pounds for drinks. Would you ask to put down the name of anybody you entertained you know.
D: I am sorry, I have forgotten. Anyway, the client's name is Limbert, Pole Limbert. He is one of building suppliers.
R: Could you spell his last name for me?
D: Limbert, yes, L-I-M-B-E-R-T.
R: Right, thanks.

答案解析

9 这段对话是 Roger 向 David 询问关于商务支出的情况。从 I am just ringing about your expenses for the business last week 一句中可以得知 Roger 打电话的目的。
10 文中 Roger 认为费用花在了商务旅行方面，而 David 进行了纠正，他说费用是花在了市场部门的会议上。
11 题目问的是花在饮料上的费用是多少，而文中之前介绍了住宾馆的费用，应该注意此干扰信息。
12 文中说到了招待宾客的姓名，而 David 只记住了一个人的姓名，从随后的拼写可以得知答案。

PART TWO

Section One

参考答案

13 B **14** C **15** F **16** G **17** D

听力原文

13
Woman: Well, no wonder the bank's returned it unpaid. Look, the figures don't match the amount in words. I expect someone was filling it in too much of a hurry. Let's see, we'd better issue another one straight away to pay Mrs. Burton, because it'll be another three weeks if we wait for the next cycle of payments. Her expenses on that sales trip were pretty high, and it wouldn't be fair to keep her waiting much longer.

14
Man: Of course, this only gives a very general picture. But as you can see, cash is a particularly healthy area. That's even when we take into account regular outgoings on loans and leasing equipment, which are included in the final totals. And even more significantly, unpaid orders are actually excluded from the final calculation. These represent a sum of approximately thirty thousand pounds. With that in mind, we can say that the company's overall position is still strong.

15
Woman: I've just asked the Arden Conference Centre about availability for our next training seminar, and they said they still haven't been paid for the one before last, which should have been dealt with six months ago. I've had to ask them to send a duplicate! We really must be careful. Arden gives us

very favorable prices, but we haven't got a contract with them — Can you deal with it straight away so we stay in their good books?

16

Man: John Woods here, phoning about the project we discussed earlier. Could you give me a ring so that we can talk about it a bit more? I've done a few calculations and I'm beginning to wonder whether it's really a practical proposition. I still think the project's got potential, but there are significant additional costs which we hadn't taken into account. So could you get back to me as soon as you can, please?

17

Woman: Yes, it was interesting... Some of it was rather obvious, of course, like dressing smartly, making sure you arrive on time, that sort of thing... But there was also quite a lot I'd never really considered... like ways to interpret what the advertisement is really asking for, reading between the lines... and a section which lists some of the harder questions they tend to ask you, with effective answers you can give.

答案解析

13 短文中多次提到了关于支付的问题，其中“we'd better issue another one straight away to pay Mrs. Burton”为关键信息句。

14 从短文中提到的关键词 loan、cash 以及 unpaid 可知谈话内容与经济有关，而从最后一句“With that in mind, we can say that the company's overall position is still strong.”可以知道，文中人物在分析公司的经济状况。

15 这段表述中，女士想为公司将要举办的培训活动预定会场，她要求提供合同的副本，其中“I've had to ask them to send a duplicate!”为关键句，duplicate 与题目选项中的 copy 意思一致，均指“副本”。故选 F 选项。

16 文中男士希望就先前讨论的项目进行更加详细的交谈，从“Could you give me a ring so that we can talk about it a bit more?”这句可以得出正确选项。

17 文中女士说到了如何穿着、按时到达、如何准备发言等，可以判断是在对某些正式场合的行为提出了一些建议，故选 D。

Section Two

参考答案

18 B **19** A **20** F **21** D **22** E

听力原文

18 Hello, Amy. This is Margaret Brock here. It's 9:30 on Wednesday morning. I'm ringing about the half-year sales report. Could you send me a copy of our department's figures, please? I'm in Helsinki until Friday. Thanks very much. Bye.

19 This is Frank Larsen from Scandinavian Conferences in Copenhagen. I'm ringing to tell you that this year's Danish Telecommunications Trade Fair's taking place in the week of November 22. If you'd like some complimentary tickets, please let me know how many you'll need. Please call me on 346766. Thank you. Bye.

20 Hi, Frida. It's Sue Mellor. How are you? I hope you're not too busy at the moment. I wanted to talk about my visit next month. You know we'd talked about the 13th? Well, I'm afraid it's not going to work out because of deadlines here. I don't suppose we could make it a week or so, could we? Give me a ring and let me know. Thanks.

21 Hi, Lilin. It's Colin. I'm on my mobile because I'm traveling to a meeting with a client but I need to talk to you urgently, so could you call me on 0486772444? It's my mobile number. I need to talk to you about that contract we're trying to get Helsinki Company because the customer accepted our proposal. I need to know whether it's all right if I just go ahead and sign the contracts or whether you want to get involved, as well. Could you call me as soon as you can? Thanks.

22 Hello, Lily. It's Steve Montgomery here. I got your proposal for the product launch and I've finally managed to have a look at it. It looks OK, but I think there could still be one or two minor problems with it. I think the time schedule looks a bit on the optimistic side, as well. I've got a couple of suggestions, so let's think about it.

答案解析

18 此人打电话的目的是了解一些销售报告的数据，从“I'm ringing about the half-year sales report. Could you send me a copy of our department's figures”可以得出答案。其中，figure 与选项中的 data 为对应的同义词，指“数据”。

19 从最后一句“If you'd like some complimentary tickets, please let me know how many you'll need. Please call me on 346766. ”可以得知此人是在提供会议的入场券。

20 根据“I don't suppose we could make it a week or so, could we? Give me a ring and let me know. Thanks. ”，我们可以了解此人不能在截止日期前进行参观访问，因此她想知道合适的时间。

21 此人打电话是想讨论关于收购公司的问题，之后说到“I need to know whether it's all right if I just go ahead and sign the contracts or whether you want to get involved, as well. Could you call me as soon as you can? Thanks. ”可以得出此人是想得到一些建议。

22 此人说他看了关于产品宣传的建议，之后谈到了一些问题，他说到“I think the time schedule looks a bit on the optimistic side, as well. I've got a couple of suggestions,”从中可以判断出他是想就销售的时间安排做些调整。其中，schedule 与 arrangement 为同义词，表示“安排”。

PART THREE

参考答案

23 B **24** B **25** B **26** A **27** B **28** C **29** B **30** A

听力原文

Marina: Hi Steve, have you got a moment?

Steve: Sure, what is it?

Marina: Well, Roberto had a word with me last night. He is worried about the level of training that new staff members have. That kitchen fire was just a silly incident but if Roberto hadn't known how to use the fire extinguisher properly and speedily, the consequences could have been much more serious.

Steve: Hmm, I agree — but isn't Jenny going to plan some Health and Safety Training for new staff?

Marina: Yes, but I think we should do some refresher training for all staff both new and old — it would be useful for everyone to remember the basics before the conference. If anything serious happened, it would be disastrous for our reputation.

Steve: You're right. Let's mention that to Jenny. Anything else?

Marina: Yes, I'd like to be able to reassure Roberto that the people he deals with during the conference will have experience in hospitality. The more I think about it, the more I don't think we should employ inexperienced students — they may work out cheaper but it's a risk, and Roberto won't be happy if things don't run smoothly, especially not after last night.

Steve: Hmm, if we hire experienced catering staff, it will definitely push our costs up.

Marina: And if we don't hire them, we could lose Roberto, and have a whole lot of problems with people who don't know what they are doing! If we are trying to make a good impression with our first big conference, we really can't afford to do that.

Steve: Well, if that's the case, we'll just have to see where we can cut corners elsewhere in our budget.

Marina: Okay, I'll look at the menu again with Roberto and see if we can find any room for savings there.

Steve: Good, and I'll tell Jenny to organize some refresher training for all of us. And I'll bring up both these points at the all-staff meeting we're having later this week.

Marina: Great, I think that we can sort something out...

(At the general meeting)

Steve: Right, okay, moving on to the last point on the agenda, and really it's over to you. Eh, if you've got any questions about the bid to host the conference, we're here to answer them. So, are there any questions?

Female staff member: Ehh, yeah. I work at housekeeping. Will we be expected to do overtime that weekend? There are going to be a lot of guests by the sound of things.

Steve: Good question. The management team — myself, Jenny and Marina that is — think that it would be better to hire extra help just for the Saturday when we would need to get a lot of rooms tidied — we'll probably hire four to five extra people for that day. Rosie the housekeeper already has a list of people who may be able to help out...

Rosie: That's right.

Steve: Then once guests are checked out, we can deal with getting the linen washed and so on in our own time. We are trying to keep our costs down in the proposal because if we win this bid, it will mean a lot more business for us in the future, and that is good for all of us. Okay?

Hotel staff: Yes... That's fine...Thanks.

Roberto: I can understand the need to keep costs down, Steve. In fact I think Marina and I have created two great menus with this in mind, but I am worried about having inexperienced people working directly with our guests. I am talking about catering staff here. If we want to offer great service, we need experienced, trained, competent waiting staff, not people who are going to cause trouble in my kitchen all the time.

Jenny: Yes. Roberto, I can answer you there. We have decided that it is best if we hire people who have catering experience, so we have chosen to employ an extra 10 waiting staff over the conference weekend from a specialist catering agency. All of them with a lot of experience, so you can put your mind at rest there.

Roberto: Oh, that's a great relief, Jenny! Thank you.

Steve: So, er... any other questions? Yes, Dave, I know you wanted...

答案解析

23 细节题。由 “Well, Roberto had a word with me last night. He is worried about the level of training that new staff members have ” 可知答案为 B。

24 Jenny 建议为新员工搞一次健康与安全培训，Marina 认为应该为新老员工都组织一次复习训练。refresher training 意思为 “复习训练”。

25 推断题。Marina 认为雇用学生工人虽然价格低，但是有风险。故可推断出雇用学生工人价格低廉，却有可能造成更多的事故。故选 B。

26 推断题。Steve认为雇用有经验的工人价格会比较高，但可以减少风险。故选C。

27 细节题。由“And I'll bring up both these points at the all-staff meeting we're having later this week”可知下周要开全体职工大会。

28 推断题。Roberto担心新雇的员工没有经验，造成麻烦。根据原文“but I am worried about having inexperienced people working directly with our guests, I am talking about catering staff here. If we want to offer great service, we need experienced, trained, competent waiting staff, not people who are going to cause trouble in my kitchen all the time.”可推断出答案为C。

29 细节题。由“it would be better to hire extra help just for the Saturday”可知会在周六雇佣房间清洁员。

30 细节题。“so we have chosen to employ an extra 10 waiting staff over the conference weekend from a specialist catering agency”此句为关键信息句，从中可得到答案。

SPEAKING 14 minutes

PART ONE（略）

PART TWO

Topic A

Main points:

When maintaining customer loyalty, one of the common practices is offering discounts to the regular customers. In this way, regular customers will keep buying. The more they buy, the more discounts they may get.

Quality product is another important factor to attract customer loyalty to one brand. Because no matter what the price is, the quality of a product should keep a relatively advantage among rivals of the same price scope. Otherwise, customers may go to the lower prices with the same quality or even better quality.

Furthermore, good after-sale service, brand culture is also key factors to keep customers loyal to the brand. Successful brand leaders will keep their products updated in time. Some of the best known brands even form a strong culture link between customers and themselves in which customers feel the concern and deep attraction from particular brand.

Topic B

Main points:

The first thing to consider in selecting marketing channel is geographic location. Nowadays many areas within a city have formed their own single or mutli-functions like CBD (central business district), bar street, etc. Therefore, selecting a good geographic location is extremely important to attract customers.

Another important factor to consider is the services provided by agencies. Because agencies are facing customers directly. Their services not only affect customers' attitude to the agencies, but also to the brand and its producer. Therefore, many successful brand makers standardize their agencies' service and other open up their own service centers to provide a best quality services to customers.

Other factors to consider include supply chain, trafficking time as well as circulation speed of the products. These factors are all important in selecting an appropriate marketing channel for a company. And in return, good marketing channel will help a company to achieve their sales goals.

Topic C

Main points:

There are many things to consider in choosing transport means for a business trip.

Firstly, we should take time-efficiency into consideration. When we are going for a business trip, especially for the urgent trip, time accounts. We need to compare the travel time and efficiency between airplanes, trains and cars.

Secondly, we would care about the costs of one transport means. It is advisable not to choose a transport whose cost is beyond your budget, since expensive transport will inevitably add costs to our business, which can even stop us from meeting our targets. Therefore, we should calculate the costs of a trip and never allow this kind of cost to ruin the whole business.

Besides, we should also take comfort and convenience into consideration. With comfortable transport, we can stretch out, lie back and even get some sleep during the trip so that we can arrive well rested and ready for our work. This is vital for the success of our business.

PART THREE

A: There are many factors to consider. First, we must consider the location. I think the supermarket should be located in the downtown area.

B: If so, then the cost of renting the space would be high, and the parking spaces would be limited. I think our supermarket can be located in the uptown area, because our supermarket may take large space, and the transport now is very convenient.

A: What about the atmosphere of the supermarket? I think we can use warm and bright colours to create a warm atmosphere.

B: It sounds good. We can also play some soft background music so that shoppers can enjoy their shopping. What's more, we must keep the supermarket clean and tidy, and goods should be displayed in a way for consumers to find easily.

A: That's true. The aisles should be wide enough for shopping trolleys to pass. Employees should be dressed in a well-designed uniform. In one word, we must make the atmosphere appealing, then shoppers would like to shop in our supermarket.

B: Should we use scrambled merchandising? I think we can offer pharmacies, and photo processing.

A: Yes, we can even offer banking services, which would be very convenient for consumers to draw money.

B: We are also given the task of offering suggestions for recruiting employees. What do you think we can do to recruit employees?

A: I think we can put an ad in a local newspaper.

B: We can also advertise the job on the Internet. Young people often go online to search for recruitment news.

A: We may also ask a recruitment company to do the recruitment job for us.

B: But we'll have to pay some money for it.

A: Well, as you know, the job of searching for, interviewing and selecting staff is difficult and time-consuming. What's more, our managers may lack the skill of finding the right people.

B: All right, we can first put a job advertisement in newspapers or on the Internet, then ask a recruitment company to recruit staff for us.

Follow-on questions

- What services do wholesalers mainly perform?
  They can absorb inventory costs for manufactures, help promote the products they sell, and provide both retailers and producers with valuable information about product demand, buying trends, and prices, etc.
- What do you think nonstore retailing includes?
  Nonstore retailing includes in-home selling, direct marketing, on-line sales and vending machines.
- What do you think are the advantages and disadvantages of vending machines?
  Vending machines offer the advantages of 24-hour-a-day operation without the need of a sales person. The main drawback includes the costs of frequent servicing and needed repairs, as well as the threat of vandalism.

- What are the types of wholesalers?
  There are merchant wholesalers, brokers and agents, manufacturers' and retailers' branches and offices, and miscellaneous wholesales.
- Do you think the location of a retail store important? (Why? / Why not?)
  The location of a retail store is very important, because a good location can guarantee high profits for the store.

Test 2 参考答案与解析

READING

PART ONE

Questions 1-7

参考答案

1 B　**2** A　**3** B　**4** D　**5** C　**6** D　**7** A

参考译文

危险的尝试

"集中注意力做你最拿手的事"这一古老的策略对微软公司在因特网多媒体软件领域的主要竞争对手 RealNetworks 网络公司十分奏效。目前，这家位于西雅图的公司正试图用一种新方法来牵制微软这个软件界巨人。10 月 29 日，这家公司发布了取得领先地位的 RealPlayer 播放器软件秘诀，即源码，并将很快对其他程序采取同样的行动——出售其知识产权的一大部分。

这听起来似乎像是 1998 年的一次危险的仿效。那年，因被微软"掐着脖子"而做生死挣扎的 Netscape 公司发表了其网络浏览器的源码（在今年 6 月它推出了真正意义上的最新版开放原码浏览器——Mozilla——之前，这种主动出击几乎没有给它带来任何实际效果）。但 RealNetworks 网络公司并不是在打防御战。它正大力创建一个对每一种文件格式和装置都适用的公共多媒体软件基础结构，这样，它就在这个很使人看好的市场上有力地牵制住了微软的野心。

该公司希望在业内其他公司（自愿参加的程序设计公司、传媒公司和硬件制造公司）将采用这种被称作 Helix DNA 的代码，对它加以改进，并在其新装置（如移动电话和家用音响等装置）上运行，最终把 RealNetworks 公司的软件变成一种行业标准。精明的许可证发放条款应保证这一标准不被像切蛋糕似的分成碎块，保证公司仍有钱可赚。

个体开发商、大学和其他非营利性组织，只要他们也能把其更改后程序的源码公布于众，可根据他们的意愿对该软件进行修改，甚至可以免费发放。这实际上是一种实物支付方式，因为到了那个时候，RealNetworks 公司也可使用这些改进的软件成果。另一方面，如果其他公司能销售 100 万以上的源码，他们须支付特许权使用费。他们还要保证他们的软件与 Helix DNA 产品兼容。软件开发业已拥有 2000 余名成员。一些硬件制造商也支持这一举动，但存在风险。由于担心被盗版，传媒组织对一切与黑客有关的举动都表示怀疑（尽管他们也不想依赖微软、向它支付技术使用费或在技术上受控于微软）。其商业产品以开放源码为基础，但具有极佳的特点。如果客户认为这些产品不值得他们额外付钱的话，那么，自我制造的竞争也可能会伤害 RealNetworks 公司。

RealNetworks 公司的举动表明了另一种迹象，即软件业正在成为混合模式。把那些源码受严格控制的专有软件成分（组件）与开放源码程序加以混合就能使公司拓展市场，集思广益，并且——他们希望——仍可赚钱。连微软公司也正以这种方式小心翼翼地行事：最近微软公司发出公告，说合伙人现在可以查看——但不能更改或重复使用——Passport（微软有争议的数字验证服务）的源码。

答案解析

第一题的句子的意思是“在 1998 年，Netscape 公司做了一次危险的模仿”。从文章的 B 段第一句中“when Netscape, struggling in Microsoft's chokehold, published the source-code of its web browser”我们可判断，RealNetworks 网络公司和 Netscape 公司的做法一样；从句子“an initiative that yielded few real results until this June, when the first serious new version of the open-source browser, Mozilla, was released.”我们可判断，Netscape 公司的做法是极不成功的，是危险的。”所以正确答案是 B。

第二题，句子的意思是“发布源码是 RealNetworks 公司对付微软的新方式”。文章在 A 段中提到“Now, the smaller Seattle-based firm is trying a novel way to contain the software giant,”目前，这家位于西雅图的公司正试图用一种新方法来牵制微软这个软件界巨人。接着就提到了发布源码的措施，“it released the underlying recipe, or source-code, of its RealPlayer software and will soon do the same for its other programs-giving away a big chunk of its intellectual property”。所以答案选择的是 A。

第三题，该句子的意思是“RealNetworks 公司期望使自己的软件成为行业标准”。与文中 B 段中的这么一句话，“The firm hopes that others in the industry (volunteer programmers, media firms and hardware makers) will take the code, called Helix DNA, improve it and make it run on new devices, such as mobile phones and home stereos, turning RealNetworks' software into an industry standard”的后半句相符。所以应该选择 B。

第四题，句子的意思是“RealNetworks 说明现在的微软市场正在成为一个混合市场”。与之相对应的是原文的 D 段中开头所提到的：“RealNetworks' move is another sign that the software industry is going hybrid.”，理解这句话的关键是要知道什么是“hybrid”。接下来的句子做出了解释“Mixing elements of proprietary software, where the source-code is tightly controlled, with open-source programs enables firms to expand a market”，在这句话中，注意词组“mix... with”。

第五题，句子的意思是“源码的发行可以带来自我竞争”。与之对应的是原文中 C 段的最后一句话：“The self-created competition could also hurt RealNetworks if customers decide its commercial products, which will be based on the open source-code but with extra features, are not worth paying extra for.”如果客户认为这些产品不值得他们额外付钱的话，那么，自我制造的竞争也可能会伤害 RealNetworks 公司。所以答案应该是 C。

第六题，句子的意思是“RealNetworks 想通过发行源码获取利润”。与之对应的是 D 段中的“Mixing elements of proprietary software, where the source-code is tightly controlled, with open-source programs enables firms to expand a market, harvest the ideas of others and, they hope, still make money,”把那些源码受严格控制的专有软件成分（组件）与开放源码程序加以混合就能使公司拓展市场，集思广益，并且——他们希望——仍可赚钱。所以正确答案是 D。

第七题的意思是“RealPlayer 公司很重视‘做你最拿手的’这一策略”。文中开头第一段，也就是 A 段第一、二句，“Focus on what you do best. This age-old strategy has worked well for Real Networks,”集中注意力做你最拿手的事这一古老的策略对 RealNetworks 网络公司十分奏效。所以正确答案是 A。

PART TWO

Questions 8-12

参考答案

Example (**0**): G

8 D　**9** B　**10** A　**11** F　**12** C

参考译文

对直觉的依赖

大部分成功的高层管理人员并不拘泥于传统的推理模式，即：首先确定目标，然后估定问题，摆出各种可能性，估计成功率，再做决定，最后才付诸行动去实施。相反，在这些人的日常决策过程中，他们靠一种定义模糊的直觉应付大量相关问题，这些问题使他们必须在一堆含糊不清、自相矛盾、奇特无比或者令人惊异的事物中做抉择，而且在考虑过程中就要有相应的行动。

管理学作品的写作者早就注意到了实践当中一些管理者对直觉依赖很强。不过总的来说，这些写作者未曾表达出什么叫作直觉。有些人将其视作理性的对立面，还有人认为它是反复无常（的做法、性格）的一个借口。

Isenberg最近对高层管理人员认知过程的研究揭示了管理者的直觉并不是上述的任何一种情况。高层管理者是在五个不同的方面使用直觉。首先，他们直觉地感到有问题存在。第二，依靠直觉，管理者们能很快表现出有教养的行为方式。这种直觉并不是任意、非理性的，而是在多年实践磨练和亲身体验培养出的技能的基础上形成的。第三，直觉把一些零散的数据和实际情况组合为一个完整画面，这经常表现为一声“Aha”式的体验。第四，有些管理者也应用直觉来检验更理性化分析的结果。大部分高层管理人员熟知传统的决策分析模式和工具，那些使用这些正式的系统化方法做出决定的人经常会对一种情况保持警惕，那就是有时此方法得出的结论和他们对正确行为的感觉不符。最后，管理者可通过直觉绕开深奥的分析而快速产生一个可能的解决办法。这么使用时，直觉几乎是一个瞬间的思维过程，这一模式为管理者所熟悉。

这些管理者应用直觉方式的一个特点是：思考和行动不能分开。由于（在这种方式中）管理者在分析和解释问题之前就已经明白应该怎么去做，他们经常是先行动，后解释。在思考—行动的循环中，分析是必不可少的。在这其中，管理者们不是靠分析他们面对的形势来思考其公司、组织的情况，而是行动和分析在高度一致地进行。

由于管理者们经常面对许多不确定的情况，他们鼓励采取各种行动来对问题做一番深入了解。他们借此对问题做出更深的体会。这种思考和行为相循环的一个特点即：行动是确定问题的一部分，而不只是解决问题的步骤。

答案解析

A 这么使用时，直觉几乎是一个瞬间的思维过程，这一模式为管理者所熟悉。
B 高层管理者是在五个不同的方面使用直觉。
C 他们借此对问题做出更深的体会。
D 还有人认为它是反复无常（的做法、性格）的一个借口。
E 市场曾预计2月份的销售量将再次小幅下滑，至485万套。
F 在思考—行动的循环中，分析是必不可少的。
G 相反，在这些人的日常决策过程中，他们靠一种定义模糊的直觉应付大量相关问题。

第八题，空的前一句提到“Some see it as the opposite of rationality”，有些人将其视作理性的对立面。所以some对应的是others，正确的选项应该是D。

第九题，空的后面列举了在直觉方面的五种不同的使用方法。所以说，空格处应该是对五种方法的综述，B刚好符合题意。

第十题，空的前一句介绍的是最后一种直觉的使用方法，所以后面的内容应该与这一方法有关。A项中刚好说的是有关使用这一方法的效果，所以A符合条件。

第十一题，空的前面说的都是思考和行动的有关信息，F项中刚好提到了thinking/acting cycle。所以说这题解决的关键在于关键词thinking/acting。

第十二题，空的前一句提到了“learn more about an issue”，而选项C中也提到了the issue。关键词相吻合，所以C选项符合条件。

PART THREE

Questions 13-18

参考答案

13 D **14** A **15** B **16** C **17** C **18** D

参考译文

视频游戏的云端转移

在媒体主管的眼中，互联网就是一个恶毒的真空吸尘器，吸食掉一个又一个的行业商机。越来越多的音乐、软件和视频都可以通过互联网得到——通常还是免费的。现在轮到视频游戏行业了。新科技和紧迫的经济形式结合在一起意味着许多的游戏都将通过互联网来玩。

在线游戏不是新东西。在互联网早期，网民们已经沉迷于那种“大规模、多玩家的角色扮演类在线游戏”——现在此类游戏借助着精美的影像而显得日益完美并仍然在流行，特别是在亚洲。另一些平台端的游戏则可以在线上玩。

以往的视频游戏行业主要是基于游戏机平台的游戏软件贩售的商业模式，然而这种模式已经开始转变成在线服务为主导的模式，这里面有几个原因可以思考。常规类游戏已经证明它未能如愿地抵挡住经济的衰退潮。

同时可选择的其他游戏方式却在快速出现。许多的个人 PC 已经有着足够的性能运行那些高速移动、高图形负荷的游戏，就像在游戏机上运行一样。因此，游戏厂商们都在提供相关游戏的线上版，它们可以通过下载客户端运行，或是通过浏览器运行。

虽然跟随着社区网络而来的社交类游戏如 Facebook 等大爆发并风行一时，但这些趋势目前都还不够强大。因为此类游戏更多的是互动类而非动作类。也就是说用户是为了一个线上扑克牌游戏或拼字游戏，或是为创立或炫耀虚拟宠物、虚拟农场等而加入他们的朋友。

该行业的经济状况因为游戏的线上转移而出现了变化。常规类的游戏需要数年时间来开发，还要花费数千万资金做市场推广，并且游戏刚上市的开始几周是否能卖个满堂红往往决定着该游戏能否收回当初的投资。这使新游戏的投产像是场赌博，类似于好莱坞的制片厂决定对一个大预算影片的制作那样。由此带来的结果也是好莱坞似的，大的游戏厂商关注的是票房保证的特技效果和动作堆叠，只有犹豫不决时才将游戏转到线上。

线上游戏，特别是社交类的，很难让游戏公司专注于此开发，Kristian Segerstrale 是这么认为的。他是排名第二的社交游戏公司 Playfish 的老板。开发一款新的线上游戏只需花几个月时间和几十万美元。游戏发布之后还可以不断改进。而虚拟化的发行更是便宜，市场营销也一样低成本，因为游戏通常在社区的朋友间大量扩散。

这中间带来的最大变化是出版商的收费方式。虽然有些游戏收取用户一定的订阅费或是出售广告，但许多出版商的收益来自管理一个线上经济模式，再加上虚拟的物品和数字货币。玩是免费的，但用户可以付费购买额外的不同物品来让游戏进行下去。

答案解析

第十三题问的是：在亚洲，什么使在线游戏依然这么流行。与之相关的是原文第二段中的倒数第二句，“a genre that, now complete with fancy graphics, is still very popular, particularly in Asia,” 现在此类游戏借助着精美的影像而显得日益完美并仍然在流行，特别是在亚洲。而 D 选项中的 perfect 和 fancy 意思相近，所以选择 D。

第十四题问的是：视频游戏将都在网上玩的主要原因是什么。原文中的第一段的最后一句，“A combination of new technology and compelling economics means that many, if not most, of them will be played online soon”，新科技和紧迫的经济形式结合在一起意味着许多的游戏都将通过互联网来玩。所以选项 A

“新技术和当前经济的结合”与题目相符。

第十五题问的是：关于线上游戏，最重要的改变是什么？根据文章中的最后一段的第一句话，“The most important change will be in the way publishers earn money”与B项的意思如出一辙，所以选择的是B。

第十六题问的是：在线游戏的经营方式从贩卖软件变为了什么？根据原文中的第三段的第一句话，“video games have begun the transition from an industry primarily based on consoles and shrink-wrapped software to one in which online services dominate”，从这句话中很明显可以看出答案是C。

第十七题问的是：社交类游戏的受喜爱趋势不够强的原因是什么？原文中第五段中有一句提到“These are more about interaction than action”，这类游戏是互动类而非动作类的。与句意相符的是选项C。

第十八题问的是：与常规的游戏相比，线上游戏的一个不同点在于什么？第七段最后一句中提到“vrtual distribution is far cheaper, and marketing tends to be too, since games often spread ‘virally’ among friends on social networks”，所以选择D。

PART FOUR

Questions 19-33

参考答案

19 C　**20** B　**21** A　**22** C　**23** A　**24** D　**25** B　**26** D　**27** D
28 D　**29** A　**30** B　**31** C　**32** D　**33** A

参考译文

规划股份投资

我们周围不乏情报贩子，向人们提供迅速发财致富的机遇。但是，如果你是一个认真的私人投资者，就把拉斯维加斯的心态留给那些有钱可供挥霍的人。认真的投资者需要一份正规的投资组合表——一种计划很周密的投资选择，结构明确，目标清晰。但是，一个股票市场的新手又如何能做到这一点呢？

如果你去向5位有威望的股票经纪人咨询，询问你应该如何使用你的资金，你很可能得到5种不同的答复，即使你提供了所有关于你的年龄、家庭、财源和你想从投资中获得的好处的信息。这是个道德问题吗？没有一种安全“正确”的方法来排列这种投资组合，然而，却毫无疑问地有几种错误的方法。可以相信5位经纪人中不会有人建议你把全部（或一部分）资金投入佩里威格斯公司。

那么你该怎么做呢？我们假定你已把基本情况弄清楚了，如抵押贷款、养老金、保险金和动用现金储备的机会。然后，你一定要建立起自己的目标。这里一方面是个人所处的环境，另一方面是心理学的问题。

比如说，如果你年纪较大，你从重大投资损失中恢复过来的时间就较少，你就很希望能够提高你的养老金收入。因此，你的首要任务就是保护你的资金和带来额外的收入。在这种情况下，你大概想制定出一份包括某些股份（但不是风险很大的股份）的投资组合，同时还有高度可靠的证券、现金储蓄，可能还有可换证券，或分割资本信托公司的所得股。

如果你年轻一些，并且经济状况可靠，你可能会采取一种积极的方式——你必须性格开朗，不会因股票价格的浮动而夜不能眠。如果你觉得你的情况是这样的话，你可在投资组合中包括几项有令人陶醉的增值前景的增长股，和其他比较平淡的投资项目放在一起。一旦你的投资目标确立以后，你就可以决定你的钱投向何处。这里的指导原则是：分散你的投资风险。如果你把所有资金投入佩里威格斯国际公司，你就把自己当成了命运的人质。

答案解析

第十九题，此题考查的是固定短语，“把……留给……”，leave something to somebody，所以选择 C 选项。

第二十题，此题考查的是 with 引导的伴随状语，所以正确答案是 B。

第二十一题，此题考查的是句子之间的关系连词。此空的前一句提到如何更好地投资，后面涉及的是新手又如何能很快地成功掌握这一点。前后是转折关系，所以选择 A。

第二十二题，此句考查的是固定短语，what 与 do with 连用，表示“处理 sth.”。D 选项中的 deal with 与 how 连用时，也可以表示“处理 sth.”。所以正确答案是 C。

第二十三题，此句考查的是考生对句子间连接词的应用。由于上下文是转折关系，并且空的后面用逗号隔开，选项 A 符合要求。既表示转折，后面又必须接逗号。

第二十四题，此题考查代词 none 的用法。根据原文的意思，这里的代词应该用否定形式的。看选项，只有 D 符合要求。所以选择 D，表示全部否定。

第二十五题，此题考查的是固定短语，suggest doing something，表示“建议做 sth.”的意思。所以选择 B。

第二十六题，此题考查的是词汇搭配。sort out 是“整理好，弄清楚”的意思。整句话的意思是“我们假定你已把基本情况弄清楚了”，所以选择 D。

第二十七题，此题考查的是词汇辨析。A、B 和 D 都表示方式、方法，但搭配同。只有 D，assess 与 to 搭配。所以选择 D。

第二十八题，考查的是词汇理解题。根据原文的意思，选择 D：“如果你年纪较大，你从重大投资损失中恢复过来的时间就较少，你就很希望能够提高你的养老金收入”。

第二十九题，考查的是连接词。or 表示选择，符合原句的意思，所以答案是 A。

第三十题，考查的是词汇。B 选项是“有进取精神的，有干劲的”，符合题意。

第三十一题，考查的是词汇。C 表示“受失眠的煎熬”。

第三十二题，考查的是固定短语 decide on，表示“做决定”，所以选择的是 D。

第三十三题，考查的是关系副词的用法。根据句意，这里应该选择的是 A：“一旦你的投资目标确立以后，你就可以决定你的钱投向何处。”

PART FIVE

Questions 34-45

参考答案

34. been	35. like	36. pessimism	37. Correct	38. and	39. company
40. that	41. recently	42. buys	43. Correct	44. with	45. got used

答案解析

第三十四题去掉 been，这句话的意思是“美国经济衰退已经结束”，无须被动语态。

第三十五题，此处应是 likely，be like 意为“像”，后接具体名词，不符合题意，应改为 be likely (to)“有可能……；有……的倾向”。这句话的意思是：“他告诉华盛顿的一个智囊团，从技术角度而言，经济衰退可能结束了。”

第三十六题，pessimism 应改为 optimism，结合后文 a steady rise 判断此句话应是正面意义。这句话的意思是“华尔街与曾在过去六个月稳定上升的道琼斯共享该乐观的状况”。

第三十七题，正确。

第三十八题去掉 and，a partner with Redpoint Ventures 与 a firm specialising in internet start-ups 都是用来修饰前文中的 Satish Dharmaraj，若用 and 则表示分别修饰两个人，因而此处的 and 多余。

第三十九题，company 应为复数形式 companies，an enormous amount 后应该修饰可数名词复数。

第四十题，that 改为 which，这句话应该是非限定定语从句，that 不可以用来引导非限定性定语从句，因此应该用 which 来指代前文中的整句话。Mr. Dharmaraj 告诉 BBC 新闻“我们正看到大量优秀公司的出现，一些优秀的人离开他们的公司加入到这项新事业中，而这通常是信心的标志。”

第四十一题，Recently 应改为 Recent，此处修饰 acquisitions，应该用形容词来修饰名词。

第四十二题，buys 应改为 buying，分析前文发现整句话中已经有谓语 include，因而此处只能做独立主格，这是由一个 Adobe 做逻辑主语、buy 做逻辑谓语的独立主格结构。

第四十三题，正确。

第四十四题，with 后加 it。分析这句话我们发现，若 the urge to splurge 做了 with 的宾语，整句话就缺失主语，因此 the urge to splurge 只能做整句话的主语，而 with 后面要用 it 来指代前文。

第四十五题，got used to，固定搭配，译为“（过去）习惯于”。

WRITING 45 minutes

PART ONE

范 文

Dear all,

We are going to launch promotional activities on a perfume product which may attract women aged 20-30. We now have a fund of 3, 000 dollars for marketing events. Please meet at the conference room at 9 a. m. on the following Monday to brainstorm ideas for possible activities.

范文解析

在本文写作中，首先要注意，本文文体类型是 Email，字数限制是 40-50 词，然后根据 email 的格式要求以及常用句式安排全文。

公司想要对新产品进行营销宣传，营销经理将产品的目标顾客、营销预算以及营销策略告知营销成员。对于本文的写作，考生要注意根据题目中的三点内容联句成文，不可漏掉题目中所给的三点信息。

PART TWO

范 文

Report on: Launching the New Car Series

Introduction

This report sets out to analyze and evaluate the possibility of launching our new car series in the targeted city and the feasibility of achieving our sales target.

Findings

The local economy, which is nearly tripled, has well-enhanced the confidence of consumers, and the size of the city itself has increased consistently with the economy. However, the number of agents of car sales has been temporarily ignored.

The desire for car purchase has been pushed up and the increase in personal income altogether makes the car more affordable for the career managers and white collars. Moreover, the further expansion of city size plus the relocation of some companies, add up to more need for vehicles.

Conclusion

The market is ready and time is appropriate.

Recommendations

We should buildup distribution channels for launching and enroll agents ahead of competitors.

范文解析

在本文写作中，首先要注意，本文文体类型是 report，字数限制是 120 ~ 140 词，然后根据 report 的格式要求以及常用句式安排全文。

公司要将新产品投放市场，在投放之前先进行了市场调查和分析，进而做可行性分析报告。题目中给出了调查得出的各项数据，以图表的形式展示，并且对相关重要内容进行标注。考生在写作时，主要注意标注的内容，其次对柱状图和表格的数据进行分析。报告的主体部分是 Findings。Findings 的第一个分析结论来自对柱状图和表格的共同分析得出，认为地方经济的发展带动了消费者的消费欲望，并且城市的大小也与经济的发展有着密切联系。(这两点根据常识也可以得出)，接着分析了目标客户对于汽车的需求(这才是报告要分析的重点)，汽车产品投放后的前景也进行了分析，对于该可行性报告，重点要分析的内容是产品投放的目标人群和目标市场的情况。

最后根据分析得出结论：产品投放的市场和时机都非常好，应该进行多渠道分销并且抢在竞争对手之前设立代理商。

LISTENING 40 minutes (including 10 minutes' transfer time)

PART ONE

Conversation One

参考答案

(1) Unit 5 (2) 10 (3) thursday (4) invoice

听力原文

A = Initial Business Suppliers B = Lacey

A: Initial Business Suppliers. Good morning.

B: Good morning. This is Lacey. I'd like to place an order, please.

A: OK. I'll just get an order form. Right now, it's Lacey?

B: That's right. We have an account with you.

A: Sorry. I didn't know. I'm new here.

B: Oh. That's OK.

A: Could you give me your address, please?

B: Yes. Of course. It's Unit 5, Hailsham Industrial Estate.

A: And that's the delivery address?

B: Yes.

A: And could I have your name, please?

B: Well. I'm Lacey, but I'd like you to address it to the "Office Manager", please.

A: OK. Fine. Now what's the order for?

B: We'd like 10 boxes of printer paper.

A: I can get it to you on Thursday, if you like.

B: That's great. Thanks.

A: And how will you be paying?

B: well. You usually send us on invoice.

A: OK. And that's to the same address?

B: That's right.

答案解析

（1） 此处需要填写地址，这段对话是女士在订购打印纸，对话中她说到“It's Unit 5, Hailsham Industrial Estate”，故可知答案。

（2） 此处填写订购产品的数量，从文中容易得到答案，“We'd like 10 boxes of printer paper”为关键句。

（3） 对话中男士说到了货物到达的时间会是周二。

（4） 说到支付方式时，女士说到“You usually send us on invoice”，可以知道是通过发票的方式。

Conversation Two

参考答案

（5） Regional Manager　（6） quality　（7） reference　（8） April 26th

听力原文

S = Sarah　D = David

S: Hello, David. It's Sarah.

D: Hello. Sarah.

S: David. I'm just going over my notes for the advertisement we're putting in the paper. There are still one or two bits of information I need.

D: OK. What do you need to know?

S: Well, you still haven't given me the final job title yet.

D: Oh, sorry. The job title should be Regional Manager.

S: And what salary should I put?

D: Well, it depends on the quality of the candidate, really. Just put "competitive salary plus benefits". What we'll ask them to do is send details of their current salary and we'll go from there.

S: So you want me to put that in the advertisement as well?

D: Yes. And it should be bit about applicants including their CVs and reference.

S: OK. And have you decided when you'll be holding interview?

D: Yes. It'll be the next week in April 25th?

S: No. I think 26th is good, actually.

D: OK.

S: Right, David. I think that's everything. Thanks.

答案解析

（5） 此段对话是两个人在谈论关于公司招聘员工的广告内容。男士说到“The job title should be Regional Manager.”可以得知他们要招聘的职位是区域经理。

（6） 在谈到什么样的薪水时，男士说到“it depends on the quality of the candidate,”是说这取决于员工的素质。

（7） 除了需要求职者的简历外，还要推荐信。其中CV译为“简历”，reference为“推荐信”。

（8） 文中男士问到面试的时间是否是4月25日时，女士提出在26日，故答案是4月26日。

Conversation Three

参考答案

(**9**) diary　　(**10**) Delorme　　(**11**) production director　　(**12**) his company

听力原文

A = Anna　　R = Roger

A: Good morning.

R: Hello, Anna,

A: Oh, hello, Roger.

R: I'm glad I caught you. Listen, I'm at the airport, and I've just realized I've left my diary in the office. You can't see it anywhere, can you?

A: Hang on. Here it is.

R: Oh, great. Now can you have a look at tomorrow? I've got an appointment at eleven-thirty with a customer. But what's the name of the woman I'm seeing?

A: It's Delorme.

R: That's it. It had gone right out of my head. Is that D-E-L-O-R-M-E?

A: That's right.

R: And what's her position of the company, exactly?

A: She's a Production Director.

R: That's it. Right. Then in the afternoon, I'm meeting Raymond at 3:30. But I can't remember whether we agreed to meet at his company or the hotel.

A: Well. There's nothing here about the hotel.

R: Right. Then it must be at his company. Sorry, Anna, I'll have to go. My plane's boarding.

A: OK, Roger. Oh, Before you go, don't forget that on Friday you'll need to confirm your flight to Rome.

R: Thanks. I'll make a note of it.

答案解析

(**9**) 这段对话是女士在上飞机前对同事安排一些工作内容，其中她说 "and I've just realized I've left my diary in the office"，可以得知她把日志忘在了办公室里。

(**10**) 女士明天要见一位顾客，从随后的拼写中我们可以得知她的姓名和职位是生产部主任。

(**11**) production director。

(**12**) 在3：30女士将见另外一个人Raymond，她忘记了在哪里见面，之后从 "A: Well. There's nothing here about the hotel. R: Right. Then it must be at his company." 这段对话可以确定是在公司见面。

PART TWO

Section One

参考答案

(**13**) B　　(**14**) A　　(**15**) D　　(**16**) G　　(**17**) E

听力原文

13 I'm interested in seeing the new mid-sized car you've been advertizing. I'm sorry I forgot the name, but I have seen it as a friend of mine has bought one. It's a racing car and it's very light, I remember. I want it in black.

14 Now, let's look at the loose filling. Oh! I'm surprised it didn't fall out, because there's a great deal of decay around it. There's also a slight cavity in another tooth. It may take considerable drilling.

15 I don't know what I'm going to find in the car. I promise that I'll check it thoroughly. For example, if your condenser becomes worn out. I'll call you and recommend that you let me put in a new one. I won't do this before we've talked about it.

16 Please take off your coat and roll up your sleeve. I want to take your blood pressure. Yes, your pressure is a little bit high. There is nothing to be alarmed about it. But you'd better get rid of those junk foods and do more exercise.

17 I represent a new but growing firm in this area. We sell all kinds of stationary supplies: various kinds of pens, pencils desk sets, file holders and whatever you mention. Here are samples of our new products. We guarantee prompt delivery and the best products.

答案解析

（**13**） 从"I'm interested in seeing the new mid-sized car you've been advertizing."一句可以得知，此人是看了广告上的汽车后进行咨询的，他是想买一辆黑色的赛车，因此可以推断出他是顾客。

（**14**） 此题很容易从 tooth 一词推断出这个人是一名牙医，他在给病人看牙。

（**15**） 从"For example, if your condenser becomes worn out , I'll call you and recommend that you let me put in a new one."这句可以推断出，此人是在讨论汽车部件的维修问题，可以判断出他是名机械工人。

（**16**） 从"Please take off your coat and roll up your sleeve. I want to take your blood pressure."这句话，我们可以得知这是医生在给病人测量血压，故选 G。

（**17**） 此人说到"I represent a new but growing firm in this area. We sell all kinds of stationary supplies"，表明他在介绍自己公司所经营的产品。可知他的身份是销售人员。

Section Two

参考答案

18 D　**19** B　**20** C　**21** F　**22** H

听力原文

18 Your car has been sluggish since it's been too long since your last tune-up. So your car doesn't really need the higher octane. You should still use regular unleaded. It won't pay to get the more expensive kind.

19 I think I'm catching a bad cold today. I have a headache. I've got a sore throat. I even cough some of the time and ache all over. Do you have a cold capsule and some cough syrup? I hope I can go to work tomorrow after taking all these. Could you recommend something?

20 These green and hard bananas aren't ripe enough to eat. These are overripe; they're soft with brown spots. The overripe ones are firm and just right for eating. If you want to cook with bananas, the overripe are fine.

21 Welcome to our chain store. We specialize in hamburgers and chicken. And we're having an introductory special. You can get free French fries with every sandwich order. Here is the coupon.

22 There are so many options to make I'm not sure which kind of glass to choose. And besides there is no specific introduction on the goods. I need to ask the seller.

答案解析

18 根据"Your car has been sluggish since it's been too long since your last tune-up"，男士说汽车从上次加油以后就变得行动迟缓，故可判断地点应该在加油站。

19 文中人物说了自己的感冒症状，之后他问到"Do you have a cold capsule and some cough syrup?"可以推断出他是在买药，因此说话地点是药店。故选 B。

20 文中介绍了香蕉的一些质量问题，可以推断此人是在食杂商店。

21 从"Welcome to our chain store. We specialize in hamburgers and chicken."这句便可得知，此人是餐馆的人员，故选 F。

22 文中人物说到有好多种类的玻璃杯，无法决定购买哪种，而且没有详细的商品介绍，可以推断出说话地点应该是在超市。

PART THREE

参考答案

23 A　**24** C　**25** B　**26** A　**27** B　**28** C　**29** A　**30** C

听力原文

Luke: Reception. Can I help you?

Male guest: Hello, yes, this is Mr. Taylor in room 418. All the lights seem to have gone out.

Luke: Yes, I am sorry about this, sir. Our electrician is investigating the problem right now. We should have normal power in a few minutes. I do apologize for any inconvenience.

Male guest: Oh, well, is there any chance of getting something to eat and drink sent up to my room whilst we're waiting for it to come back on?

Luke : Well, I'm not sure if we have any power to do any hot food sir, but I can certainly send some sandwiches up to your room now... Oh, there we are sir, the emergency generator has kicked in now — the lights are back on. So, er, what exactly would you like sent up sir?

Male guest: Well, can I have some smoked salmon sandwiches (we don't need anything hot right now) and a nice cold bottle of Chablis, please, and two glasses, please.

Luke: Yes, of course, sir, smoked salmon sandwiches and a bottle of our Chablis. I'll get that organized right away. Thanks very much sir. Bye bye.

Luke: Hello, Madam, can I help you?

Female guest: Yes, I'd like to check in, can I? Is there a problem?

Luke: I'm afraid we've just had a temporary problem with our electricity supply madam, so our computers are down at the moment. That means I can't give you your room card until the computers are back on again, but in the meantime, would you mind filling in this form?

Female guest: Okay, but what am I going to do? I don't want to hang around waiting for your computers to come back on.

Luke: No, of course not, madam. Please accept my apologies for the inconvenience. May I suggest that you relax in the main bar with a drink of your choice, compliments of the hotel? I'll phone through to our bar staff to make sure they don't charge you. And I'll come and call you when the computers are back on and we can check you in properly.

Female guest: That's a good idea. Thank you!

Luke: You're more than welcome, madam. And I do apologize again.

(The female guest leaves and then a male guest arrives at the reception)

Luke: Yes, sir?

Male guest: Hello, I've just come down from room 208. There are still no towels in my room I'm afraid. I did call you about it earlier.

Luke: Yes, indeed, sir. I'll get onto housekeeping about it right away.

Male guest: And I'm wanting to have a look around the town. Have you any suggestions where I should start.

Luke: Well, here is a map of the town sir. You're very welcome to this. Now we are here, you see, and if I were you, I would go along to the front... here... and walk along until you come to the main pier. That's quite interesting in itself — it's got a funfair on it and lots of rides and games.

Male guest: Er, no... I... I don't think that's quite me.

答案解析

23 细节题。由“this is Mr. Taylor in room 418”可知。

24 细节题。由“All the lights seem to have gone out.”可知，C项是主要原因，文中也提及A、B项，但并不是主要原因，因此最佳答案为C。

25 由“a nice cold bottle of Chablis, please, and two glasses, please.”可知，Mr. Taylor想要一瓶酒，两个玻璃杯。

26 细节题。由“I'm afraid we've just had a temporary problem with our electricity supply madam, so our computers are down at the moment.”可知。

27 由“May I suggest that you relax in the main bar with a drink of your choice”可知答案为B，女客人不想徘徊等待，所以Luck建议去大厅休息一下。

28 由“May I suggest that you relax in the main bar with a drink of your choice, compliments of the hotel?”可知，饮品由酒店免费提供，作为停电给顾客带来不便的赔偿。

29 细节题。由“Hello, I've just come down from room 208. There are still no towels in my room I'm afraid. I did call you about it earlier.”可知。

30 由“I'm wanting to have a look around the town. Have you any suggestions where I should start.”可知答案为C。A项不选，因为文中直说没有毛巾，并没有提及要洗澡。B项的酒是Mr. Taylor要的，也就是在418房间的男客人，不是208房间的。

SPEAKING 14 minutes

PART ONE（略）

PART TWO

Topic A

Main points:

One important factor in choosing a hotel on a business trip is the location. It depends on the purpose of your trip and your personal preference: if you travel a lot within a city, you will find a hotel with facilitate transport connections quite convenient for you; but on the other hand, a hotel in a central business district may be noisy, and most of the time, you may have to face traffic jam on your way in and out.

Facilities provided are another important factor to consider. The hotel you choose should come equipped to handle standard business needs, such as telephones, Internet access, data/fax modem ports and meeting rooms. These facilities can guarantee you the normal business activities.

Of course, besides the factors above, there are other things you may care like a timely dry-cleaning service, workout facilities and maybe delicious foods to your taste.

Topic B

Main points:

First of all, we have to be clear about the purpose of our trip. Then we can prepare for the trip accordingly. For example, if it is a business visit to another company for a potential contract, we'll have to think beforehand who we're going to meet with, what to discuss and how to promote our business.

Secondly, travel arrangement is very important. If time allowed, we'd book the tickets in advance to avoid some unnecessary worry especially when a transfer occurs. If we can make sure the exact returning date we can book the return air tickets, which can also save us some trouble and money.

In addition, we should also give a thought to the luggage we take with ourselves. We should keep our luggage light and secured. Well-prepared and travelling light, we can make our business trip both rewarding and delight.

Topic C

Main points:

In selecting a travel agency for business trips, what counts is the reputation of an agency. Whether the agency is reliable and offers high-quality service are essential for the success of your business trip. So you need to find out the specialties and experience of an agency before making the decision.

Speed of service is also very important. Speed means you can save some valuable time in business, which also means business opportunities. Sometimes when an urgent trip is to make, you will need a quick-response travel agency to deal with a last-minute airline booking for you.

Discounts are always something preferable. This can minimize your travel expenses without sacrificing comfort and efficiency.

PART THREE

A: You know our company is planning to reduce the travel budget. Do you have any suggestions on that?

B: Yes, I think that's because we spent too much on travel when we could have spent less.

A: In my opinion, one of the best ways to cut the costs of business trips is not to take some trips in the first place.

B: You mean reducing the total number of business trips?

A: Indeed, some of the trips are not that necessary. I think we should stop participating the unnecessary conferences, and we can avoid many of the traveling if we make full use of the modern high-tech such as videoconferencing can save lots of the travel budgets for our company.

B: Exactly. You know, some of the face-to-face talks may simply be replaced by a conference call and some travels can be arranged at a later date in conjunction with other trips.

A: For some trips we have to make, there are also some ways to reduce the costs.

B: Yeah. In my opinion, saving should start from choosing the right transportation means in the first place. We should always consider the cheaper ways of getting around by train and bus. When we have to travel by plane, avoid a last-minute booking could also enable us to select a cheaper ticket.

A: I see what you mean. Generally, the cheaper the air ticket, the less flexible it is. The cheapest fares do not allow one to make any changes to his booking. So we can save some money by planning business trips ahead and using a less flexible ticket.

B: You're right. Accomodation is also a major travel expense. I think our company should encourage our staff to stay in nice hotels instead of expensive ones, which can save us a lot of the travel budget.

A: When it comes to local transport, I think we could still save some budget by taking a taxi instead of a chauffeured car.

B: Yes. If we could all keep in mind of saving, I believe we can reduce our travel costs substantially.

Follow-on questions

- Do you think there will be any negative effect on a company's performance if there is a reduction in business travel (Why? / Why not)?
  Well, I don't think a little reduction in business travel will make much difference since many contacts with the clients can be done through phone calls or e-mails.
  That depends. In countries like China where people strongly believe in personal contact, a reduction in business travel may bring about some negative effects.
- How to prevent employees spending more than they are supposed to during business travel?
  An effective way would be to have one set procedure for all employees to follow for business travel expenses. Pick a simplest financial software system that serves your business travel needs and then have everyone from the top down follow it exactly.
- Do you think companies are willing to pay extra for business class travel (Why? / Why not)?
  Yes, especially for their executives. Business class is a symbol of status and strength and may enhance the company image.
  No, I don't think so. Unless when it is necessary, no companies would be willing to pay extra for business class travel since it means increase of costs.
- How important is it to plan the itinerary before starting a business trip? (Why?)
  It's very important. A well-planned itinerary enables a traveller to make the best possible use of time on travel.
- What's the most cost-effective way to reduce costs for business travellers?
  I think the most cost-effective way would be to look for better-value hotels as well as cheaper flights.

附录 II　听力中常见英语单词

abroad *adv*. 在国外，出国；广泛流传
absence *n*. 缺席，离开
absent *adj*. 不在的，不参与的
absenteeism *n*. 旷工，旷职
absorb *v*. 吸收；减轻（冲击、困难等）
abstract *n*. 摘要
access *n*. 接近（或进入）的机会，享用权
accommodation *n*. 设施；住宿
account *n*. 会计账目
accountancy *n*. 会计工作
accountant *n*. 会计
accounts *n*. 往来账目
account for 解释，说明
account executive（广告公司）客户经理
accrual *n*. 增值，增长
achieve *v*. 获得，达到，实现，完成
acknowledge *v*. 承认；告知已收到（某物）
acquire *v*. 获得，得到
acquisition *n*. 收购；被收购的公司或股份
acting *adj*. 代理的
activity *n*. 业务类型
actual *adj*. 实在的，实际的，确实的
adapt *v*. 修改，适应
adjust *v*. 整理，使适应
administration *n*. 实施；经营；行政
administer *v*. 管理，实施
adopt *v*. 采纳，批准；挑选某人做候选人
advertise *v*. 公布，做广告
ad *n*. 广告
advertisement *n*. 出公告，做广告
advertising *n*. 广告业
after-sales service 售后服务
agenda *n*. 议事日程
agent *n*. 代理人，经纪人
allocate *v*. 分配，配给
amalgamation *n*. 合并，重组
ambition *n*. 强烈的欲望，野心
amortize *v*. 摊还
analyze *v*. 分析，研究
analysis *n*. 分析，分析结果的报告
analyst *n*. 分析家，化验员
annual *adj*. 每年的，按年度计算的
annual general meeting（AGM）股东年会
anticipate *v*. 期望
anticipated *adj*. 期待的
appeal *n*. 吸引力
apply *v*. 申请，请求；应用，运用
applicant *n*. 申请人
application *n*. 申请，施用，实施
appointee *n*. 被任命人
appraisal *n*. 估量，估价
appreciate *v*. 赏识；体谅；增值
appropriate *v*. 拨出（款项）
approve *v*. 赞成，同意，批准
aptitude *n*. 天资，才能
arbitrage *n*. 套利
arbitration *n*. 仲裁
arrears *n*. 欠账
assemble *v*. 收集，集合
assembly-line *n*. 装配线，流水作业线
assess *v*. 评定，估价
asset *n*. 资产
　current assets 流动资产
　fixed assets 固定资产
　frozen assets 冻结资产
　intangible assets 无形资产
　liquid assets 速动资产
　tangible assets 有形资产
assist *v*. 援助，协助，出席
audit *n*. 查账，审计

automate *v.* 使某事物自动操作
average *n.* 平均，平均水准
awareness *n.* 意识；警觉

B

backing *n.* 财务支持，赞助
backhander *n.* 贿赂
backlog *n.* 积压（工作或订货）
bad debt 死账（无法收回的欠款）
balance *n.* 收支差额，余额
balance of payments 贸易支付差额
balance sheet 资产负债表
bankrupt *adj.* 破产的
bankruptcy *n.* 破产
bank statement *n.* 银行结算清单，对账单
bar chart 条形图，柱状图
bargain *v.* 谈判，讲价
base *n.* 基地，根据地
batch *n.* 一批，一组，一群
batch production 批量生产
bear market 熊市
beat *v.* 超过，胜过
behave *v.* 表现；运转
behaviour *n.* 举止，行为；运转情况
benchmark *n.* 衡量标准
benefit *n.* 利益，补助金，保险金得益
  fringe benefits 附加福利
  sickness benefit 疾病补助费
bid *n.* 出价，投标
takeover bid 盘进，出价
bill *n.* 账单，票据
billboard *n.*（路边）广告牌，招贴板
black *adj.* 违法的
  in the black 有盈余
black list 黑名单，禁止贸易的名单
Black Monday 黑色星期一（指1987年10月国际股票市场崩溃的日子）
blue chips 蓝筹股，绩优股
blue-collar *adj.* 蓝领（工人）的
Board of Directors 董事会
bond *n.* 债券
bonus *n.* 津贴，红利
books *n.* 公司账目
book value 账面价值，（公司或股票）净值
bookkeeper *n.* 簿记员，记账人
boom *n.* 繁荣，暴涨
boost *v.* 提高，增加，宣扬
bottleneck *n.* 瓶颈，窄路，阻碍
bottom *adj.* 最后的，根本的
brainstorm *n.* /*v.* 点子会议；献计献策
branch *n.* 分支，分部
brand *n.* 商标，品牌
brand leader 占市场最大份额的品牌，名牌
brand loyalty（消费者）对品牌的忠实
break even 收支相抵，不亏不盈
break even point 收支相抵点，盈亏平衡点
breakthrough *n.* 突破
brief *n.* 摘要
brochure *n.* 小册子
broker *n.* 经纪人，代理人
bull market 牛市
budget *n.* 预算
bulk *n.* 大量（货物） *adj.* 大量的
bust *adj.* 破了产的
buyout *n.* 买下全部产权

C

CAD 计算机辅助设计
call *n.* 打电话
call on *v.* 呼吁；约请；拜访
campaign *n.* 战役，运动
candidate *n.* 求职者，候选人
canteen *n.* 食堂
canvass *v.* 征求意见，劝说
capacity *n.* 生产额，（最大）产量
caption *n.*（照片或图片下的）简短说明
capital *n.* 资本，资金
capture *v.* 赢得
cash *n.* 现金，现付款 *v.* 兑现
cash flow 现金流量
case study 案例分析
catalogue *n.* 目录，产品目录
catastrophe *n.* 大灾难，大祸
CEO（Chief Executive Officer）（美）总经理
chain *n.* 连锁店
challenger *n.* 挑战者
channel *n.*（商品流通的）渠道
charge *v.* 使承担；要（价）
chart *n.* 图表
checkout *n.* 付款台

chief *adj.* 主要的，首席的，总的
CIF, c. i. f. 成本保险费加运费
circular *n.* 传阅的小册子（传单等）
circulate *v.* 传阅
claim *n.* /*v.* 要求，索赔
client *n.* 委托人，顾客
cold *adj.* 没人找上门来的，生意清淡的
commercialise *v.* 使商品化
commission *n.* 佣金
commitment *n.* 承诺
commodity *n.* 商品，货物
company *n.* 公司
limited company（Ltd.）股份有限公司
public limited company 股票上市公司
compensate *v.* 补偿，酬报
compensation *n.* 补偿，酬金
compete *v.* 比赛，竞争
competition *n.* 比赛，竞争
competitor *n.* 竞争者，对手
competitive *adj.* 竞争性的
component *n.* 机器元件，组件，部件，部分
concentrated marketing 集中营销策略
condition *n.* 条件，状况
configuration *n.* 设备的结构，组合
conflict *n.* 冲突，争论
conglomerate *n.* 综合商社，多元化集团公司
consolidate *v.* 账目合并
consortium *n.* 财团
constant *adj.* 恒定的，不断的，经常的
consultant *n.* 咨询人员，顾问，会诊医生
consumables *n.* 消耗品
consumer durables 耐用消费品
consumer goods *n.* 消费品，生活资料
contingency *n.* 意外事件
continuum *n.* 连续时间
contract *n.* 合同，契约
contractor *n.* 承办商，承建人
contribute *v.* 提供，捐献
contribution *n.* 贡献，捐献，税
conversion *n.* 改装，改造
conveyor *n.* 运送，传递，转让
core time（弹性工作制的）基本上班时间
cost *n.* 成本
  fixed costs 固定成本
  running costs 日常管理费用
  variable costs 可变成本
cost-effective *adj.* 合算的，有效益的
costing *n.* 成本计算，成本会计
credit *n.* 赊购，赊购制度
  credit control 赊销管理
  letter of credit 信用证
  credit limit 赊销限额
  credit rating 信贷的信用等级，信誉评价
creditor *n.* 债权人，贷方
creditworthiness *n.* 信贷价值，信贷信用
crisis *n.* 危机，转折点
critical *adj.* 关键的
critical path analysis 关键途径分析法
currency *n.* 货币，流通
current *adj.* 通用的，现行的
  current account 往来账户，活期（存款）户
  current assets 流动资产
  current liabilities 流动负债
customise *v.* 按顾客的具体要求制造
cut-throat *adj.* 残酷的，激烈的
cut-price *adj.* 削价（出售）的
CV（=curriculum vitae）简历，履历
cycle time 循环时间

D

damages *n.* 损害，损失
deadline *n.* 最后期限
deal *n.* 营业协议；数量 *v.* 交易
dealer *n.* 商人
debit *n.* 借方，欠的钱
debt *n.* 欠款，债务
  to get into debt 负债
  to be out of debt 不欠债
  to pay off a debt 还清债务
debtor *n.* 债务人
  aged debtors 长期债务人
declare *v.* 申报，声明
decline *n.* /*v.* 衰退，缓慢，下降
decrease *v.* 减少
deduct *v.* 扣除，减去
default *n.* 违约，未履行
defect *n.* 缺陷
defective *adj.* 有缺点的
defer *v.* 推迟
deferred payments 延期支付

deficit *n.* 赤字
delivery cycle 交货周期
demand management 需求规划
demotivated *adj.* 消极的，冷淡的
deposit *n.* 储蓄，预付（定金）
depot *n.* 仓库
depreciate *v.* 贬值，（对资产）折旧
depressing *adj.* 令人沮丧的
deputy *n.* 代理人，副职，代理
devalue *v.* 货币贬值（相对于其他货币）
diet *n.* 饮食，食物，特种饮食
differentiation *n.* 区分，鉴别
dimensions *n.* 尺寸，面积，规模
direct *v.* 管理，指导
director *n.* 经理，主管
Managing Director 总经理，业务主任
direct cost 直接成本
direct mail 直接邮件
direct selling 直销，直接销售
directory *n.* 指南，号码簿
discount *n.* 折扣，贴现
dismiss *v.* 让……离开，打发走
dismissal *n.* 打发走
dispatch *n.*/*v.* 调遣
display *n.*/*v.* 展出，显示
dispose *v.* 安排，处理（事务）
dispose of 去掉，清除
distribution *n.* 分配，分发，分送产品
diversify *v.* 从事多种经营；多样化
divest *v.* 剥夺
dividend *n.* 股息，红利，年息
division *n.* 部门
dog *n.* 滞销品
down-market *a.*/*ad.* 低档商品的
down-time/downtime *n.* 设备闲置期
DP（=Data Processing）计算机数据处理
dramatic *adj.* 戏剧性的
drive *n.* 积极性，能动性
due *adj.* 应付的，预期的
dynamic *adj.* 有活力的

E

earnings *n.* 工资
efficiency *n.* 效率
endorse *v.* 背书，接受
engage *v.* 雇用
entitle *v.* 授权
entitlement *n.* 应得的权利
holiday entitlement 休假权
equity *n.* 股东权益
equity capital 股本
equities 普通股，股票
estimated demand 估计需求
evaluate *v.* 估价，评价
eventual *adj.* 最终的
exaggerate *v.* 夸张
exceed *v.* 超过
exhibit *n.* 展览，表现
expenditure *n.* 花费，支出额
expense *n.* 费用，支出
expense account 费用账户
expenses *n.* 费用，业务津贴
expertise *n.* 专长，专门知识和技能
exposure *n.* 公众对某一产品或公司的知悉

F

facilities *n.* 用于生产的设备，器材
facilities layout 设备的布局规划、计划
facilities location 设备安置
factoring *n.* 折价购买债券
fail-safe system 安全系统
feedback *n.* 反馈，反馈的信息
field *n.* 办公室外边，具体业务
file *n.* 文件集，卷宗，档案，文件
fill *v.* 充任
finance *n.* 资金，财政　*v.* 提供资金
financial *adj.* 财政的
financing *n.* 提供资金，筹措资金
finished goods 制成品
firm *n.* 公司
fire *v.* 解雇
fix *v.* 确定，使固定在
fix up 解决，商妥
fiscal *adj.* 国库的；财政的
flexible *adj.* 有弹性的，灵活的
flextime *n.* 弹性工作时间制
flier（=flyer）*n.* 促销传单
float *v.* 发行；漂浮，飘动
flop *n.* 失败
shop *n.* 车间

fluctuate *v.* 波动，涨落，起伏
FOB, *f. o. b.* 离岸价
follow-up *n.* 细节落实；接连要做的事
forecast *v.* 预测
framework *n.* 框架，结构
franchise *n.* 特许经销权
franchisee *n.* 特许经营人
franchiser *n.* 授予特许经营权者
fraud *n.* 欺骗
freebie *n.* （非正式的）赠品
futures *n.* 期货交易

G

gap *n.* 缺口，空隙
gearing *n.* 配称（即定息债务与股份资本之间的比率）
gimmick *n.* 好主意，好点子
goal *n.* 目标
going *adj.* 进行的，运转中的
going rate 产品的市场价格
goods *n.* 货物，商品
goodwill *n.* 声誉
go public 首次公开发行股票
grapple with 与……搏斗，尽力解决
grievance *n.* 申诉，抱怨
gross *adj.* 总的，毛的
gross margin 毛利率
gross profit 毛利
gross yield 毛收益
gradually *adv.* 逐渐地
group *n.* （由若干公司联合而成的）集团
grow *v.* 增长，扩大
growth *n.* 增长，发展
guarantee *n.* 保证，保单
guidelines *n.* 指导方针，准则

H

hand in 呈送
handle *v.* 经营
hands on 用手操作，手控地
hard sell 强行推销
hazard *n.* 危险，危害行为
head *n.* 主管，负责
health and safety 健康和安全
hedge *n.* 套期保值
hidden *adj.* 隐藏的，不明显的
hierarchy *n.* 等级制度，统治集团，领导层
hire *v.* 雇用
hire purchase *n.* 分期付款购物法
hit *v.* 击中，到达
holder *n.* 持有者
holding company 控股公司
hostile *adj.* 不友好的，恶意的
HRD 人力资源发展部
human resources 人力资源
hype *n.* 天花乱坠的（夸张）广告宣传

I

impact *n.* 冲击，强烈影响
implement *v.* 实施，执行
implication *n.* 隐含意义
incentive *n.* 刺激；鼓励
income *n.* 工资或薪金收入
earned income 劳动收入，劳动所得
unearned income 非劳动收入，投资所得
increment *v.* 定期增加
incur *v.* 招致；承担
index *n.* 指数，索引
retail price index 零售价格指数
indirect costs 间接成本
industrial *adj.* 工业的
industrial action（罢工、怠工）劳工行动
industrial relations 劳资关系
inefficiency *n.* 低效率，不称职
inflate *v.* 抬高（物价），（使通货等）膨胀
inflation *n.* 通货膨胀
infringe *v.* 违法，违章
initial *adj.* 初步的
innovate *v.* 革新
input *n.* 投入
installment *n.* 部分，分期付款
insure *v.* 给……保险，投保
insurance *n.* 保险
interest *n.* 利息，兴趣
interest rate 利率
interim *n.* 中期，过渡期间
intermittent production 阶段性生产
interview *n.* /*v.* 面试
interviewee *n.* 被面试的人
interviewer *n.* 主持面试的人，招聘者

introduce *v.* 介绍；提出
inventory *n.* 库存
buffer inventory 应付突发性需求的存货
capacity inventory 用于将来使用的存货
cycle inventory 循环盘存
decoupling inventory 保险性存货
finished goods inventory 制成品存货（盘存）
pipeline inventory 在途存货
raw materials inventory 原材料存货
invest *v.* 投资
investment *n.* 投资
investor *n.* 投资者
invoice *n.* 发票
irrevocable *adj.* 不可撤销的，不能改变的
issue *n.* 发行股票
rights issue 优先认股权
IT = Information Technology 信息技术
item *n.* 货物；条目，条款

J

job *n.* 工作
job description 工作说明，职务说明
job mobility 工作流动
job rotation 工作轮换
rotation of crops 庄稼轮作
job satisfaction 工作的满意感（自豪感）
joint *adj.* 联合的
joint bank account（几个人的）联合银行存款账户
journal *n.* 专业杂志
jurisdiction *n.* 管辖（权）
junk bonds 低档（风险）债券，垃圾债券
junk mail（未经收信人要求的）直接邮寄的广告宣传
just-in-time *n.* 无库存制度，准时制生产

K

key *adj.* 主要的，关键的
knockdown *adj.*（价格）很低的
know-how *n.* 专门技术，诀窍

L

label *n.* 标签，标牌 *v.* 加标签，加上标牌
labour *n.* 劳动，工作，劳动力
labour market 劳动力市场
labour relations 劳资关系
labour shortage 劳动力短缺
launch *v.* 在市场上推出一种新产品 *n.* 新产品的推出
lay-off/layoff *n.*/*v.* 临时解雇
layout *n.* 工厂的布局
lead *v.* 领先，领导
lead time 完成某项活动所需的时间
leaflet *n.* 广告印刷传单
lease *n.* 租借，租赁物
right to lease or rent 出租权
legal *adj.* 合法的
lend *v.* 出借，贷款
lessee *n.* 承租人
lessor *n.* 出租人
ledger *n.* 分类账
nominal ledger 记名账
purchase ledger 进货
sales ledger 销货账
leverage *n.* 杠杆比率
liability *n.* 负债
liabilities *n.* 债务
licence（US: license）*n.* 许可证
license *v.* 许可，批准
life cycle 寿命周期
likely *adj.* 可能的
line process 流水线（组装）
link *n.* 关系，联系，环
liquid *adj.* 易转换成现款的
liquidate *v.* 清算
liquidity *n.* 拥有变现力
liquidation *n.* 清理（关闭公司），清算
liquidator *n.* 清算人，公司资产清理人
listed *adj.* 登记注册的
listing *n.* 上市公司名录
literature *n.* 印刷品，宣传品
litigate *v.* 提出诉讼
loan *n.*/*v.* 贷款，暂借
logo *n.* 企业的特有标记
lose *v.* 亏损
loser *n.* 失败者
loss *n.* 损失

lot *n.* 批，量
loyalty *n.* 忠诚，忠实

M

magazine *n.* 杂志，期刊
mailshot *n.* 邮购
maintain *v.* 维持，保持
maintenance *n.* 维持，坚持
major *adj.* 重大的，主要的，较大的
majority shareholding 绝对控股
make *n.* 产品的牌子或型号
management *n.* 管理，管理部门
managerial *adj.* 管理人员的
manager *n.* 经理
plant manager 工厂负责人
line manager 基层负责人
staff manager 部门经理助理
management accounts 管理账目
matrix management 矩阵管理
manning *n.* 人员配备
manpower *n.* 劳动力
manpower resources 劳动力资源
manual *adj.* 体力的，人工的，蓝领的
manufacture *v.* （用机器）制造
manufacturer *n.* 制造者（厂、商、公司）
manufacturing *adj.* 制造的
manufacturing industry 制造业
margin *n.* 利润
gross margin 毛利率
net margin 净利润
mark-up *v.* 标高售价，加价
market *n.* 市场；产品可能的销量
down market 低档市场
up market 高档市场
marketing mix 综合营销策略
market leader 市场上的主导公司
market niche 小摊位
market penetration 市场渗入
market segmentation 市场划分
market share 市场占有率，市场份额
mass-marketing *n.* 大众营销术
master production schedule 生产计划
materials handling 材料管理，材料控制
maximise *v.* 使增至最大限度
measure *n.* 措施，步骤
media *n.* 新闻工具，传媒
mass media 大众传媒（如电视、广播、报纸）
merge *v.* 联合，合并
merger *n.* （公司、企业等的）合并
merit *n.* 优点，值得，应受
method study 方法研究
middleman *n.* 中间人，经纪人
full milk 全脂牛奶
skimmed milk 脱脂乳
minimise *v.* 使减至最小限度，最小化
mission *n.* 公司的长期目标和原则
mobility *n.* 流动性，可移性
moderately *adv.* 中等地，适度地
monopoly *n.* 垄断，独占
mortgage *n.*/*v.* 抵押
motivate *v.* 激励，激发……的积极性
motivated *adj.* 有积极性的
motivation *n.* 提供动机，积极性，动力
motive *n.* 动机

N

negotiate *v.* 谈判
negotiable *adj.* 可谈判的，可转让的
net *adj.* 净的，纯的
network *n.* 网络
niche *n.* 专业市场中的小摊位
notice *n.* 通知，辞职申请，离职通知

O

objective *n.* 目标，目的
obsolete *adj.* 过时的，淘汰的，废弃的
offer *n.* 报价，发盘
offer *v.* 开价
off-season *adj.*/*adv.* 淡季的（地）
off-the-shelf *adj.* 非专门设计的
off-the-peg *adj.* 标准的，非顾客化的
opening *n.* 空位
operate *v.* 操作，经营，管理
operating profits 营业利润
operations chart 经营（管理）表
operations scheduling 生产经营进度表
opportunity *n.* 机会
optimize *v.* 优化
option *n.* 选择权
share option 期权

organigram *n.* 组织图
organisation chart 公司组织机构图
orient *v.* 定向，指引
orientation *n.* 倾向，方向
outcome *n.* 结果
outlay *n.* 开销，支出，费用
outlet *n.* 商店
a retail outlet 零售店
outgoings *n.* 开支，开销
outlined *adj.* 概括的，勾勒的
output *n.* 产量
outstanding *adj.* 未付款的，应收的
over-demand *n.* 求过于供
overdraft *n.* 透支
overdraft facility 透支限额
overdraw *v.* 透支
overhead costs 营业成本
overheads *n.* 企业一般管理费用
overpay *n.* 多付（款）
overtime *n.* 加班
overview *n.* 概述，概观
owe *v.* 欠钱，应付

P

p. a. （=per annum）每年
packaging *n.* 包装物；包装
parent company *n.* 母公司，总公司
part-time *adj.* 部分时间工作的，业余的
participate *v.* 参加，分享（in）
partnership *n.* 合伙（关系）
patent *n.* 专利
pay *n.* 工资，酬金 *v.* 付钱，付报酬
take-home pay 实得工资
payroll *n.* 雇员名单，工资表
peak *n.* 峰值，顶点
penetrate *v.* 渗透，打入（市场）
penetration *n.* 目标市场的占有份额
pension *n.* 养老金，退休金
perform *v.* 表现，执行
performance 进行，表现工作情况
performance appraisal 工作情况评估
perk *n.* 额外待遇（交通、保健、保险等）
personnel *n.* 员工，人员
petty cash 零用现金
phase out 分阶段停止使用
pie chart 饼形图
pilot 小规模试验
pipeline *n.* 管道，渠道
plant capacity 生产规模，生产能力
plot *v.* 标绘，策划
point of sale（POS）销售点
policy *n.* 政策，规定；保险单
portfolio *n.*（投资）组合
post *n.* 邮件，邮局；职位
position *n.* 职位
potential *n.* 潜在力，潜势
power *n.* 能力
purchasing power 购买力
PR = Public Relations 公共关系
preference shares 优先股
price *n.* 价格
market price 市场价，市价
retail price 零售价
probation *n.* 试用期
product *n.* 产品
production cycle 生产周期
production schedule 生产计划
product life cycle 产品生命周期
product mix 产品组合
productive *adj.* 生产的，多产的
profile *n.* 简介形象特征
profit *n.* 利润
operating profit 营业利润
profit and loss account 损益账户
project *v.* 预测
promote *v.* 推销
promotion *n.* 提升，升级
proposal *n.* 建议，计划
prospect *n.* 预期，展望
prospectus *n.* 计划书，说明书
prosperity *n.* 繁荣，兴隆
prototype *n.* 原型，样品
publicity *n.* 引起公众注意
public *adj.* 公众的，公开的
public sector 公有企业
publicity *n.* 公开场合；名声；宣传
publics *n.* 公众
punctual *adj.* 准时的
punctuality *n.* 准时
purchase *v./n.* 购买

purchaser *n.* 买主，采购人

Q

QC（=Quality Circle）质检人员
qualify *v.* 有资格，胜任
qualified *adj.* 有资格的，胜任的，合格的
qualification *n.* 资格，资格证明
quality *n.* 质量
quality assurance 质量保证
quality control 质量控制，质量管理
quarterly *adj.*/*adv.* 季度的；按季度
questionnaire *n.* 调查表，问卷
quote *n.* 报价，股票牌价
quotation *n.* 报价，股票牌价

R

Research and Development 研究与开发
radically *adv.* 根本地，彻底地
raise *n.*（美）增加薪金
range *n.* 系列产品
rank *n.*/*v.* 排名
rapport *n.* 密切的关系，轻松愉快的气氛
rate *n.* 比率，费用
fixed rate 固定费用，固定汇率
going rate 现行利率，现行汇率
rating *n.* 评定结果
ratio *n.* 比率
rationalise *v.* 使更有效，使更合理
raw *adj.* 原料状态的，未加工的
raw material 原材料
receive *v.* 得到
receipt *n.* 收据
receiver *n.* 接管人，清算人
accounts receivable 应收账
receivership *n.* 破产管理
recession *n.* 萧条
reckon *v.* 估算，认为
recognise *v.* 承认
recoup *v.* 扣除，赔偿
recover *v.* 重新获得，恢复
recovery *n.* 重获，恢复
recruit *v.* 招聘，征募 *n.* 新招收的人员
recruitment *n.* 新成员的吸收
red *n.* 红色
in the red 赤字，负债
reduce *v.* 减少
reduction *n.* 减少
redundant *adj.* 过多的，被解雇的
redundancy *n.* 裁员，解雇
reference *n.* 参考，参考资料
refund *n.*/*v.* 归还，偿还
region *n.* 地区
reimburse *v.* 偿还，报销
reject *n.*/*v.* 拒绝
reliability *n.* 可靠性
relief *n.* 减轻，解除，救济
relocate *v.* 调动，重新安置
remuneration *n.* 酬报，酬金
rent *v.* 租 *n.* 租金
rep *n.* 代表（缩写）
report to 隶属，从属
reposition *v.*（为商品）重新定位
represent *v.* 代表，代理
representative *n.* 代理人，代表
reputation *n.* 名声，声望
reputable *adj.* 名声（名誉）好的
reserves *n.* 储量金，准备金
resign *v.* 放弃，辞去
resignation *n.* 辞职
resistance *n.* 阻力，抵触情绪
respond *v.* 回答，答复
response *n.* 回答，答复
restore *v.* 恢复
result/results *n.* 结果，效果
retail *n.*/*v.* 零售
retailer *n.* 零售商
retained earnings 留存收益
retire *v.* 退休
retirement *n.* 退休
return *n.* 投资报酬
revenue *n.* 岁入，税收
review *v.*/*n.* 检查
reward *n.*/*v.* 报答，报酬，奖赏
rework *v.*（因劣质而）重作
risk capital 风险资本
rival *n.* 竞争者，对手
rocket *v.* 急速上升，直线上升，飞升
ROI（Return on Investment）投资利润
roughly *adv.* 粗略地
round *adj.* 整数表示的，大约

round trip 往返的行程
royalty *n.* 特许权，专利权税
run *v.* 管理，经营
running *adj.* 运转的

S

sack *v.* 解雇
sales force 销售人员
sample *n.* 样品
saturation *n.* 饱和
saturate *v.* 饱和
save *v.* 节省，储蓄
savings *n.* 存款
scale *n.* 刻度，层次
scapegoat *n.* 替罪羊
scare *adj.* 缺乏的，不足的
scrap *n.* 废料，废品
seasonal *adj.* 季节性的
section *n.* 部门
sector *n.* 部门
securities *n.* 债券及有价证券
segment *n.* 部分　*v.* 将市场划分成不同的部分
segmentation *n.* 市场划分
semi-skilled *adj.* 半熟练的
settle *v.* 解决，决定
settlement *n.* 解决，清偿，支付
service *n.* 服务，帮佣
services *n.* 专业服务
settle *v.* 安排，支付
set up *v.* 创立
share *n.* 股份
shareholder *n.* 股东
shelf-life *n.* 货架期
shift *n.* 轮班
showroom *n.* 陈列室
simulation *n.* 模拟
shop *n.* 商店
closed shop 限制行业
open shop 开放行业
shop steward 工会管事
shopfloor *n.* 生产场所
sick *adj.* 病的
sick leave 病假
sick note 病假条
sick pay 病假工资
sickness 生病
skill *n.* 技能，熟巧
skilled employee 熟练工人
skimming *n.* 高额定价
slogan *n.* 销售口号
slump *n.* 暴跌
a slump in sales 销售暴跌
software *n.* 软件
sole *adj.* 仅有的，单独的
sole distributor 独家分销商
solvent *adj.* 有偿付能力的
sourcing *n.* 得到供货
spare part 零部件
specification *n.* 产品说明
split *v.* 分离
spokesman *n.* 发言人
sponsor *n.* 赞助者
spread *n.* 股票差额
stable *adj.* 稳定的
staff *n.* 职员
stag *n.* 投机认股者
stagnant *adj.* 停滞的，萧条的
statute *n.* 成文法
statutory *adj.* 法定的
steadily *adv.* 稳定地，平稳地
stock *n.* 库存，股票
stock exchange 证券交易所
stockbroker *n.* 股票经纪人
stock controller 库房管理者
storage *n.* 贮藏，库存量
strategy *n.* 战略
streamline *v.* 精简机构，提高效率
stress *n.* 压力，紧迫
strike *n.* 罢工
structure *n.* 结构，设备
subcontract *v.* 分包（工程项目），转包
subordinate *n.* 下级
subscribe *v.* 认购
subsidiary *n.* 子公司
subsidise *v.* 补贴，资助
subsidy *n.* 补助金
substantially *adv.* 大量地，大幅度地
summarise *v.* 概括，总结
superior *n.* 上级，长官
supervisor *n.* 监督人，管理人

supervisory *adj.* 监督的，管理的
supply *n.*/*v.* 供给，提供
survey *n.* 调查
synergy *n.* 协作

T

tactic *n.* 战术，兵法
tailor *v.* 特制产品
tailor made products 特制产品
take on 雇用
takeover *n.* 接管
target *n.* 目标
tariff *n.* 关税；价目表
task *n.* 任务，工作
tax *n.* 税，税金
capital gains tax 资本收益税
corporation tax 公司税，法人税
income tax 所得税
value added tax 增值税
tax allowance 免减税
tax avoidance 避税
taxable 可征税的
taxation 征税
telesales *n.* 电话销售，电话售货
temporary *adj.* 暂时的
temporary post 临时职位
tender *n.*/*v.* 投标
territory *n.* （销售）区域
tie *n.* 关系，联系
throughput *n.* 工厂的总产量
TQC 全面质量管理
track record 追踪记录，业绩
trade *n.*/*v.* 商业，生意；交易，经商
balance of trade 贸易平衡
trading profit 贸易利润
insider trading 内部交易
trade mark 商标
trade union 工会
trainee *n.* 受培训者
transaction *n.* 交易，业务
transfer *n.*/*v.* 传输，转让
transformation *n.* 加工
transparency *n.* （投影用）透明胶片
treasurer *n.* 司库，掌管财务的人
treasury *n.* 国库，财政部
trend *n.* 趋势，时尚
trouble-shooting *n.* 解决问题
turnover *n.* 营业额，员工流动的比率
staff turnover 人员换手率
stock turnover 股票换手率

U

undertake *v.* 从事；同意做某事
uneconomical *adj.* 不经济的，浪费的
unemployment *n.* 失业
unemployment benefit 失业津贴
unit *n.* 单位
unit cost 单位成本
update *v.* 使现代化
up to date *adj.*/*adv.* 流行的（地），现行的（地），时髦的（地）
upgrade *v.* 升级，增加
upturn *n.* 使向上，使朝上
USP 唯一的销售计划

V

vacancy *n.* 空缺
vacant *adj.* 空缺的
value *n.*/*v.* 价值，估价
valuation *n.* 价值
value-added *n.* 增加值
variable *n.* 可变物
variation *n.* 变化，变更
variety *n.* 多样化
a variety of 多种多样的
vary *v.* 改变，修改
VAT（Value Added Tax）增值税
vendor *n.* 卖主（公司或个人）
venture *n.* 冒险，投机
venue *n.* 地点，集合地点
viable *adj.* 可行的
viability *n.* 可行性
vision *n.* 设想；公司的长期目标
vocation *n.* 行业，职业
vocational *adj.* 行业的，职业的

W

wage *n.* （周）工资
wage freeze 工资冻结
warehouse *n.* 仓库，货栈

wealth *n.* 财富，资源
wealthy *adj.* 富裕的，丰富的
welfare *n.* 福利
white-collar *n.* 白领阶层
wholesaler *n.* 批发商
wind up 关闭公司
withdraw *v.* 拿走，收回，退出
withdrawal *n.* 拿走，收回，退出
wholesale *n./a.* 批发（的）
wholesaler *n.* 批发商
work *n.* 工作
working conditions 工作条件
work-in-progress *n.* 工作过程
workload *n.* 工作量
work station 工作位置
working capital 营运资本，营运资金
write off 取消
write-off *n.* 债务的取消

Y

yield *n.* 有效产量

Z

zero defect 合格产品，零缺陷
zero inventory 零存货